The Complete Book of
Baskets and Basketry

The Complete Book of
BASKETS AND BASKETRY

Dorothy Wright

With 281 illustrations including 12 in colour;
line illustrations by David Button, Susan Smith and
Malcolm Couch

CHARLES SCRIBNER'S SONS · NEW YORK

© Dorothy Wright 1977

Copyright under the Berne Convention

All rights reserved. No part of this book
may be reproduced in any form without the
permission of Charles Scribner's Sons.

1 3 5 7 9 11 13 15 17 19 I/C 20 18 16 14 12 10 8 6 4 2

Printed in Great Britain
Library of Congress Catalog Card Number 77-92088
ISBN 0-684-15644-X

Contents

1

Introduction

The history of basket and mat making is the longest of any of the crafts, longer than pottery or the carving of stone, for the one great practical reason that no man likes to sit or sleep on the bare ground. As early man moved from place to place he needed receptacles to carry his belongings and others in which to collect seeds and berries. When he began to think about the hereafter, he put food and household goods in baskets and mats in the graves of his dead.

As he grew more accomplished he began to trap fish, not just with nets but in most elaborate constructions made of branches and twigs. This he does still. In quiet corners of nearly every country in the world men still make fish traps although few people think to enquire how the eels and langoustes, the salmon and lobsters and lesser delicacies, come to be on marble slab and restaurant table. We generally ignore the traps and mats and baskets, even when they are there.

Sophisticated man making journeys by sea and air no longer carries his goods in baskets; but men living and travelling in jungle and forest still use them as their primary luggage, lightness with strength being the first essential of portability. This is a major reason for the universality of basket techniques as well as for their age. This can be better understood when one remembers not only the sea traffic of the past but also the caravan routes over which came dates and spices, jewels, silks and gold from Africa and the East. Everything was wrapped in mats and baskets. Many Indonesian plaiting techniques are found in Spain and Portugal; Portugal was the first European country to colonise the Malayan archipelago in the first quarter of the sixteenth century.

Chariots were anciently made of wicker on a wooden frame, and were used for hunting as well as for war. From the Bible come examples, possibly poetic: Jabin, King of Canaan, had 900; David took 700 from the Kings of Syria and 1,000 from the King of Zobah; Solomon owned 1,400. Chariots and carts with basket sides appear on the bas-reliefs of ancient Egypt, Assyria, Etruria and Greece. Julius Caesar described the wicker-sided war chariots of Britain as very light and fast and capable of swift manoeuvre over rough ground.

It was this lightness combined with strength which made the first aviators turn to baskets. James Sadler, an Oxford confectioner, was in 1784 the first Englishman to ascend in a Montgolfière balloon. The tiny basket – gondola, cradle or car – was elaborately decorated but must have been terrifying. Scotts, basketmakers of Soho, made one for him the following year that was 30in (76cm) long, 12in (30cm) deep at its deepest point, and boat-shaped. Aeroplane seats made for the Royal Flying Corps in 1915 resembled cane chairs without legs. Passenger seats were slightly different from that of the pilot and some, not surprisingly, had hand-holds.

The most numerous and certainly one of the most important baskets ever made in the United Kingdom was the airborne pannier (Illus 1) for air supply of our forces during World War II. Two million were made to be dropped by parachute.

The making of baskets is not only the earliest

of the hand-crafts but may well be the last to resist the machine. It holds a curious position among the crafts since it depends on utility and skill alone for its value, the materials being almost valueless in themselves, the end-product short-lived. Probably no professional basketmaker ever set himself up as an artist-craftsman, and were one to make such a claim he might be considered absurd, particularly by his peers. Value judgements of his work, deeper than the immediately visual, can only be made by those who understand something of the many traditional and ancient techniques he may use in his basketmaking. These techniques vary with the materials used and in different parts of the globe, so an English willow basket cannot be compared with a North American Indian coiled basket or a Japanese bamboo one.

Every year the baskets of the world grow fewer, not only in the developed countries. There are now so many substitutes that even unsophisticated peoples are beginning to think it a waste of time to make extremely complicated things where the preparation of material alone takes hours of cutting up, splitting,

Illus 1 Airborne pannier. World War II brought to Great Britain an extraordinary demand for 2 million airborne panniers to be dropped to her armies in the field. Every available basketmaker was ordered to make them, and willows were specially imported as there were not enough home-grown ones. The panniers are no longer Army issue.

The larger or top half measured 36 × 22 × 16½in (91 × 56 × 42cm), the lower one 34 × 20 × 16½in (86 × 51 × 42cm) *Imperial War Museum*

---

beating and even chewing. In times past boredom was probably the main reason for the patient creation of such exquisitely fine and time-consuming artifacts; now the whole world has other ways to counter tedium, though less tasteful, more ephemoral and probably less successful. But since mankind cannot go backwards there must be fewer and less good baskets.

Nevertheless many of us do cultivate basketmaking as a recreation and a pleasure. Some of us seem to be born with the need to use our hands in a creative way and without satisfying this need we feel incomplete and deprived of a part of our humanity. In a world where leisure time is increasingly given over to looking on at others playing games or pursuing the arts or just endeavouring to entertain the rest of us, crafts hold a satisfaction as old as man himself, the satisfaction of moulding a natural material with one's hands. Many factors come into this: the development of the five senses, an exploration of a special facet of one's own personality, the finding of a peculiar calm and contentment in a noisy world, and sharing all these with the like-minded.

In all crafts the important sense is, to some extent, tactile, in basketmaking particularly so – a reason why it can be followed by the blind whose sense of touch must be developed above all the others. But to the rest of us the training of the eye is just as important – here the blind must use special rulers and aids – and eye and hand work in unison to create a shape, to think and form it far more slowly than a potter shapes a pot.

Basketmaking is still a profession in many countries. A century ago thousands made it their living, now the numbers have shrunk to hundreds. Because the best baskets are made by professionals, this book contains many pictures of traditional working baskets. Many are outside the scope of the amateur as they stand, but the sections on techniques set out ways in which some of them can be made, and though mainly intended for the amateur it is hoped that the information in them will prove useful to professional workers too, particularly to the younger ones whose training is not as detailed as it used to be.

The book covers materials and the five main techniques, also the working of rush which involves several so that it has to have a section to itself. Each technique includes instructions for making, and photographs of, other baskets in that technique. A chapter is devoted to the baskets of America: the ones made by settlers from Europe and their descendants, and those made by Indians. As well there are pictures and notes which have slipped from the strict confines of a particular technique to stand on their own: strange woven articles connected with the sowing and harvesting of corn, delicious fussy bits of Victoriana, some Italian baskets of special interest and English fishing baskets. Concluding chapters give information about the care and repair of baskets and on the quality of modern basket design, there is a list of the curious words used in the pursuance of the craft and a bibliography indicating the particular value of many of the books mentioned.

It may strike the reader that few baskets in the book are of any great age, none in fact older than the end of the eighteenth century. This is because the materials are fragile and do not survive long in temperate climates, nor indeed anywhere except in dry sand or undisturbed water. Also they are difficult to draw and artists of the distant past either did not try or did so rather badly. What is more, very old baskets, unlike very old people, do not make good photographs. But many of the baskets here have a long ancestry and all have something to say and teach anyone who is ready to listen, look and learn.

2

Materials and their Preparation

The form and type of baskets in any part of the world is largely determined by the plants growing in the area. Necessity has always been the mother of invention where baskets are concerned. If there is only straw or grass available then it is coiled and sewn with roots or creepers, and however short and brittle the fibres they will hold together. Weaving and plaiting flourish in kinder climates, and the greater choice of materials there has made man selective. In tropical and sub-tropical climates there are many palms; these are sometimes coiled but are mostly plaited. Some baskets have not changed at all in 1,800 years. Esparto grass, used for coiled baskets in Tutankhamen's tomb, is still the primary material used in Egypt, southern Spain, Algeria and Morocco.

Almost all the cultivated cereals have been used for baskets since earliest times, and wild reeds, rushes, grasses and sedges in infinite variety. Bamboos and canes are the materials of south-east Asia: Burma uses mostly bamboo and some cane; Sarawak uses more cane then bamboo. Taiwan uses nearly all bamboo, which is also much used in south China and in Japan where it has long been the foundation of fine lacquer ware. Far Eastern cane has become a universal material for heavy commercial baskets and furniture, and centre cane is exported in great quantities as the favourite material, because the most accessible, of the amateur the world over.

But in the New World in particular there is now a longing among those who have access to the countryside, to use native materials. The old methods of splitting saplings into their yearly rings and then cutting them into splints or skeins were used in Britain in medieval times, and it appears that the North American Indians knew them too, possibly having learnt from Scandinavian travellers. Laborious but satisfying is the verdict of those who follow these methods today and many fine frame or ribbed baskets have been made from white oak and ash, drawing on Indian designs and copying baskets and techniques brought in by settlers from Europe.

Willow

The first material of northern and western Europe is the osier or basket willow. The *Salix* family is an enormous one including many species and varieties of which the osiers are only one branch. Even at the time of Pliny eight useful osier species were named though it is difficult to identify them exactly. The most important species grown for making baskets are:

(a) *Salix triandra* which produces high-quality rods an average of 7ft (2m) long

(b) *Salix viminalis* gives a stouter type of rod, up to 12ft (3.6m) long, which is used in coarser basketry such as hurdles and agricultural baskets

(c) *Salix purpurea* which is not much grown now. It gives a small, slender, very tough rod up to 4ft (1.20m) long, which does not buff well and was used for small, fine high-class basketware.

There is an old saying that 'land that will bear fat beasts will bear good willows'. The main willow-growing area in England is now in Somerset, in the rich alluvial 'moors' drained by the rivers Parrett, Yeo and Tone. The main centre is Langport and the Paddington–Penzance railway line runs through the willow beds, so that any interested traveller can see the industry being carried on. The moors are flat and have to be well drained by a maze of ditches, because of seasonal flooding. Modern pumping-stations have greatly improved the drainage.

Willows need rich, deep and well-drained soil, especially clay and silt mixtures. There must be abundant water with good drainage, though *Salix viminalis* will grow in poor soil and *S. purpurea* is said to prefer a sandy soil. In the past willows were also grown in large numbers in west Lancashire, the Trent Valley, in Nottingham and East Anglia and the Thames Valley, but since 1925 the area of land under willow cultivation has decreased everywhere. The disastrous East Coast floods of 1953, caused by an exceptional combination of tide and weather, wiped out many willow beds which have never been replanted.

Wild willows are said to have no 'nature' or, if they have, it is not 'kind'. 'Nature' may be defined as strength and elasticity – a good skein has such a nature that you could lace your boots with it. 'Kindness' is harder to define, but any worker with willow or cane knows what it is. One might call it co-operation. Nevertheless one of the best basketmakers of the recent past, William Shelley, was taught as a boy to use wild willows grown for duck cover. His father got them for nothing and their workshop used them for farm baskets. So the amateur, if he can get permission to cut from a pollarded tree or even from old osiers which have grown free, will find they certainly serve for bottom sticks and, with judicious cutting, for siding too.

CULTIVATION

The life of a willow bed varies between 20 and 50 years, and the first saleable crop is obtained in the third season after planting.

Planting is usually done in March or April, in clean land. Cuttings or sets 9–15in (23–38cm) in length are made from 1 year old rods, and pushed into the ground until approximately one-third of their length is showing, buds upward. Rows are carefully measured, and a spacing of 27in (69cm) between rows and 14in (36cm) between cuttings in the row allows room for power-driven cultivators. One acre so spaced requires about 16,500 cuttings, or just over 40,000 per hectare.

During the first two seasons after planting the new bed must be carefully and frequently weeded. The shoots, though not commercially usable, must be cut annually in winter or early spring to encourage new growth. A mature bed also requires weeding but no fertiliser, because of the heavy leaf-fall.

Harvesting is done annually, any time during the winter or spring before the sap rises. Cutting is a highly skilled job done with a heavy sickle (Illus 2).

Illus 2

Rods are tied into bundles immediately after cutting. A traditional bundle measured an old English ell – 45in (115cm) – around, measured 1ft (30cm) up from the butts. In Somerset however, today a bundle of *processed S. triandra*

MR. THOMAS COWLEY'S
Annual Sale of Willows,

On Monday, November 17th, 1913.

SALE TO COMMENCE AT 11-0 O'CLOCK PROMPT.
JOHN CRITCHLEY, Auctioneer, LEYLAND.

Lot	Rows		Lot	Rows		Lot	Rows	
1	46	Moss Redbuds	84	14	Orchardhey Redbuds	167	40	No. 4 Field Redbuds
2	16	ditto	85	14	ditto	168	40	ditto
3	16	ditto	86	15	ditto	169	40	ditto
4	16	ditto	87	15	ditto	170	40	ditto
5	16	ditto	88	18	ditto	171	40	ditto
6	44	First Year's Redbuds	89	17	Barnhey Redbuds	172	40	ditto
7	18	Redbuds	90	17	ditto	173	40	ditto
8	18	ditto	91	22	ditto	174	40	ditto
9	19	ditto	92	22	ditto	175	144	ditto
10	7	Mawdesley's Bows	93	20	ditto	176	10	No. 5 Field Bows
11	7	ditto	94	20	ditto	177	10	ditto
12	7	ditto	95	16	ditto	178	10	ditto
13	6	ditto	96	15	ditto	179	10	ditto
14	6	ditto	97	21	ditto	180	10	ditto
15	10	Mawdesley's Scanes	98	22	ditto	181	10	ditto
16	10	ditto	99	24	ditto	182	10	ditto
17	10	ditto	100	25	Outlet Redbuds	183	10	ditto
18	10	ditto	101	24	ditto	184	24	ditto
19	10	ditto	102	24	ditto	185	11	No. 6 Field two-year-olds
20	10	ditto	103	25	ditto	186	11	ditto
21	11	Long Scanes	104	15	Hill Cottage Bows	187	12	ditto
22	12	ditto	105	15	ditto	188	10	ditto
23	15	ditto	106	15	ditto	189	10	ditto
24	20	ditto	107	15	ditto	190	10	ditto
25	37	ditto	108	16	Mawdesley's Bows	192	10	ditto
26	14	Redbuds	109	16	ditto	193	10	ditto
27	14	ditto	110	16	ditto	194	10	ditto
28	15	ditto	111	25	ditto	195	10	ditto
29	25	Gale's Bows	112	The Field First-year's Scanes		196	10	ditto
30	15	ditto	113	10	Blackmoor Black Scanes	197	10	ditto
31	15	ditto	114	10	ditto	198	17	ditto
32	15	ditto	115	10	ditto	199	40	ditto
33	13	ditto	116	10	ditto	200	5	No. 7 Field two-year-olds
34	13	ditto	117	10	ditto	201	5	ditto
35	35	Gale's Redbuds	118	15	ditto	202	5	ditto
36	35	ditto	119	11	Ashcroft's Field Black Scanes	203	5	ditto
37	35	ditto	120	11	ditto	204	5	ditto
38	35	ditto	121	11	ditto	206	5	ditto
39	43	ditto	122	11	ditto	207	5	ditto
40		Two-year-olds	123	11	ditto	208	5	ditto
41	18	Big Brook Redbuds	124	10	ditto	209	5	ditto
42	12	ditto	125	10	ditto	210	5	ditto
43	11	ditto	126	10	ditto	211	5	ditto
44	11	ditto	127	10	ditto	212	27	No. 8 Field Redbuds
45	11	ditto	128	11	ditto	213	27	ditto
46	11	ditto	129	21	Ashcroft's Field Redbuds	214	27	ditto
47	11	ditto	130	21	ditto	215	27	ditto
48	11	ditto	131	21	ditto	216	27	ditto
49	11	ditto	132	21	ditto	217	27	ditto
50	11	ditto	133	20	ditto	218	27	ditto
51	11	ditto				219	34	ditto
52	11	ditto				220	15	No. 9 Field two-year-olds
53	11	ditto	Lots 100 to 133 will be sold on samples			221	8	ditto
54	15	Little Brook Redbuds	at Walmsley Fold.			222	8	ditto
55	15	ditto				223	8	ditto
56	16	ditto	134	17	Lowmeadow No. 1 Field Scanes	223	8	ditto
57	16	ditto	135	34	ditto	224	8	ditto
58	16	ditto	136	33	ditto	225	8	ditto
59	21	Copy Redbuds	137	32	ditto	226	9	ditto
60	21	ditto	138	34	ditto	227	8	ditto
61	21	ditto	139	33	ditto	228	8	ditto
62	20	ditto	140	35	ditto	229	9	ditto
63	20	ditto	142	33	ditto	230	9	No. 9 Field Scanes
64	20	ditto	143	34	ditto	231	8	ditto
65	20	ditto	144	33	ditto	232	8	ditto
66	20	ditto	145	73	ditto	233	12	Mawdesleys
67	20	ditto	146	18	No. 2 Field Mawdesley's Scanes	234	12	ditto
68	17	Orchardhey Bows	147	18	ditto	235	16	ditto
69	8	ditto	148	14	ditto	236	16	ditto
70	8	ditto	149	15	ditto	237	179	Rows Blackrods
71	8	ditto	150	16	ditto	238	191	Rows Blackrods
72	7	ditto	151	16	ditto			
73	7	ditto	152	12	ditto			
74	7	ditto	153	13	ditto			
75	7	ditto	154	14	ditto	15 Tons of Black one-year-olds grow-		
76	7	ditto	155	13	ditto	ing at Ainsdale and 80 tons Mawdesley's		
77	7	ditto	160	13	ditto	one-year-olds and other kinds, will be		
78	6	ditto	161	23	ditto	sold on samples, after lot 238.		
79	6	ditto	162	12	No. 3 Field Scanes			
80	15	Orchardhey Redbuds	163	12	ditto			
81	15	ditto	164	11	ditto	Sale to commence at 11 prompt.		
82	15	ditto	165	11	ditto	Luncheon at One o'clock at Walmsley		
83	14	ditto	166	12	ditto	Fold.		

Illus 3 Sale notice of Mr Thomas Cowley of Mawdesley, Lancashire

measures 37in (95cm) in circumference 2in (5cm) from the base. Approximate weight is 26lb (12kg). The traditional bundle has three ties, the ell band, one closer to the butt ends than the ell band and the other well above it. An acre (0.4ha) of the most useful willow grown in Somerset, the Black Maul variety of *S. triandra*, will produce an average yield of 200 bundles, weighing approximately 6 tons, the equivalent of 16.1 tonnes per hectare.

PROCESSING AND MARKETING

Autumn was the time when willow auctions were held, though these are now occasions of the past. Illus 3 shows the notice of Mr Thomas Cowley of Mawdesley's annual sale in 1913 and it will be seen how great was the quantity sold by one firm alone in the Lancashire area not far from Preston. The osiers grown in the land which had been the estuary of the Ribble, only drained in 1800, were very fine and small and of the best quality. Buyers came from all over England. Varieties of *Salix purpurea* in particular grew very well in this area, they seem to be even more salt-tolerant than most willows, and the reclaimed estuary was ideal for their growth.

After cutting, the bundles of willows are graded by standing them in a tub and selecting them against a measuring stick. The rods are graded in 1ft (30cm) lengths from 3ft (91cm) upwards.

Brown Willows are rods dried and used with the bark on.

White Willows are rods peeled without boiling just before they break into leaf. In most cases bundles for 'peeling for white' are 'pitted', ie stood in 6in (15cm) of water, either in ditches or concrete pits. In spring they begin to break into leaf and must be peeled by the end of June.

Buff Willows are brown rods that have been boiled in tanks for several hours and then peeled, giving a red-brown colour. This colour varies considerably according to the kind of willow and also the time when it is 'buffed'. A paler colour known as 'harvest buff' (see colour illustration on p 51) is obtained by cutting the willows in winter, stacking them in the open to dry until summer, when they are boiled and peeled. The darker colours come from boiling

and peeling in winter, soon after cutting.

Peeling used to be done by hand, but the bulk of the crop is now machine-peeled, only a few whites being done manually. In both cases a device called a willow-brake is used (Illus 4).

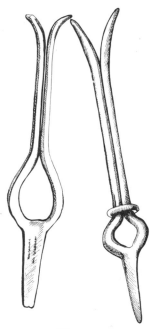

Illus 4

Two smooth metal rods are sprung together and the willow rod is drawn between them, stripping off the bark (Illus 5). After peeling, the rods are dried in the open air spread out along hedges, fences and walls, a characteristic sight throughout willow country.

IMPORTED WILLOWS

Insufficient willows are grown in England today to keep basketmakers supplied. West Country baskets are mostly made of Somerset willows, but basketmakers in the cities in Scotland, the Midlands and East Anglia, if they are unable to get local willows, are compelled to use imported ones.

Excellent white or buff willows are coming in from Spain, the Netherlands, Argentina, Belgium, Poland, Portugal, Madeira, Austria, Hungary and Germany. These willows are often better graded and cheaper than Somerset willows, but there is no doubt that English basketmakers prefer native material when they

can get it. At least one Somerset man who has emigrated to New Zealand is getting his local buff willows shipped out to him.

PREPARATION FOR WORKING

Materials should be prepared and sorted beforehand. Osiers, as already mentioned, are bought by length only. All have a long taper but the thickness will vary, and when choosing rods for a particular basket one tries to match stakes with some care so that the parts used for the border will be fairly even. Only in the very finest professional work are rods precisely matched.

Bottom sticks should be approximately three times stouter than stakes, and will therefore have to come from a very long rod. Stakes and liners are stouter than wale, and waling rods stouter than side rods. Material for randing is naturally stouter than that for slewing, for which the tips will come in useful so that the stuff (as the basketmaker calls it) is not wasted.

A stout rod is one that has a big taper (Illus 6). The taper of willow rods is perhaps the greatest difference there is in the working of willow and cane. The use of willows is so much a matter of eye and of experience because, like

Illus 5 An old print of a willow grower and his family with journeymen and an apprentice working with harvested withies. On the far left these are being bundled or graded into lengths. The next man is batting down the butts of tied bundles, and the master, right centre, also appears to be sorting or grading. The central figure is stripping the withies at one of a pair of standing brakes and behind these a girl has paused in splitting a thick rod with a knife while she talks to an older man. The apprentice on the right is also stripping at a brake we cannot see, and there are children about who no doubt are helping now and then and keeping out of their elders' way. A 'doctor's basket' probably holds some provisions and the can shows that it is thirsty work

———————————

rushes, they are natural materials which, though cultivated, are not machine processed. In making a willow basket it is well to remember that you are making something that cannot be made by machine.

Willows are worked in a damp or mellow condition which means that they must be soaked in cold or warm water (never hot) and then allowed to lie covered in a cool place.

The times for soaking vary according to the thickness and type of willow and are largely gauged by experience. A rough table is:

tip →

← belly

back →

butt

Illus 6 The willow rod or withy. The four parts should be remembered in working

Brown rods

3–5ft (90–150cm)	2–3 days
5–7ft (1.5–2.1m)	3–4 days
7–8ft (2.1–2.5m)	4–5 days
8ft (2.5m)	1 week–10 days

Professional basketmakers in a hurry will sometimes steam brown rods for a couple of hours to make them supple but this turns them a hard dark brown instead of the soft greenish brown that is their natural colour.

White and buff rods

up to 4ft (1.2m)	$\frac{1}{2}$ hour
4–6ft (1.2–1.8m)	$\frac{1}{2}$–1 hour
6–8ft (1.8–2.5m)	2–3 hours
8ft (2.5m) and longer	3–4 hours
skeins	merely dipped

In all cases, the stuff, after being taken from the water, should be laid down in a sheltered place for a night or some hours to mellow, care being taken not to prepare more white or buff than is needed for one or two days' work.

Skeining is the use of thin strips of the skin of

a white or buff willow, prepared with the tools in Illus 25, 26 and 27.

N.B. Though willows are usually thought of as being plants of water and wet places they must be stored dry, and dried out again thoroughly after they have been wetted for working. Like any other damp wood they will go rotten if stored without good circulation of air round them. Any basket must also be allowed to dry out after it has been made, and certainly before it is varnished.

The State School of Basketmaking and Willow Culture at Fayl-Billot in France hardly ever uses buff or brown willows, their baskets are a shining white, not varnished but, when finished, put for some hours into a kiln in which sulphur is burning (Illus 65).

WILLOWS FOR THE AMATEUR CRAFTSMAN

The amateur craftsman in England or elsewhere may well have read the past few pages feeling that they had little bearing on his situation as a would-be willow worker. It has long been difficult and expensive to obtain the processed material and impossible, certainly outside the United Kingdom, to buy willows in the green state for planting and growing oneself. The most severe quarantine regulations govern the import of green willows in many countries. Happily the situation has now changed and is becoming easier, not because of a pressing desire to grow willows for basketmaking but because the versatile genus *Salix* is proving useful in many other ways, for windbreaks, water control, papermaking and cricket bats among others.

In England, Long Ashton Research Station near Bristol has a long history of interest in basket-willow growing and breeding, and is the first place any willow grower should contact for information. The willow officer has knowledge of the whole *Salix* family, not just of those which grow in Europe or the United Kingdom. There are over 260 different European willows growing in the Salicetum at Long Ashton, planted in 1971. To anyone interested in their history it is fascinating to see the old names of hybrids and varieties of osiers that were being grown in the eighteenth century and probably long before.

In New Zealand there is very considerable interest in willows, mainly for river defence work, and people are working on introduced willows and methods of establishing them for control of river erosion. This has come about through the scientist in charge of the Plant Materials Centre at the Ministry of Works and Development, Palmerston North, New Zealand, where there is a small research section investigating breeding and selection of willows of special interest to them. It is mainly the European and South American willows that are proving the most valuable.

When willows first come into New Zealand they go to the plant quarantine laboratories where they stay for two years. If nothing untoward develops they are sent out into the field. This is general practice today with many plants and trees, and also in the United States of America and Canada where quarantine has always been very strict. Long Ashton is able to pass on requests for cuttings from Australia to New Zealand knowing that they can benefit from the very satisfactory quarantine regulations there and also be in phase with the correct planting seasons. Australia is interested in willows for planting along watercourses and also to provide fodder for cattle. It would seem very possible that basket-willows could be cultivated too.

Long Ashton does supply planting material for the United Kingdom but it really exists for research and trial purposes. On the other hand the willow officer will give names and addresses of willow growers who can supply processed osiers for basketmaking and cuttings for planting, and of nurserymen supplying willows for amenity planting particularly on a commercial basis. He will also give advice to would-be growers of basket willows.

Cane

Calamus – cane or rattan – is the generic name for the many varieties of cane palm growing in the jungle and virgin forest of tropical countries. No cane grows in the British Isles, except at Kew. The trade names of the best known varieties used in industry are:

Tohiti. A thick cane 12mm to 30mm in diameter, used for furniture.

Malacca. The cane associated with walking sticks and umbrella handles. Also used for furniture frames.

Kubu. A yellow soft-natured variety, used for heavy industrial baskets, from 5mm to 12mm in diameter.

Palembang. A small smooth reddish cane 3mm to 8mm in diameter, tougher than processed cane and useful for smaller hampers and industrial baskets. It splits well and can be used by the amateur in this state.

Sarawak and *Segah*. The varieties from which chair seating and centre canes are manufactured.

Whangee. The nobbed yellow cane popular for umbrella and bag handles.

CULTIVATION AND MARKETING

The best cane grows in Malaya, Borneo, Sarawak, Java and Celebes. It is also found in Burma, Indo-China, Australia, Africa and China. The plant cannot be said to be cultivated as it grows wild and needs no attention. Single canes grow to enormous lengths, up to 600ft (180m), but the average diameter is under 1in (2.5cm). It is difficult to harvest because the outer skin is covered with hooked thorns. Natives work in heavy gloves with axes. After cutting, the canes are left to dry where they grew and the spiny covering can then be stripped off. The inner bark, shiny and hard, is the surface we know in glossy lapping, and chair cane.

After the outer bark is removed the canes are cut into 12–30ft (4–9m) lengths, tied in bundles, and sent by water to Singapore, Hong Kong and other South-East Asian parts which are the world centres for cane production and marketing.

PROCESSING

After washing, the outer surface is split off by machine and this is made into various thicknesses and grades of lapping and chair-seating cane. The tough cream fibrous core is known in this country as pulp or centre cane, in Australia as pith or rattan-core, and in the United States as reed. It is cut with circular knives into various

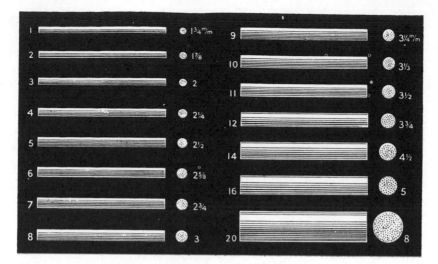

1		⊙ $1\frac{3}{4}$ m/m	9		⊙ $3\frac{1}{4}$ m/m
2		⊙ $1\frac{7}{8}$	10		⊙ $3\frac{1}{3}$
3		⊙ 2	11		⊙ $3\frac{1}{2}$
4		⊙ $2\frac{1}{4}$	12		⊙ $3\frac{3}{4}$
5		⊙ $2\frac{1}{2}$	14		⊙ $4\frac{1}{2}$
6		⊙ $2\frac{5}{8}$	16		⊙ 5
7		⊙ $2\frac{3}{4}$			
8		⊙ 3	20		⊙ 8

Illus 7 Handle cane for basketry is generally 8mm in centre cane, and from 6 to 10mm in glossy. Chair-seating cane runs from No 1 (very fine) to No 6

diameters sold in this country by numbers ranging from 000 to 15. The measures are in millimetres, and the information in Illus 7 may be useful in copying foreign pattern books.

GRADING AND QUALITY

Until about 1970, the processing of high quality centre cane, lapping and chair seating canes was done in Europe, raw cane being shipped mainly from Singapore. This was known as 'Continental' quality, as opposed to the 'Far Eastern' cane, processed in the country of origin. Now Singapore and Hong Kong have taken over the high quality trade, producing the same two grades for the world market under the same names. Japan is said to be the most discriminating buyer.

At one time there was a system of coloured strings to tie up 1lb (0.5kg) bundles of different grades, but this is no longer either clear or reliable, particularly since the advent of bleached centre cane.

Since the war, West German processing firms have invented a method of bleaching the dark portions of the cane core which previously were unusable for basketry. This renders the cane very soft, more like macaroni when damp. This may be an advantage in therapy, but the resulting work is neither strong nor lively to look at and has a dead antiseptic air. It colours with age as cream cane does, but is cheaper.

PREPARATION

Long soaking of centre cane is to be deprecated. It spoils the quality and can even turn it black. Use damp weaving canes and, if they dry, pass them through water. Dry cane will not shape well.

Approximate Times in Water

8mm and 5mm handle cane	20–30 minutes
Nos 14–10	15 minutes
Nos 9–7	10 minutes
Nos 6–4	5 minutes
Nos 3 and under	pass through water

Where it is possible to let the canes lie under a wet cloth or sack, soaking of canes smaller than No 9 will not be needed at all. They need simply to be dipped in water first.

It is a good rule not to wet stakes and liners after they have been upsett, unless a very marked curve is to be made, until the border is reached.

Palembang has a hard outer skin and requires several hours in water but, when split, the exposed core quickly absorbs water. Sizes 3–5 require 10–15 minutes. Lengths of palembang may be split by holding the cane under the left arm, making a split in the end with a knife and pulling the two pieces apart. When one splits thinner than the other, bend the thicker one away from it. This requires a little practice but is not difficult. Palembang makes a strong resilient basket. Split the cane when dry.

Shiny handle cane requires longer soaking than the matt sort.

Rush

The plaiting or braiding of some of the large family of European rushes and sedges is an ancient technique. Pre-Iron Age rush matting has been found at Mere in Somerset. In Saxon times bundles of rushes were gathered and strewn on the hall floors of great houses for warmth. They were changed perhaps twice or three times a year and naturally became extremely foul. By the sixteenth century rush matting had begun to be used in the smaller rooms of larger houses. Today, the National Trust in Britain keeps a small country industry going in East Anglia making rush matting for the old houses in its care.

Poor people lay on mattresses stuffed with rushes, so did the sick. Church monuments from the sixteenth to the nineteenth centuries show the noble and gentle dead lying on plaited rushes. Baskets were sometimes made by sewing rush plaits together (Illus 197), but the method of making baskets shown in the illustration is probably not older than the late-nineteenth century.

Rush is a soft material, easily broken when dry, but strong when damp. In weaving, some of the same strokes and borders are used as for cane and willow, but the handling is very different and, to anyone used to working with centre cane, rush presents problems as well as charm. The colours are beautiful though all will fade in time to a uniform soft brown. Correctly prepared rushes are almost silky to the touch, but there are great variations in length, thickness and hardness. The plant shares its characteristic taper with willows and many other rods, so that one has to work for the look of smoothness and harmony, often using two rushes to match one and hiding the ends away, which might seem like cheating to a cane worker. Rush is worked damp and shrinks as it dries, therefore it must be worked tightly and firmly and this requires practice.

CULTIVATION

Rushes grow all over the temperate parts of the world. There are many different kinds and they are most difficult to identify botanically, though it is now generally accepted that the most important for use in basketry and seating is *Scirpus lacustris* the club rush or, as some say, the true bullrush. A smaller one, not suitable for seating, is *Juncus effusis*. Both are common and grow wild by fresh water, and small industries have generally sprung up in areas where *Scirpus lacustris* grows in quantity.

Rushes are bought either from a grower or from a retailer (who may also sell imported ones) by the bolt – a large bundle up to 10ft (3m) high and roughly 40in (1m) round the base.

Scirpus lacustris grows 6–9ft (1.8–2.7m) out of the water. The stem is tapering, leafless, round, spongy and bright green, quickly identifiable by the terminating bunch of brown flowerets. Rushes are cut every other year in high summer, as near the root as possible. The butt is the strongest and thickest part. After careful washing, the stems kept straight, the rushes are laid out on the grass to dry for several days. They must be turned so that they dry evenly and are then ready to be tied in bundles or bolts. These stand upright in the open air but must be protected from sun and rain which spots them. Artificial drying is not satisfactory and the loss of weight must be total before storage (Illus 8).

PREPARATION FOR WORKING

Before use rushes must be wetted, laid either in a bath or on a lawn and watered with a can, for 10 minutes; then they are wrapped in a damp cloth or sack and left overnight to mellow. Each rush is then wiped from tip to butt with a damp cloth to remove mud and expel air, which may come out with a satisfying crack. They lie under the damp cloth until needed.

N.B. Rushes should never be kept damp for more than 48 hours; they get sticky. Dry and damp again.

Raffia

Raffia is a product of a palm *Raphia ruffia* which grows in Madagascar. The leaves are cut before they uncurl and the tough underside is stripped off, dried and split into various widths. For sale in craft shops raffia is graded and made up into small hanks and sometimes treated with

Illus 8 Rushes from the river Stour are cut in high summer and are shown drying outside the Deben Rush Weavers' factory at Debenham in Suffolk, England (*Author's Collection*)

glycerine, but the bundles sold for garden use are quite satisfactory and very much cheaper if one is going to use it for a whole basket.

In the garden-bundles pieces vary considerably, some being soft and wide and others hard and thin. The latter are used to form a coil and the soft wide ones for oversewing it. The bundles are tied at one end and should be hung up by the knot, from which the pieces are drawn out singly. When sewing it is the ends at the knot which should be threaded through the needle.

PREPARATION FOR WORKING

Little has to be done, raffia is good-tempered stuff and very strong. It may be used as it is, or soaked for a few minutes in water in which a little glycerine has been stirred, about ½ teaspoonful to 1 pint.

Raffia takes dyes quite well. It is often sold ready dyed, but it can be dyed at home, using the methods for dyeing materials such as wool and cotton. It will retain vegetable dyes if mordanted, and chemical ones such as Dylon, without more preparation than careful washing with soap and water. It should be tied lightly in one or two places and go wet into any dye-bath where it may need rather longer immersion than wool or cotton. Stirring should be gentle so as not to tangle it, and it should be hung up to dry.

Straw

Straw of all the food grains may be used to make coiled baskets, but it must be long and of good quality; threshed straw that is cracked and broken will not do. There is no preparation except to strip off the leaves and ears.

Straw was once much used for plaiting to make hats and baskets but this industry has almost died out except in some Mediterranean countries, the Far East and the West Indies where tourists like to buy ethnic objects. It is still possible to buy plaited straw by the yard or metre, imported from the Far East where it is made by the Chinese. It may be woven into baskets or sewn together.

Grasses and Creepers

The different grasses which have been or still are used to make baskets are so numerous that their gathering and preparation must be left to those who use them. They are not exported in the raw state and even museums find it hard to identify them. The rattans, a commercial crop, are dealt with under the heading of Cane (p. 16).

The same comments apply to creepers, vines and brambles.

Palms

There are over 130 genera of the Palmaceae found in tropical and sub-tropical climates. The doum palm, *Hyphaene thebaica*, was used for the sewing of coiled baskets and the date

---

Illus 9 This *gerla* from Lake Como, northern Italy, is a back basket for carrying hay on the steep slopes of the mountain meadows. It is made of sweet chestnut, split lengthways and the top wale is split hazel. The rope is a twisted grapevine which is strong enough to carry its load (*Collected by Randolph Langenbach in October 1976; Author's Collection*)

palm, *Phoenix dactylifera* has also been identified in basketmaking. Probably more and cheaper baskets made of some kind or other of palm are exported all over the world than any others.

Coppice Woods

These are trees or shrubs of temperate climates. *Chestnut, sweet or Spanish, Castanea sativa*, is a European tree which is cultivated as a coppice wood for making such items as poles and fences as well as for making spale or splint baskets (see the Italian ones in Illus 261 and 262). In France also it has many uses in the making of heavier baskets, in particular those of the countryside such as the back baskets of the mountain regions. A similar type from northern Italy is shown in Illus 9. It is also used as a reinforcement of osier baskets and to replace malacca cane in wicker furniture.

It is easily grown; in the Alps and Pyrenees it grows up to elevations of 2,800ft (850m) and it is also found in Asia Minor and the Caucasus. In Italy in particular there are great forests of chestnut trees on the slopes of the Apennines.

As a coppice wood it is grown on a rotation of 3–5 years when it attains a basal diameter of 2–2½in (5–6cm). It splits very easily and requires no special treatment.

Oak, Quercus pedunculata, when grown as a coppice wood, is given a rotation of 15–30 years. If used for the making of baskets it requires soaking and boiling before it can be split into spale (Illus 10).

Hazel, Corylus avellana, never attains the stature of a tree. It grows wild in temperate areas of Europe and Asia and its flexible stems are used for hurdle making, and for the frames, rims and handles of coarse basketry. Coal-, iron- and lead-mining baskets used before 1875 in the north of England and the Midlands were made entirely of hazel, and great quantities were grown in what is now Cumbria solely for making corves – enormous baskets for hauling both men and minerals up and down the mine shafts. The hazel coppices of Hampshire, Dorset and south-east England supplied rods for the pottery crates of Staffordshire, originally designed by Josiah Wedgwood. These hazels were cut by itinerant crate-rodmakers. Few of

Illus 10 Swill makers at Low Cunsey Mill *c* 1860 (watercolour). A swill was one name for the frame or ribbed basket made in Cumbria and nearby Lancashire from split oak saplings, known as 'spale' or 'spelk'. The rims may be oak, ash or hazel. One family, the Aireys of Storth, believed that they had been making swills for 300 years.

Our picture shows the saplings stored in the rafters of the workshop on the right, and on the left is the bricked boiler where the saplings are boiled. The rims of the baskets are shown hanging up to dry. Vats for soaking would be outside. The man on the right is seated at the foot-vice trimming and finishing the oak strips which the other two men are working over the rims. No nails or pegs are used.

The makers were known in Cumbria as swillers. The rims were boiled to make them pliable, and the stripped oak for the spales, the ribs and the weaving strips, known here as 'taws' or 'tyres', were also boiled for twenty-four hours before trimming and dressing. The tyres, being thinner got further trimming on the padded knee of the worker with a sharp knife. A swiller might spend a day in the week preparing his material.

When the rim had been shaped the first rib was tied and knotted with a tyre at each side of the rim, and another rib was added to each side of it. Further ribs to fill the space were set into the rim with the point of a bodkin as the weaving proceeded, a slightly more complicated method than most frame baskets and differing in this from the Worcestershire scuttle. The weaving was carried out in the usual way, beginning at either side.

Swills were made in varying sizes, from very large ones used in the coal pits of Cumberland to others convenient for the coaling of ships or building work. At one time many swills went over the border into the Scottish Lowlands for seeding and harvesting potatoes and local farmers used them for feeding stock. Others were bobbin baskets in the mills of Lancashire, now replaced by plastic and hardboard. Sometimes upright garden baskets with wooden bottoms and the sides made of spelks can be found. They last many years.

There are also varieties in shape from round to oval or kidney shape, the last used to be for sowing before mechanical methods came in. They still have an occasional use on an awkward hillside or garden where a machine would not do.

In medieval times the use of split 'underwoods' for making baskets, as well as for wattling and fencing, was much more general. Pollarded willows, even after the true osier was specially cultivated, were used for farm baskets as well as for implements, but they do not grow everywhere, and it is evident from some illuminated manuscripts that the material used is wide and flat, so it must have been spelk (*Abbot Hall Museum of Lakeland Life and Industry, Kendal*)

these workers are now left, and their production is used for other things.

Ash, Fraxinus excelsior, cut into flat slats was used as a foundation for a few specialist agricultural baskets such as the winnowing fan (Illus 250).

Woods for veneer baskets – or chips and punnets as they are known in England – were poplar, fir, lime and willow. The wood had to be fresh-felled and received no treatment except rotary sawing into thin slips of various widths from 1in (2.5cm) upwards. When local wood was not available the factories used imported wood. Cardboard and plastic has replaced veneer.

The Sussex trug, called a basket though it is not woven, is made of split willow, ash and chestnut.

White oak, Quercus alba, is made into splints for the ubiquitous frame or ribbed baskets of rural America, particularly in the Appalachian Mountains. Splint corresponds to spale or spelk in Britain and the making of it by hand is much the same and a hard labour.

As preparation, 5–6ft (1.5–1.8m) clear length of sapling is split into quarters or eighths and the outer bark removed. A cleaving tool and mallet are used to remove the heartwood (often used for ribs and handles) and to split each piece into four at right-angles to the growth rings. If a shaving horse (Illus 10) is available this is used with a drawknife to trim the pieces to the required width of the splint. After this, using a knife to start the splitting, the wood is split down the growth rings, using the hands. The final polish is given with the knife, holding the splints against the thigh – protected by a piece of leather.

The wood is split immediately after felling, or left soaking until it can be split. It is also wetted as the basket is being made to keep it pliable.

Ash, Black and White, Fraxinus nigra, F. americana is more used for baskets in New England than further south. It is more amenable to soaking than is white oak, and billets can with advantage be soaked for a month, preferably in running water, to separate the growth rings. After removing the bark the billet is pounded with a heavy wooden maul along its length which will separate the outer layers. The surface is then scored longways at the width wanted, and the splints peeled off. Only as much material as is needed is taken, and the billet is then put back to soak.

Hickory, Carya spp., was used by the people of the Appalachians. It is a wonderfully resilient wood and makes baskets with a very long life, but it is difficult to split.

Machine-made splints can now be bought in the United States, and many craft-workers there also use flat lapping cane, wider and stronger than is generally available in Europe.

Other Materials

The Women's Institutes in England make what we call hedgerow baskets and have also tried out the leaves of tall garden plants, such as irises and Montbretia, which turn beautiful colours in the autumn. When dried for a few weeks and then prepared like rush, they will plait like rushes or can be coiled and sewn into baskets. To avoid disappointment, experiments should at first be simple research projects. Some plants shrink too much, some become brittle and hard, and nearly always one needs large quantities to make even one basket. But there is great pleasure and excitement to be gained by making a small mat from wild or garden material collected and processed by oneself.

3
Techniques

There are many different ways of making or weaving baskets but they can be roughly divided into five types for the explanation and teaching of technique:

Stake-and-Strand (known in America as 'wickering'). The bottom and sides of the

---

Illus 11 A Somerset-made log basket of brown and white willow. Curved sides are difficult to make in willow since the material does not have the elasticity of cane, but once it is kinked there it will stay, and the final result is a strong and graceful basket (*CoSIRA*)

basket are made of a framework of radiating or, in the case of a rectangular basket, straight sticks and stakes of rigid material interwoven with more pliable material passing over and under, building up from the bottom (Illus, 11, 12).

Frame or Ribbed. Baskets built on a rigid frame or hoop: circular, oval, rectangular or rarely half-hoop in shape with, if required, a handle ring crossing the frame and going underneath. Ribs are added during the weaving which is put on from the edge of the frame downwards, unlike stake-and-strand (Illus 13, 14).

Illus 12 Made by Mr W. H. Sandling of Stroud, Gloucestershire, this tea basket is in buff willow. It measures 7 × 20 × 14in (18 × 51 × 36cm) and is a typical rectangular willow basket. More elaborate picnic baskets have trunk covers, and fastenings vary according to type and price. They were developed at the beginning of this century when the advent of the bicycle and then the car made outdoor meals a general pleasure (CoSIRA)

Illus 13 Potato skip, made by Gwylm Jones, Llandyssul, Dyfed, Wales, of white willow; 22in (56cm) diameter, 10½in (27cm) high.

Baskets of this type are still made occasionally in Scotland, Ireland and Wales, though it is doubtful if one as fine as this was ever used for harvesting roots. The two or three that the author knows of, made by the same man, are regarded as works of art by their owners and are indeed a lesson in the use of the osier or basket willow. The rods are perfectly matched, the ribs shaped with a knife and the whole basket is a pleasure to look at and handle. Notice that the weave is not continuous; on both sides of the basket the butts of the rods are laid to the inside of the second rib down, and go across and round the rim on the opposite side, their tips ending in the centre of the belly (Museum of English Rural Life)

Illus 14 Traditional fish creel and baskets from Arbroath, Angus. These, and the sculls (Illus 257) were collected by the late Dr Evelyn Baxter, author and ornithologist, and may be seen at the Shandwick Place gallery of the National Museum of Antiquities of Scotland in Edinburgh. The creels, as supreme examples of the art of basketmaking, were shown at the Living Traditions exhibition in Edinburgh in 1951.

Frame or ribbed baskets are probably one of the oldest types in Britain, and were seldom, if ever, made by professional basketmakers. Fishermen, farmers and other country people made them for their own use, and some people believe that they are Celtic in origin. Certainly they were, and still are, made in Scotland, Ireland and Wales rather more than by the English, and emigrants from these countries undoubtedly introduced this type of basket to North America and the Caribbean, where they are still being made.

There are many forms of frame basket and a recipe for the simplest is on page 125.

The Arbroath baskets illustrated are of fine Kubu or heavy Palembang cane with hoops probably of hazel (National Museum of Antiquities of Scotland)

Coiled. A simple but laborious construction where a single length or a bunch of plant material is sewn in concentric rings, one to another, with thinner materials. It allows the introduction of much colour and design (see colour illustration on p 104).

Plaited. Baskets and mats are made with flexible materials such as rushes, palms, grasses and split rattans and bamboos. At its most elaborate it is nearer to textile weaving than any of the other techniques, but braided narrow lengths may be coiled and sewn, or laid flat to make mats (see colour illustration on p 34).

Twined. In this both uprights and weavers are soft – straw, bast, rush or grasses being used. At its simplest only two weavers are used, but many and various decorative features may be introduced. It is probably the oldest technique of all (see colour illustrations on p 52 and 85).

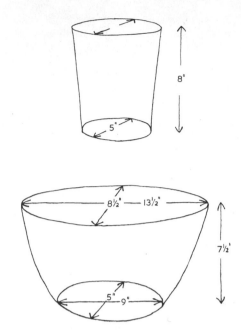

Illus 15

Stake-and-Strand

DESIGNING

The term 'stake-and-strand' covers willow and cane in the European tradition, some splint as worked in the United States of America, and in part rush as worked in the methods included here.

To design such baskets one usually begins with a rough drawing or plan of base, top and sides (Illus 15) followed by a list of dimensions. As an example:

Round

Base	5in (13cm) diameter
Top	6½in (16.5cm) diameter
Height	6½in (16.5cm)

The number of bottom sticks is in proportion to the diameters, and the number of stakes is usually two to each end of a bottom stick, adding or subtracting one if the weave requires an odd number, as in randing with cane or slewing with cane or willow.

The type of border, the type of handle suitable to the basket's proposed use, and the height in proportion to the whole, have also to be considered.

For the weaving, *round rods* may seem heavier than the basket requires, in this case

they may be split in half down the length with a knife, or in three if a cleave (Illus 25) is available. The pith should be removed either with knife or shave (Illus 26). The time taken to make the basket will be a bit longer, but less material will be used.

Materials. The choice of the sizes of *cane* may be helped by a simple rule:

Bottom sticks 4 or more sizes thicker than the stakes
Stakes and liners twice as thick as the wales
Wales twice as thick as the weavers
Translated into centre cane:

Bottom sticks of No 12	No 10
Stakes and liners of No 8	No 6
Wales of No 6	No 4
Weavers of No 4	No 2

A perfectly satisfactory basket can be made with wales and weavers of the same size.

The weavers must never master the stakes and no beginner should attempt to make a basket with stakes and weavers the same thickness.

In slewing with *cane* (Illus 82) it is better to use a thinner cane than for randing, unless the stakes and liners are exceptionally strong.

The overall choice will be determined by the size of the projected basket, its ultimate use and the sort of wear it is likely to get. The general rules for working *willow* are on pp 14–15.

A Round Basket

Bottom Sticks. There is no rule about numbers.

A small *willow* shopper might have a 5in (13cm) base for which cut 5 sticks 7in (18cm) long from the butts of 2–3ft (60–90cm) willows.

A small *cane* shopper might have 8 sticks 7in (18cm) long cut from No 12 cane.

Stakes. The *number* of stakes for a round basket is usually four times the number of sticks plus or minus 1, to give an uneven number.

Their *length* is determined by:

Insertion into the base	2in (5cm)
Height of finished basket, eg	8in (20cm)
Extra for any curve or flow	1in (3cm)
Border (see p 45), eg	9in (23cm)
	—
Total length	20in (51cm)

In a *cane* basket the stakes are cut exactly to size, with an inch or two extra. In a *willow* one the rods must be of the right size to have the required length without using the tips.

Weaving Materials. The amount required is a question of practical experience rather than rule. In preparing materials for a willow basket it is better to have too much than too little because of the time required for mellowing.

A study of the Recipe section (see p 50) will give a fair idea.

An Oval Basket

The design of an oval basket is more complicated than a round one. Everything depends on the base and the design of the slath. For this there are no set rules. The simplest and most usual type is the one at Illus 104.

The number of bottom sticks also determines the number of stakes and since there is always more flow at the ends than the sides, there must be more stakes at the ends. Otherwise by the time the top is reached the end stakes will be further apart than the side ones and the border

will be uneven. It will be seen that the oval slath consists of a number of short stakes having a lesser number of long ones put through them. An oval basket with wide ends should have perhaps 4 long sticks and a group of 3 short ones at either end with single ones between (Illus 16). A more upright basket should have 3 long stakes and 2 or 3 short ones in the end groups (Illus 17).

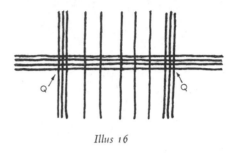

Illus 16

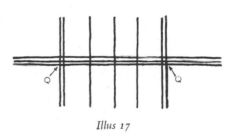

Illus 17

A base measuring 9in × 6in (23 × 15cm) will have long sticks 10½in (27cm) and short ones 7½in (19cm), allowing 1½in (4cm) to spare. To make the base illustrated in Illus 104 (without the league X), 3 long sticks and 7 short ones are needed. The *vital measurement* in making any oval base is that of the length of the slath, Q to Q in Illus 16 and 17, when the only known measurement is the final size of the base (9in × 6in, 23 × 15cm). It is obtained thus:

(a) Place the long sticks together side by side and measure them. In No 12 cane they measure ½in (1.3cm).

(b) The width of the finished base is 6in (15cm), and it is made up of 5½in (14cm) of weaving + ½in (1.3cm) as at (a).

(c) Since there will be the same amount of weaving all the way round the base, that is at the ends as well as the sides, the length of

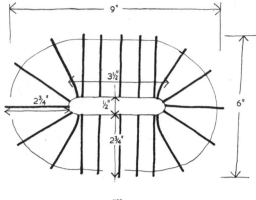

Illus 18

Any extra for curve or flow
Border

A cane basket may have liners to the stakes. If these are to be cut off before bordering they should be calculated by:

The height of the finished basket
Extra for curve or flow
1in (2.5cm) or so of spare

If they are to be used in the border, make them the same length as the stakes, less the part inserted into the base.

These stake and liner measurements would be the same for *a wooden base* with holes but an extra 3in (8cm) or more would be added for working the foot border (see p 49). For another oval base used for heavier willow see p 42.

Weaves, Handles, Colour (Decorative Weaves) and Ties and Trimmings. All these are at the designer's will and are discussed under their own headings. Fancy weaves are always shown off at their best by large areas of plain randing. A fancy band is usually offset by two or three rounds of waling above and below it. It should be remembered that an unprotected stake is always a weakness. A cane basket when it breaks will go at the place where the stakes are woven with weaker material. The ends of a trac border break off or a scalloped one come out. Fitching is weaker than solid weaving.

Proportion. Here one can only repeat the remarks made about *Shape* on p 174. The height of a narrow straight shape such as a linen basket will deceive the eye. The top should be an inch or two bigger than the bottom, or it will appear to run in.

Q–Q must be 9in, less 5½in, ie 3½in (23cm, less 14cm, i.e 9cm).

(d) The make-up of the base is shown at Illus 18.

Do not be confused by the figure 2¾in (7cm); 2¾in is half 5½in (14cm). There is 2¾in of weaving on each side and at each end.

Staking-up and the Number of Stakes and Liners (Illus 19). Again there are no hard and fast rules about staking-up an oval basket, but a simple one to remember is that the bottom sticks at the sides of the base each have 1 stake (the Xs), and those at the ends have 2, 1 on either side (the Os). Illus 19 has a total of 30 stakes.

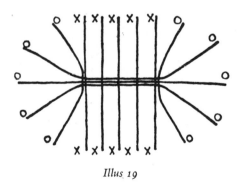

Illus 19

A boat-shaped oval will have longer stakes at the ends. A cradle, with a hood, will have longer stakes at one end. As for a round basket, the *length* of the stakes is calculated by:

Inserted part into the base
Height of the finished basket

Willow

Tools

It is possible to make a willow basket with no more than a pocket knife, but a few other tools are normally needed.

Garden shears with points will do most cutting and picking.

Bodkins (Hamlet's kind, not for threading ribbon). Two are enough and one must be heavy. The point on a scout knife is better than nothing (Illus 20).

An *Iron* with a thick and thin edge to be used for coarse or fine work. A smith could make it. If it has a ring at the end this is useful for straightening thick rods. It is used for tapping down the weaving, hammering down crams etc (Illus 21).

Illus 20

Grease Horn. Ideally a cow's horn nearly full of tallow and horse or cow's hair. Some lubricant is needed for the bodkin, driving stakes into the base or a handle bow into the sides, so a substitute could be a plastic detergent bottle cut off at the neck and half-filled with soap jelly or soft soap (Illus 22).

Weights to keep a basket still in the making. Kitchen weights, flat-irons, lead-type etc. Wrap in plastic if rusty.

A *stiff 3-ft (100cm) Rule* is an essential and can be made from dowel.

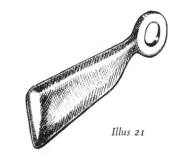

Illus 21

Block for making square bases and lids. Two pieces of close-grained wood 3ft long × 3in wide × 2½in deep (91 × 7.5 × 6.5cm). When laid side-by-side, two long carriage bolts with thumb screws are run through about 6in (15cm) from the ends. When the screws are closed the block measures 6in across × 2½in deep (15 × 6.5cm) (Illus 23).

Lap-Board A deal board about 2ft 9in × 20 or 24in wide (84 × 51 or 61cm) tilted by a strip of wood about 3in (7.5cm) deep, fixed across one end. A smaller board can be used by a worker sitting at a table (Illus 24 and 78).

Illus 22

Tank. It is essential to soak the full length of willow rods and the ideal is a galvanised iron tank about 6ft (180cm) long with a lip. Planks may be wedged under the lip to keep the rods from floating. But one may use a stream, pond or domestic bath, though half the length may

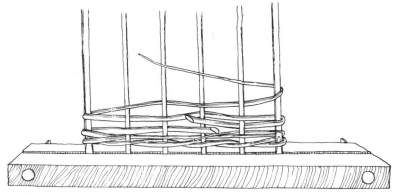

Illus 23

29

Illus 24 G. W. Scott & Sons basket workshop, London. Young apprentices sitting at the plank with the lapboard in use are making sieves. This is the standard position for making a heavy basket; a higher basket might mean sitting on the box, now behind the worker.

The bushel basket or sieve is the traditional basket that Covent Garden fruit and vegetable market porters carried piled on their heads. There were races to see who could run fastest with the greatest number. There used to be smaller sizes but the standard became 12in (30.5cm) high and 18in (46cm) diameter. The boy in the foreground is laying down the 5-behind-2 border and using the shop iron (see page 29).

Scott's was founded in 1661 and closed in 1967. Their daybooks and accounts are extant from 1704 and are preserved in County Hall Record Office, Westminster. Every sort of basket was made, from simple sieves to silver baskets for Buckingham Palace. Scott's also did much trade with the London silversmiths covering the handles of silver coffee and teapots (see page 81). This is called wickering.

After the Crimean War (1854-6) Scott's made cane frames for the bearskins of the Brigade of Guards. They invented the picnic basket in 1851 and showed it at the Great Exhibition. Until they closed they made stage properties for many London theatres and Covent Garden Opera House, and also had a considerable hand in the decorations of the Battersea Pleasure Gardens for the Festival of Britain in 1951. interpreting the designs of John Piper, Osbert Lancaster and Ursula Earle. Cane furniture was one of their specialities (*Museum of English Rural Life*)

have to soak at a time. When the wetting time is up (see p 15), the willows are mellowed.

Moulds are used in many countries to make certain curved willow baskets, though this is never done in Britain. French and Italian basketmakers use wooden ones made in three or four sections. These have an indefinite life and ensure that exact copies are made. Everyone uses hoops of heavy cane as patterns in making frame or ribbed baskets.

Cleave for splitting dry rods to make skeins. To make three clefts the cleave has three 'fins'. It is held in the right hand while the left hand guides the rod. The clefts run up through the fingers of the right hand (Illus 25).

Shave. The cleft is drawn through, pith side upwards, with the right hand, while the left hand holds it down on the far side of the blade. (A thumb guard should be worn.) First the butt end is shaved; then the cleft is turned and the rest shaved. The thickness of the skein is determined by the number of times it is taken through the shave and the adjustment of the blade by the screw (Illus 26).

Upright. When very fine and even skeins are wanted they are drawn through the twin blades, which are adjusted by the screw. The skein is held in the same way as when using the shave. An uprighted skein has no butt or tip (Illus 27).

Picking Knife. The curved tip is used for picking (Illus 28).

The tools used in *cane* basketry and shown in Illus 66–79 are used in willow work, with the exception of 68, 69, 71 and 76. Heavier shears than the pair shown at 70 are used, and a heavier iron than that at 73, but the illustrated tools will serve for fine willow work.

Working

Willows have no elasticity and where they are kinked there they will stay. That is their strength. Unlike cane, they cannot be undone and woven again. Their stiffness can be somewhat modified by careful twisting (see p 36). Stakes are rarely cut to length, the whole rod is used and the tips are cut off when the border is finished. Tips over 1ft (30cm) long should be saved and used for slewing and randing.

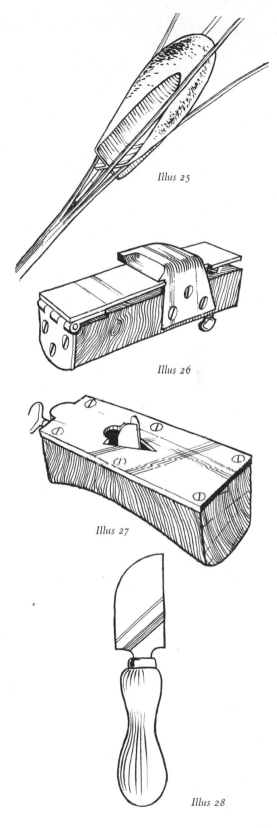

Illus 25

Illus 26

Illus 27

Illus 28

Sequence of Making a Stake-and-Strand Willow Basket

(1) A round base or bottom is made over 4 or more sticks about 2in (5cm) longer than the diameter of the basket, cut from the butts of stout rods. These are tied together with thinner rods, opened out and woven until they have the required diameter (see Bases, p 41). An oval base is made differently (see Bases), but the staking, upsetting, siding and bordering are as now described for a round basket.

(2) The ends of the sticks are then cut off and the butts of the stakes are inserted by the sides of the sticks and are then 'pricked-up' with the point of the knife or bent over its blunt edge. The belly of the rod is generally set to the outside of the basket. A ring of willow is put over the stakes to hold them in position (Illus 107). The number of the stakes is determined by the type of basket and the number of sticks; distances between them should be fairly even.

(3) The stakes are then upsett, that is, woven round with 3 rods in a wale of two or three rounds to set them up in their places to make the shape required. The most usual is: one round of 4-rod, drop one and finish with 3-rod (see Weaves, p 40).

(4) The basket is now sided with any suitable weave and shaped as it goes. When nearly high enough a top wale is worked, the border is put on and the stakes cut off.

(5) A handle is added if necessary.

(6) A round or oval lid or cover is generally made much like a base and border stakes are added when it is the right diameter. If it is to fit over the basket – a trunk cover – these stakes are turned down to make a shallow rim and then bordered (Illus 169).

Square or Rectangular Basket. This is made on the same principle except that the base is made with the sticks set in a block, thicker ones at the ends (Illus 23). The weaving begins and ends with a row of pairing, the rest being randed or slewed. There may be an even or an odd number of sticks. All ends of the weaving rods are on the underside (see Bases, p 43).

When finished the stakes are driven into the ends, pricked-up and put into a ring. Those at the sides may be scallomed on (Illus 29) or slyped and driven into holes made for them

Colour Plate 1
Sarawak plaited carrying baskets. These two bags or baskets were made by the Kenyah people of the Baram river in the interior of Sarawak, now East Malaysia, in 1952. They are not meant for heavy loads, but for little things, rather as we in the West use handbags, leaving the hands free. They are most practical, so elastic that they will hold anything from an umbrella to a water-melon.

Both are made of split cane though the complicated base of the child's one contains some very fine round cane. The larger one demonstrates in a more elaborate pattern our drawing on page 134. There is no border because the opening must be as elastic as the whole, so the long lengths of cane are taken up to the top, woven in fours over small plaited rings and down again to be woven into the base. There are no joins anywhere, both ends of each cane being firmly and invisibly hidden in the base.

Canes of the child's bag are $\frac{1}{16}$in (1.5mm) wide and the sides have a chequered pattern of black and natural which begins at the bottom with a 10-petalled flower.

Shoulder straps are complicated braids all made for adequate strength, combined with a technique which ensures their never coming undone in use. Women make these lovely things.

As it stands the larger is 16in (41cm) tall and the little one 10in (25cm) (*Jerome Dessain*)

with a bodkin along the thicker sticks of the base (Illus 109). Corner stakes may be in pairs the same thickness as the rest. Upsett and siding are as other baskets. A single much thicker corner post is not driven in but is held upright by the weaving round it. It is cut off on a level with the top wale and one or two extra stakes are driven down beside it to be worked into the border. Borders have some modifications (see Borders, p 44).

N.B. It is a bad technique to have many ends in one place and in siding a rectangular basket one should never begin or end a rod at a corner stake.

Cutting the Rods. The trimming of the ends on a willow basket is called picking. The general rule is to pick the base when it is finished, and to pick the sides when the basket is finished. A sensible rule is to cut off ends when they get in the way or are in danger of being broken off, or if they cannot be got at later. Use shears or a knife.

N.B. When picking, cut as short as you dare and slightly on the slant, but never leave an end without either a stake, stick or the rod beneath it to rest on.

A *slype* (Illus 29) is a slanting cut made with a sharp knife (in one slice if possible). It is made at

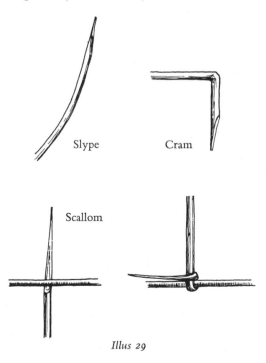

Slype   Cram

Scallom

Illus 29

Colour Plate 2
Melanu baskets from Sarawak. These plaited or woven baskets are made in quantity by the people living in the coastal areas of Sarawak, East Malaysia, from Bemban ayer (*Donax arundastratum*), a plant growing by water. Only the outer rind of the long stalks is used, and this material provides baskets and mats throughout Indonesia and Malaysia. The colours are all natural ones, and are applied mixed with resin to the dried outer surface of the stalk before it is shaved into strands.

The rims, inside and out, and the feet are made of cane – rattan – dyed in the same way. Sewing and decorating is done with fine cane, similar to that sold all over the world for caning chairs, but most of it far finer than what we see in the West.

The weave or plait begins at the centre of the bottom (see Illus 228) but it is a plain twill – over and under in twos and then dividing the twos. A little way up the sides come the patterns which would take a book in themselves to describe and draw.

This fine and delicate basketry can be matched in Guyana, on the north-east coast of the South American continent, where the cassava baskets made by the Amerindians are remarkably similar in pattern and finish (*Jerome Dessain*)

Colour Plate 3
Rush baskets (see recipes on pages 113 and 114)

Illus 30 A workbasket of skeined buff willow made by Miss F. N. Hyde of Worcester, England, who comes from an old basketmaking family. It shows that fine willow work is not too heavy for women's hands if they have the skill. The side has a 4-rod upsett and 3 rounds of 3-rod wale and afterwards is randed with skein and finished with a 5-pair plait (see Illus 130–5). The lid sticks are tied at the centre with the pattern shown in Illus 100 and the stroke on the lid is rib-randing first with skein and then with round rods and a simple border. There is probably a ledge (Illus 158) inside for it to rest on (*CoSIRA*)

---

various times, eg when putting the butt of a stake into a base, and the back of the rod is cut; when putting a handle bow into a basket; when 'cramming-down' during bordering and some-times when weaving – meaning turning the slyped end of a rod at a right-angle and knocking it down by a stake.

A *scallom* (Illus 29) is a long slanting cut made on the back of a butt to make a tongue. The rod is a stake if turned round the frame or square base stick, or may act as a stick. Its length depends on the travel. It may be 6 or 8in (15 or 20cm) long. The tip will always be held by the next scallom and may be held by a second and third as well (see also Illus 105).

Twisting. It is essential to know how to twist a willow rod or withy, which must be of good quality, damp and mellow. The butt must already be firmly fixed in the work, so that both hands are free.

The left hand holds the rod upright while the right thumb and first finger grip the tip, giving it a little twist from left to right. The rod is then twisted by making a cranking movement with the right hand and wrist. As this goes on, both hands slide down the rod until the whole length is twisted. The left hand holds while the right hand cranks. With thin withies this is quite a light movement.

If you find it easier, begin at the butt of the rod and work upwards working in exactly the same way. No illustration can give a true idea of this movement and practice will bring success. Once the twisting has been done, the withy can be left still damp, and can be tightened quite easily when the twist is to be permanent.

(above)
Illus 31 William Shelley of Salisbury, England, made this basket. It is a table basket to hold eggs or rolls or fruit, and is found all over the world in willow, as here, or cane. In England the technique is called a Madeira side, the French call it a Monaco border. It is just one of those pretty but not very strong techniques to which one can give neither source nor date (*CoSIRA*)

Illus 32 Birdcage made by Leslie Maltby in white willow. Country people in the eighteenth century used to hang such a cage by their doors and keep a blackbird or a starling to sing to them. The little platform would have a turf on it to hold worms for food.

To make it: 6½ bottom sticks, 25 stakes, 24 bye-stakes. Diameter of bottom: 10in (25cm); 4 rounds upsett, 2 fitches on the side; diameter at second fitch inside, 16in (41cm); height at second fitch 13in (33cm). 5-rod wale above second fitch; 2 fitches on the spire, and cut off some bye-stakes above the top one. Total height 24in (61cm). Make a twisted handle and bind in with the stakes with a twisted rod. Door between first and second fitches and a feeding platform above upsett. Perch across first fitch (*Museum of English Rural Life*)

Weaves

English Randing p 86 (top) Randing with willow rods is quite different in appearance from randing with long lengths of cane (Illus 80). On the side of a willow basket there should be an even number of stakes for this weave. The butts of the weavers lie inside and the tips outside. The rods are woven out to the ends of the tips and each round is made with a single rod, the tip never ending beyond the butt. The second rod will go in one stake to the right of the first and end as before, butt inside and tip outside. The third rod goes in by the next rod to the right and so on all round. The side will look odd and uneven on the way up but, by the top of the basket, it will have evened out.

The edge of the hand is used to beat the weave down lightly as it progresses, but for close randing the iron is used instead.

Illus 33 This oval shopper of brown and white willow was made by Finch of Gloucester, England. The side stakes are scallomed to the frame base, see Illus 29. The border is 5-behind-2 (*CoSIRA*)

Illus 34 and 35 Dolls' furniture. These beautifully made buff willow toys belong to Henry Rothschild of Primavera, Cambridge. In the days when basket-makers had more time and pay was better there was nothing a skilled man enjoyed more than making miniatures. Many were the children's chairs, dolls' chairs, shopping baskets and little plate baskets for dolls' houses; a few years ago you could find them among the bric-à-brac in back-street antique dealers. Now they have become museum pieces.

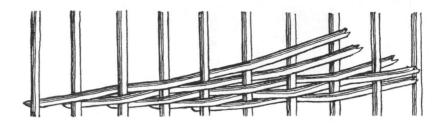

Illus 37 Kentish kibsey. A fruit-harvesting basket made for the fruit farmers of Kent. The back is flat and has two slits so that it may be strapped round the waist, leaving both hands free. The border is 5 behind 2. The upsett and the rope handle are brown willow, the rest is white.

This size is for 2gal (9l) of cherries, and measures 10½in (27cm) diameter top, 7½in (19cm) diameter bottom. It stands 9in (23cm) high.

There are other sizes: 1gal (4.5l) for soft fruit, 2gal (9l) plain round for cherries; 3gal (13.5l) flat-backed for plums and pears, and round for the same; 6gal (27l) for apples and pears.

There are many fruit-picking baskets, but most are round with strong roped handles. All the types mentioned were being made in Canterbury by G. T. H. Nason in 1965. They were known in 1500 and the name is Kentish slang, 'kip' being a Gipsy word for basket (*Museum of English Rural Life*)

French Randing (Illus 36). In this weave there may be any number of stakes. As far as possible rods should be the same length and stoutness. Butts lie inside at the start and rods are worked out to the useful parts of the tips which also end inside. A second set may be needed to make the height. The hand is used to beat as in English randing. This stroke is not so strong.

Slewing (Illus 82). The slew needs an odd number of stakes and may be two or more rods in width. On the side of the basket the butts go to the inside and the tips to the outside. When working a slew with three rods, the first rod begins by itself and goes over one and under one with a third of its length before the second one goes in, and they are worked together one on top of another. The third goes in when a third of the length of the second one has been worked. Then all three are worked together.

The first rod to come to an end of its tip will naturally be the first one that went in, and it will be below the other two. The new rod will go in on top of the second and third rods, butt first. All new rods are joined in this way. Thus there are no gaps in the weaving (Illus 37).

Wale (Illus 85, 86). Using tapered rods the stroke begins with the tips and ends with the butts, each round of wale being completed. A further round starts in another place.

The bottom wale or upsett of a round or oval basket is usually a round of 4-rod followed by one or more rounds of 3-rod. The butts of the four rods are driven down behind the stakes into the base. This first round covers the bends of the stakes and gives the basket a firm stance. When it is completed drop one rod and cut it off and work the next round of the wale with the remaining three.

Sometimes the bottom wale on a square basket runs only halfway round and stops with

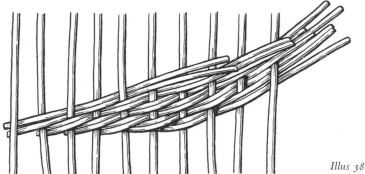

Illus 38

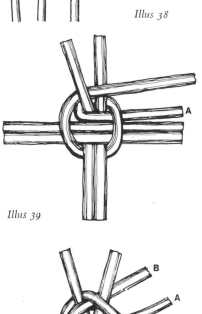

Illus 39

the long butts pointing outwards. A second wale is begun (with the tips) on the far side of the basket and, when it meets the first set of rods, they take over and go half round to the second set. In this way the lowest complete round of the upsett is fine all round and there are no gaps. This fine round may be pushed well down to cover the kinks of the pricked-up stakes.

N.B. This shows how the taper of willow rods is used to advantage.

The 4, 5, 6-rod, chain and double-chain wales (see pp 64, 65) all follow the same rules. Illus 92 does not apply to willow.

Pairing (Illus 93) is begun by doubling a rod round a stake. The reverse or fitch follows the same rule.

A French Slew (Illus 38) is worked like a French rand (Illus 36), but the rods are in pairs.

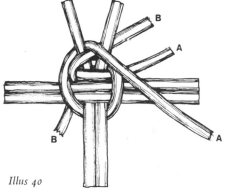

Illus 40

Bases

Round Bases. Illus 96 and 99 apply to the use of willow. The most usual strokes are pairing and slewing. The centre and opening-out is always paired, beginning with the butts of two rods which are worked out to their tips. Two more tips are joined and worked out and a further two making six rods in all. If the basket is then to be slewed an extra stake must have been provided (Illus 39, 40, 41). The final round must be paired. In heavy work the butts are slyped and driven down beside the sticks. Some fine French bases are French-randed, beginning with the tips, after the centre pairing.

Round bases should be domed to give an inverted saucer shape.

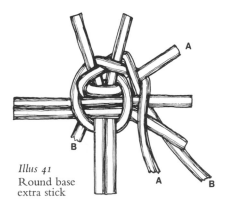

*Illus 41
Round base
extra stick*

Oval Bases. The oval base in Illus 104 may be used on fine willow baskets but without the crosses and winding, unless skeins are used. The slath should be paired using one fine rod bent near the centre. French basketmakers use this base for all oval baskets.

English basketmakers have several ways of making oval willow bases, these may vary according to the district and certainly according to the type and size of basket. The following is a simple method useful for heavier baskets. It is made flat on the ground.

Cut three sticks the width of the base plus 2 or 3in (5–8cm), from the stoutish butts of prepared willows, and slype them at one side.

Take four long pliable rods and place the butts of two of them A and B, under the left foot (Illus 42). Lift up one rod and put a stick under it with the slype upwards, about 3in (8cm) away from the butts. Lift up the second rod and put another stick under that a short distance away from the first. Lift up the first rod and put in the third stick in the same way.

Now take the second pair of long rods C

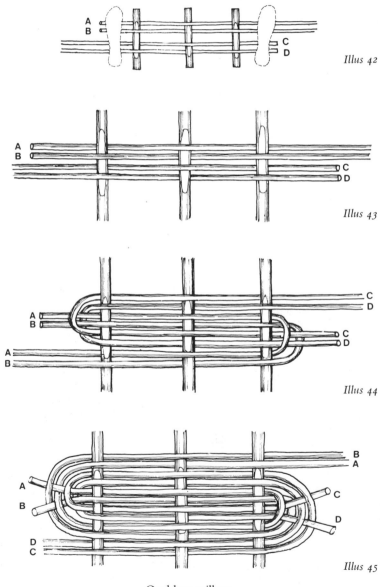

Illus 42

Illus 43

Illus 44

Illus 45

Oval base willow

and D, and, starting at the other end, work them in with the sticks in the same way, using the right foot. When this is done the construction should look like Illus 43 but closer together.

The area between the two outside sticks is called the slath and in calculating the size a good estimate is that the slath should measure half the finished base.

The second stage is to weave the first pair of rods up the sticks in the same way in front and behind, to their short ends, and go round them and down again, at the same time spreading the short ends apart. Then do the same with the second pair of rods (Illus 44).

The third stage is the same movement except that the long rods now divide the spread short ends, in this way randing all round the base (Illus 45). More rods are pieced in as needed

---

Illus 46 Bottle basket of buff and white willow made by Blackall of Chasney Bassett, Wantage, England. Baskets of this type are known as Winchesters and vary in size to suit the different trades which use them. The side is English-randed and the corners are soft. The partitions are made afterwards and tied in (CoSIRA)

and the weaving continues until the base is the required size. Many heavy bases are slewed and to do this the long rods are doubled after the end sticks have been worked over singly.

N.B. The base must be tightly made or otherwise the finished basket will sag. A crown or dome should be made by pulling up the ends of the sticks a little.

A stronger base can be made by doubling the sticks and setting them in pairs. If the ends of the basket are to have more flow, and therefore need more stakes, separate the sticks of the end pairs. This will give four radials instead of two.

Square or rectangular is the easiest of the willow bases though a square basket is the most difficult to make. It needs four or more sticks about 2in (5cm) longer than the finished bottom, two of which are thicker. One end is slyped and set into the block (Illus 23).

The number of sticks is determined by the spacing between the stakes all round the basket. To get the odd number for a slewed basket it may be better to double-stake one stick.

The first and last lines on a square base are always paired, the rest may be plain-randed or slewed. Begin by bending the middle of a rod round an outside stick, pair across and bring the butt round the outside stick and inside to lie

against the next one. Rand or slew with the tip going across and back again, joining butts to tips and letting all ends lie on the inside, ie away from you, and always against one of the middle sticks. This will be the bottom side. After the final pairing take the last butt round the end stick, slype and cram it down by the last-but-one stick. Cut off the ends when the base is finished.

N.B. The beginner's base will tend to get narrower at the top, particularly when slewing. This must be corrected by setting the outside sticks slightly outwards and holding firmly as the rod is turned round them.

Staking-up

Oval Baskets. There are many different ways of staking-up oval willow baskets. A study of actual baskets is helpful and interesting. A usual way is for stakes to be put in one on either side of the sticks at the ends and two to each pair of sticks at the sides unless long rods (leagues) have been used. These serve as stakes. If the basket is to have a handle there must be a central stake at each side – or end. If an extra stake is wanted to make an uneven number it will probably go in at one shoulder.

Square or Rectangular Baskets. There are two ways of doing these:

(1) The end stakes are slyped on the back, put down by the sticks and pricked-up. At the sides, holes are made with the bodkin (using the grease horn first) driven into the outside sticks of the base at an angle of 45° and the slyped ends of the stakes pushed in, pricked-up and hammered home with the iron.

(2) The stakes go into the ends as in (1). Some authorities consider it easier to scallom the side stakes on to the outside sticks (see p 36). Be sure that the scallom is cut long enough to be held by the next two. On reaching the left-hand end lay the last two scalloms behind and in front of the end stakes.

Corners may be 'soft', ie having two stakes the same stoutness as the rest (Illus 46), or true square, having a single much thicker rod which will not be worked into the border and which may act as a foot for the basket to stand on. It is held in position by wale and siding.

Borders

Tracs (Illus 113 and 114). The finish requires care. The rods should be slightly twisted to stop them from cracking and kinked about ¾in (2cm) above the wale. About 6in (15cm) of standing stake, cut before working, is needed for Illus 14 if stakes are 1in (2.5cm) apart.

Three-rod Plain (Illus 117–20). It is usual to cram down A, B and C instead of working them through. They are kinked at a point just to the left of the next stake and slyped for about 1in (2.5cm) below the kink. This short slyped end is inserted into the weave to the left and beside the stake and tapped down with the iron (Illus 29).

Three-rod Plain with a Back-trac (Illus 122). This may be done on a fine willow basket.

Four-rod Plain (Illus 123). It may also be worked by bringing down four stakes behind two before the first one goes in front of three and behind one. Stakes are kinked about ½in (1.3cm) up. The working is in other respects the same as Illus 117–20, ending with cramming down (see p 35); 5- and 6-rod may also be worked.

Bordering a Square Basket. But the bordering of the corners of a square basket needs some modification if the corners are 'soft', ie have two corner stakes (Illus 47). When the front pair is behind the first of the two corner stakes, F and G, bring the next one to come forward in front of 3 and behind the two corner stakes and leave it, 5. Then (Illus 48) kink the next two standing stakes, D and E and bring them down together as a pair, between the two corner stakes. Cut off E, it goes no further. Bring the next one A forward in front of 3 and behind one (G, the second corner stake) and bend and twist the first corner stake F down with it (Illus 49). The next one B to come forward will go in front of 3 and behind one (Illus 50). It has no stake down with it but counts as a pair.

Bring the next one C, forward in front of 3 and behind one and the second corner stake down with it (behind 2). Do this again with D (Illus 51). There are now four pairs again as there should be. The second of them is the single one B that counts as a pair. A distinct kink should be made as each rod goes round the corner stakes.

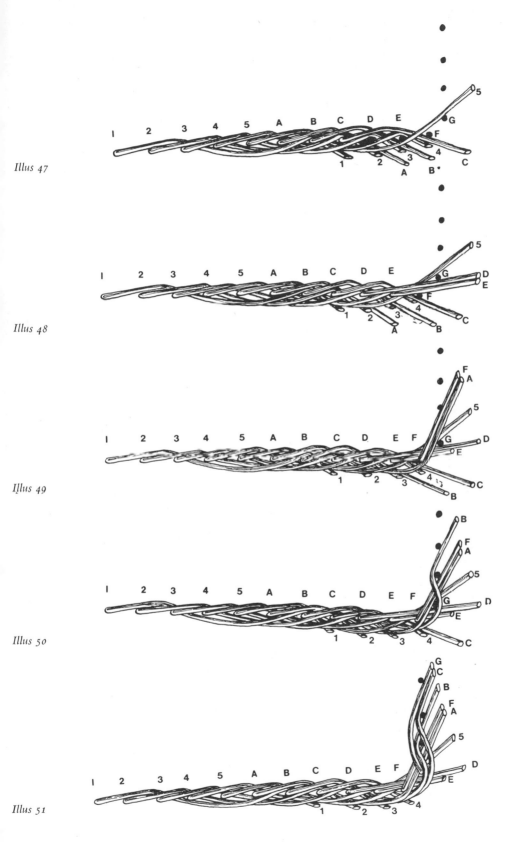

Illus 47

Illus 48

Illus 49

Illus 50

Illus 51

Should the basket have a single thick corner stake not intended to be woven into the border, it is cut off level with the work and two stakes are slyped and pushed down into the wale on either side of it. The above corner is then worked and covers the stump.

Three-pair Plait (Illus 124–8). This border worked in willow will retain the three extra stakes, so Illus 129 does not apply. Instead of threading away the last three long ends it is easier to cut, slype, kink, and cram them down by the appropriate stakes.

Madeira Border (Illus 136 and 137) is seldom used now on willow baskets, but was used on wicker chairs.

Handles

Rope or Twisted Handle (Illus 52). A bow and 8 well-mellowed rods are needed. Put the butts of three rods down by one end of the bow to its left, and one rod to its right. Bring this last one round the back of the bow to join the others and take all, lying flat, over to the right, round and under; go once over the side, once over the top, once over the side and down with the other end of the bow, and leave them.

N.B. This sounds easy but requires great care that the willows do not twist or kink.

The other four rods are put in at the far side and fill the spaces left by the first four (Illus 53). Take three rods only through to the left side of the bow, under border and wale to the inside bringing them out again on the same side, round the bow to the front and down under the start from left to right. Cut off on the slant and cut the fourth rod with them. For clarity the drawing shows only the first set of four rods in position.

To hold the handle while it dries a tie may be put across the inside of the basket from border to border. If a twisted rod is used the twist should go the opposite way to the twist of the handle.

Another Rope Handle. This is suitable for a stronger basket as it uses a thicker bow and thicker rods.

The bow is driven well down on either side of the basket. Four rods are needed for the rope, these are 5–6ft (1.5–1.8m) rods. Two are slyped and driven well down by the left of the

Illus 52

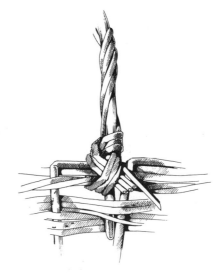

Illus 53

bow. They are then taken together and twisted over and round the bow three times. At the far side they go through below the border and are twisted over and back to their own side again and left.

The second pair are driven in at the opposite side and twisted over and back in exactly the same way, and the ends of the first pair are held under the loop they make as they come through and back again.

Illus 54 Garden basket. Graceful and pretty though this willow basket is, it is intended for hard use. The foundation is of wooden slats or spales, with bottom and side in one. Eight bye-stakes have been added on the way up the side to keep the distances between the spales even. A rim is sewn on with wire. The cross handle is twisted over a bow and a small twisted handle (see above) is worked at one end for using the basket as a scoop for vegetables and fruit (*CoSIRA*)

N.B. Care must be taken to keep the rope in sequence and not to cross the pairs over each other, nor to kink them.

When the second pair return to their own side they are pulled through the loop made by the first pair and cut off.

This handle is complete in itself but for extra strength and long wear it may have a tie as shown in Illus 60 at either side, made thus:

Push the butt of a flexible rod down by the bow and twist it on itself (p 36). Wind it tightly six or eight times up the roped handle. Take the last wind but one through two of the rope twists on the inside of the handle using the bodkin, and bring the rod round again through the same place. Pull tight and cut the end off short.

Small Twisted Handle Made from One Rod. A stout smooth rod 4ft 6in (137cm) is needed. Slype the butt and put it down by a stake.

(left)

Illus 55 Malt skip, once used for shovelling barley during brewing. This one was made by the late William Shelley of Salisbury. Like the garden basket in Illus 54, this is made on a foundation of ash spelks. One side has been pulled out to make a lip, 8 extra bye-stakes being added. There is no border but a cane hoop has been lapped on with skeined willow and over the pulled side is a tinned iron lip sewn on with wire. There are two twisted handles below the rim. It measures 19in × 17in (48 × 43cm) at the mouth, and is 11½in (29cm) deep *(Museum of English Rural Life)*

(below)

Illus 56 A skeined buff willow tray made by William Shelley of Salisbury. It is rib-randed, the side being a 5-pair plait; twisted handles. This is not an old idea, and seems to have occurred to willow workers throughout Europe during the present century *(Primavera Ltd, Cambridge)*

Twist the whole rod (see p 36) and then put the tip through under the border and pull it until it makes an arc the size of the handle, from outside to inside. Bring it forward again over the border and twist it round the arc from left to right three times and take it through on the right of the slyped end, out again and twist it back to the other end. Draw the tip through under the turn and cut it off. The twist of the rod itself must be maintained as you make the handle (see front handle in Illus 54.)

Double Twisted Handle Made with Two Rods. This is made with two 5–6ft (1.5–1.8m) rods and is worked on the opposite side of the basket which is held between the knees. The larger of the two rods A is slyped and inserted to the left of one stake and B, the smaller of the two, by a stake the distance away that is equal to the diameter of the finished handle.

A is then drawn through, *untwisted*, under the border and to the right beyond B's stake, from the outside to the inside, and left. This makes the bow of the handle.

B rod is now twisted on itself (p 36), and two or three turns are made with it round the bow (A) going to the left, starting from inside to outside. Take it through under the border and then twist it back again, laying it closely by the side of its first twist. This is repeated back again and B is now left on the inside having done its work.

The long end of A is now twisted on itself and then twisted across and over the bow. As A comes through the border, B is held firmly between it and the bow and is afterwards cut off here. A is twisted back again once or, if the bow is not covered, a third time, and then pulled through the loops to the left and cut off (Illus 55 and 56).

Such handles on heavy baskets are often made with Kubu cane

Lapped and Listed Handle. This handle, shown at Illus 141, is also suitable for fine willow baskets.

Making a Foot
Working a foot on a willow basket is done by turning the finished basket upside down. Insert the thicker ends of rods cut off the border by the side of the stakes, and work a simple border

such as 3 behind 2. Two rounds of wale before bordering will make the foot higher.

Illus 57 Basket from Egmond-aan-Zee, north of Amsterdam, Holland. This is called a *draagmand*, a 'carrying basket', by the fishermen of this village by the dunes, who carried it on their backs for selling fish and for beachcombing until 1945 at least. The farmers, on the east of the dunes, call it a *kriel*. So we have the English words 'maund', generally a basket of this shape, and 'creel' which may be of many shapes and techniques.

There were three sizes of this basket and the smallest was used for selling blackberries picked on the dunes by the women. They were made of brown and white willow by basketmakers in the nearby town of Alkmaar. The photograph shows a strong oval bottom and an exceptionally good foot.

Few baskets are made in Holland today but their tradition embraces the finest willow work, as one can see by looking at Dutch paintings, particularly those of the seventeenth century – by Vermeer of Delft and Gerard Dou for instance.

A Dutch willow cradle for the first Pilgrim baby, Peregrine White, crossed the Atlantic in the *Mayflower* and may still be seen in the museum at Plymouth, Mass. It was probably first used as a trunk (*Mevrouw Pot van Regteren Altena*).

Recipes

CHERRY BASKET (Illus 58)
(White Willow)

Simple baskets like this used to be sold full of
fruit and were non-returnable. Its capacity is
1½–2lb (0.7–0.9kg).
Material:
White willow
Measurements:
Depth: 6½in (16.5cm)
Width bottom: 5½in (14cm)
Width top: 6in (15cm)
5½ bottom sticks, 7 stakes, 6½ cover sticks
Method:
Slewed bottom, sides and cover.
2 rounds upsett starting with the butts.
Border 3 behind 1 (Illus 117–19).
The cover has no border, and the final round is
pairing; randed at the centre.
Handle, twist of 3, no bow. It goes through the
cover at one side.

Without the cover this would make a small
wastepaper basket.

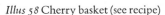

Illus 58 Cherry basket (see recipe)

Colour Plate 4
Somerset willybutt. This is a strong all-purpose
basket for farm and garden, made of three colours of
willow – white, brown and buff. The buff is known as
'harvest buff' (see p 13). This use of colour is not
arbitrary but traditional and, if the basket were made
otherwise, should not have this name.
To make it:
7½ bottom sticks, 29 stakes, white.
Diameter of bottom inside: 13in (33cm).
Bottom slewed with white.
Upsett buff: 1 round 4-rod and 3 rounds 3-rod.
Sides slewed buff up to 12in (30.5cm), then 3 rounds
slewed brown; 3 rounds slewed white and one round
pairing.
Border: 4 behind 2, tied on either side with a twisted
white rod.
Diameter of the top inside: 17in (43cm).
Height inside: 16in (41cm).
Two small white twisted handles are upright on the
border (*Jerome Dessain*)

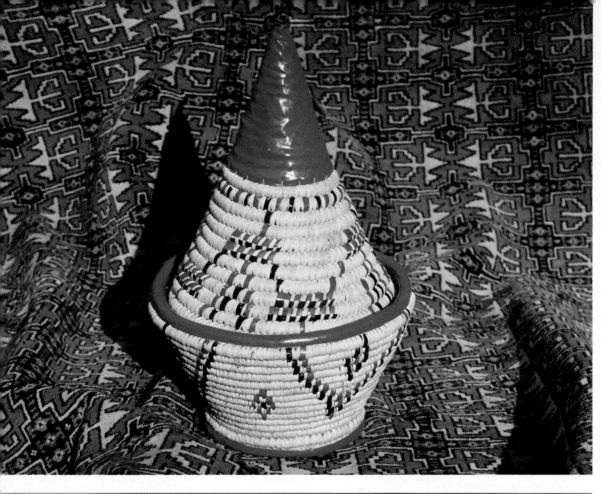

Colour Plate 5
Coiled basket for storing flour, Tangier. Bought in a street market in Tangier, these traditional Arab baskets are sold for the storage of flour. The coloured top to the conical lid and the bindings on the basket itself were once made of leather, now they are plastic, and strips of coloured polythene are woven in with the coiled palm for decoration. Height 22in (56cm) (*Jerome Dessain*)

Colour Plate 6
Chinese twined workbaskets. These baskets are included in the hope that our Western eyes may be newly opened to appreciate them. They are made in China and sold all over the world for ridiculously low prices; we are so used to them that we do not really look at them at all. Yet they are beautifully made and finished and the technique is the oldest, the same as that of the Indian baskets of the north-western seaboard of America which are now so highly valued by collectors.

There is of course no real comparison – the Chinese baskets are not made to last, and the merest fraction of making-time was expended on them. The material from which they are made is plentiful and needs little preparation. We can be sure too that no status, and only the barest living, is enjoyed by the countless basketmakers in the vast population of China.

These are made of a fine rush which is considerably thicker than the straw, and of course very much thicker than the fine spruce roots used in the Tlingit basket (Illus 235). The 'spider' base is used but the centre is decorated. The borders are treble tracs with the ends outside.

The gold pair (see colour illustration on p 85) are the more closely woven of straw, and the base and lid stakes are tied together at the centre much like the 'spider' base in English rushwork (p 108). The borders are a double trac, over one, with ends inside (p 72) (*Jerome Dessain*)

SQUARE SHOPPER OF BUFF WILLOW (Illus 59)

Materials:
Some 6–7ft (2m) buff willows
6 sticks 12in (30cm), 2 of these are thicker for the outside of the base.
1 handle bow
Base:
Set the sticks evenly in the block with the outside ones 7in (18cm) apart (outside measurement).
One round pairing then rand until 11in (28cm) high.
Complete with 1 round of pairing.
Sides:
31 stakes: 2 at each corner, 5 at one end and 4 at the other between them, and 7 at each side.
Side stakes may be driven in (Illus 109) or scallomed on (Illus 33 and 105) to give a centre stake at each side.
Upsett with 4 rounds 3-rod wale (Illus 85 and p 40), beginning with the tips.
   Slew until 5½in (14cm) high and then work 1 round 3-rod wale.
Border:
Before bordering beat down the corners well.

This will give a slight lift to the centres of the sides. The border is 3 behind 2, with soft corners (Illus 47–51).
Handle:
Side to side, roped (Illus 52 and 53).
Measurements:
Inside bottom: 11 × 7in (28 × 18cm)
Inside top: 13½ × 9½in (34 × 24cm)
Height: 7in (18cm)
Height to top of handle: 11in (28cm)

Illus 59 Square shopper (see recipe)

OVAL GARDEN OR AGRICULTURAL BASKET
(White Willow Illus 60)

This is a strong basket made of stout rods and should not be undertaken by anyone without strong hands and some knowledge of the craft (see p 31).

Materials:
7–8ft (2.20–2.50m) white or buff willows, prepared
3 pairs of sticks.
1 handle bow.

Base:
This is made by the method described on pages 42 and 43 and in Illus 42–5. It is randed. When finished the base measures 12 × 9in (30.5 × 23cm), and the end pairs of sticks are 5in (12.5cm) apart, and are separated to give 4 radials at each end.

Sides:
28 stakes, 2 on either side of each stick.
Upsett with one round of 5-rod wale. To begin this the butts of the 5 rods are crammed down beside the sticks and when the round is finished 2 are crammed down and the other 3 continue to work 3 rounds of 3-rod wale.

The measurements will show that the basket has a considerable flow at the ends and some at the middle. It is English-randed (p 38) until 5in (12.5cm) high, but the 2 middle stakes at either side are treated as one. This allows room for the ends of the handle bow.
2 rounds of 3-rod wale complete it.

Border:
5-behind-2 (in front of 5 and behind 2). It is begun at one side.

Handle:
The bow goes down to the bottom of the randing.
Work the second rope handle on page 46. The twisted ties may be omitted.
The border may be further strengthened by twisted ties over each end.

Measurements:
Base of finished basket: 13 × 10in
  (33 × 25.5cm)
Top of basket inside: 16 × 12in (41 × 30.5cm)
Top of basket outside: 18½ × 14½ (47 × 37 cm)
Height inside: 6in (15cm)
Height to top of handle: 12in (30.5cm)

Illus 60 Oval garden or agricultural basket (see recipe)

For other illustrations of stake-and-strand willow work see Illus 61–5 and the colour illustration on p 86. The colour illustration on p 103 shows a Chinese bamboo basket in stake-and-strand technique.

Illus 61 The 'Stanley' cycle crate. The advent of the bicycle was a minor revolution, it meant that people, previously unable to travel, became mobile. Some took their machines by train, so cycle crates were developed, some to take a single bicycle, others to take half a dozen or more. The Stanley Cycle Crate, made by the great firm of Scott, was obviously all that a cycle crate should be.

Even the early motor car sometimes used basketry in its construction following the tradition of the horse-drawn governess cart and the light carriages of the early nineteenth century which had panels of cane-work for lightness and ornament, later to be imitated in cane and veneer. Special baskets were made to be strapped to the sides of the early motor car. What these baskets held the catalogues do not tell us – elaborate fittings for picnics, or wine and cigars? Or merely tools? (*Author's Collection*)

Illus 62 A buff willow cat basket from Somerset. This is a standard shape for both cats and dogs, though there are different sizes. This one has diameter of top 18in (46cm), height of back 7in (18cm), height at front 5in (13cm). Bottom and side below the notch (see p 87) are slewed; randed above (*CoSIRA*)

Illus 63 This buff willow cradle is a Government basket and may only be reproduced by permission of the Controller, HM Stationery Office, Crown copyright reserved. It is made to specification for the use of Service personnel.

It is a fine example of fitching, and the measurements are: bottom $26\frac{1}{2} \times 14$in (67×36cm), top 33×18in (84×46cm), height of head $14\frac{1}{2}$in (37cm), height of foot 12in (30cm) (HMSO)

(*below*)
Illus 65 French white willow baskets. The teaching of willow basketry and furniture-making in France is now in the hands of the National School of Basket-making and Osier Growing at Fayl-Billot in the Department of Haute Marne, under the Ministry of Agriculture, and anyone who has taken the full 3-year course there is a true professional. Three of the professors who teach there have written an excellent 2-volume manual *La Vannerie* (see Duchesne in the bibliography), unfortunately only available in French. The baskets illustrated are all made by men trained at the school.

The basket on the left is called a *panier ovale à jour*, literally an oval openwork or, as we would say, fitched basket. It has a base of wooden slats tied to a rim to which are scallomed the stakes (see p 35). There are two fitches, the top one has two rounds of 4-rod wale worked in front of 2 and behind 2 so that it is the same on both sides, followed by a border in front of 4 and behind 2. It has a heavy bow covered by a twist or rope. The measurements are: bottom $11\frac{3}{4} \times 6\frac{3}{4}$in (30 × 17cm), height $6\frac{3}{4}$in (17cm), top inside $14\frac{1}{2} \times 9\frac{1}{2}$in (37 × 24cm). It came from the co-

operative at Bussières-les-Belmonts near Fayl-Billot, which specialises in openwork or fitching.

The large shopping basket on the right is a *vendéen* and is made on a 5-piece wooden mould. There are several variations of this basket and this one has a roped or corded border and handle. It is found mostly in the west of France – La Vendée – where it undoubtedly originated. The bottom is made of round rods but the side is skeined. It is very strong and does well for collecting windfall apples. Its measurements are: bottom $9\frac{1}{2} \times 6$in (24×15cm); top inside $13\frac{1}{2} \times 9\frac{1}{2}$in ($34 \times 24$cm); height at ends 11in (28cm), at centre $8\frac{1}{4}$in (21cm); height to top of handle 17in (43cm).

The tray leaning against the *vendéen* is a *volette de patissier*, much used by pastrycook shops in France and also for cakes and rolls on the domestic table. The cross rods are scallomed on to the rim at both sides and a line of fitching goes across the centre. The diameter may be anything from 8–20in (20 to 50cm). Larger sizes have two or more fitches. This one came from Bussières in 1976; its diameter is 12in (30cm).

The two table mats look simple enough, but are beautifully made. Their diameter is $8\frac{1}{2}$in (22cm). There are 8 sticks, paired in fours three times and in twos once. 16 fine rods French-rand the mat, beginning at their tips. Border stakes are put down, one to each stick, and a 3-rod plain border is worked on the wrong side. These also came from the co-operative at Bussières.

The round basket at the front has no particular name and is not in *La Vannerie*. It was made for the co-operative at Bussières, and is a basket for the table. It could no doubt be made in smaller sizes; this one has a diameter of $11\frac{3}{4}$in (30cm) and a depth inside of $2\frac{3}{4}$in (7cm). The bottom is slightly domed. There are 8 sticks, paired over until the diameter is $2\frac{3}{4}$in (7cm). The bottom is completed by French randing beginning with the butts of the rods and 1 round of pairing. The stakes are butts split in half with the round side facing inwards, and 8 rounds of 3-rod wale over them. The stakes are then bent over sharply and the ends are pushed back into the base with the first ends.

Another basket co-operative society is centered at Villaines-les-Rochers, in Indre-et-Loire 1 mile (2km) from the town of Azay-le-Rideau. This supplies dealers in the Loire valley. The work here is also varied and excellent, but visitors to Villaines, where the 120 workers have their workshops in limestone caves, should avoid grape-harvest time as this has priority over basketmaking (*Author's Collection*)

Cane

The grades and sizes of cane, and the preparation for working will be found on pp 16–17.

Many of the weaves and some of the methods of construction used for cane or willow and shown here are common to basket types other than stake-and-strand. Such techniques are not described or illustrated a second time elsewhere but references are made to this section.

A few of the cane recipes at the end of this section use some willow in their making but only for sticks, stakes and liners and not in weaving.

Tools

The minimum essentials are marked ★

★*Long Bodkin* for the insertion of handles (Illus 66).

Medium Bodkin for working borders, insertion of stakes etc (Illus 67).

Fine Bodkin for fine work. The bodkin is in constant use and saves time and work (Illus 68).

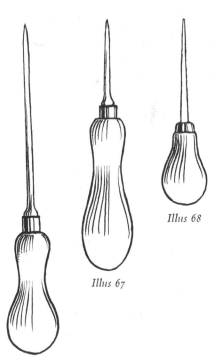

Illus 68

Illus 67

Illus 66

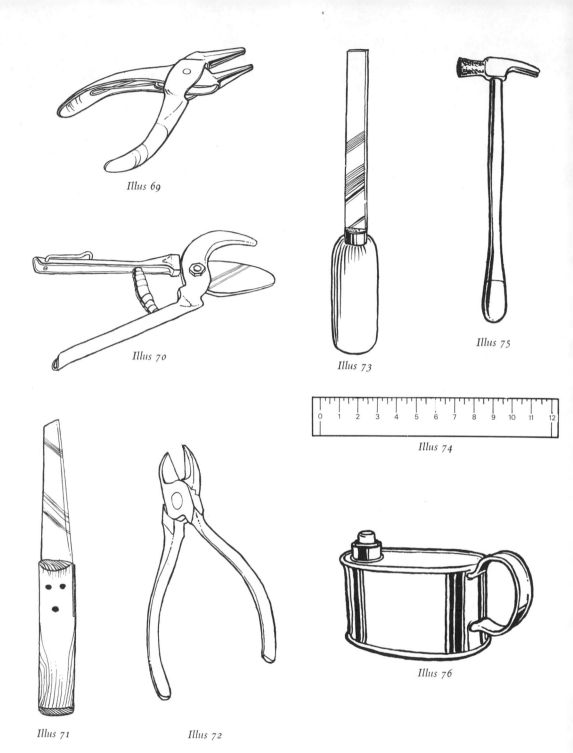

Illus 69

Illus 70

Illus 73

Illus 75

Illus 74

Illus 71

Illus 72

Illus 76

Round-nosed Pliers for squeezing canes so that they may bend at an angle without cracking (Illus 69).

Secateurs for cutting handle and heavier cane (Illus 70).

Knife for slyping (Illus 71).

Sidecutters for all general cutting and picking (Illus 72).

Rapping Iron for tapping down weaving to keep it even (Illus 73).

60

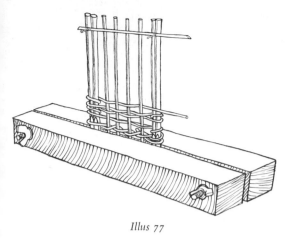

Illus 77

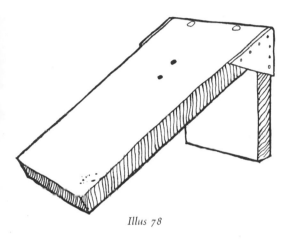

Illus 78

Illus 79

Hammer for use in nailing handles, frames etc (Illus 75).

Ruler for constant checking during work. A flexible steel rule is also useful (Illus 74).

Cane Spirit Lamp for singeing off the hairs on a cane basket after completion (Illus 76).

Screw Block, the foundation in making a rectangular base or lid (Illus 77).

Workboard (Illus 78). The basket is pinned to it with a *Bradawl* (Illus 79), and revolves in work (see *Weights*, below).

Extras:

Long-nosed Pliers will hold an end that fingers cannot reach, and are also useful in nailing.

Assorted Basketry Nails may be obtained in ¼lb packets of mixed sizes. Used in making frames and in nailing two or more handle bows together before lapping.

Weights. Where a workboard is unobtainable or unsuitable, a 1 or 2lb weight, an old hammer-head or even half a brick or a screw-top jar of water will steady a basket on the table.

Clothes Pegs are a great help, particularly to the disabled, as a 'third hand', when starting a large wale or as a guide to a starting place or one to be watched.

Jam Jar. It is helpful to rib-rand (Illus 84) a lid on the top of a jam jar. A good dome may be made and the lid swings round fast in weaving.

Sellotape is a useful tie for fine work but will not hold on wet material.

Sharpening Stone for knives.

Soft Soap or *Tallow*. The bodkin is dipped in this before making a place for a handle, or being inserted into a rectangular base when staking-up.

String. May help an amateur to tie stakes in position or mark a place to be watched.

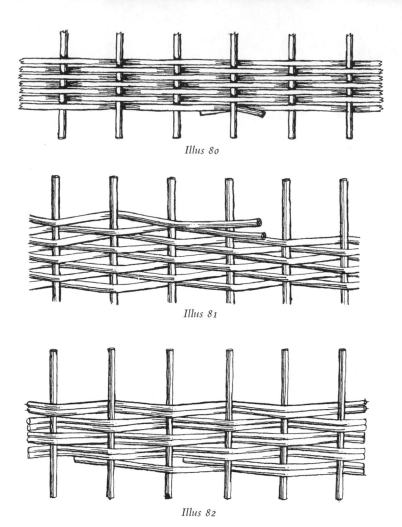

Illus 80

Illus 81

Illus 82

Illus 83

Weaves

Randing (Illus 80). To join cane, the old and new weavers lie behind the same stake. (When randing with willow the butt of a rod is laid between two stakes and worked over and under to its top. The next rod is laid in between the next stakes to the right and worked the same).

Randing with two weavers when there is an even number of stakes (Illus 81). Sometimes called chasing.

Slewing (Illus 82). Randing with two or more weavers together. The start and the finish are graded so that there is no gap.

Spiral Slewing (Illus 83). This needs a num-

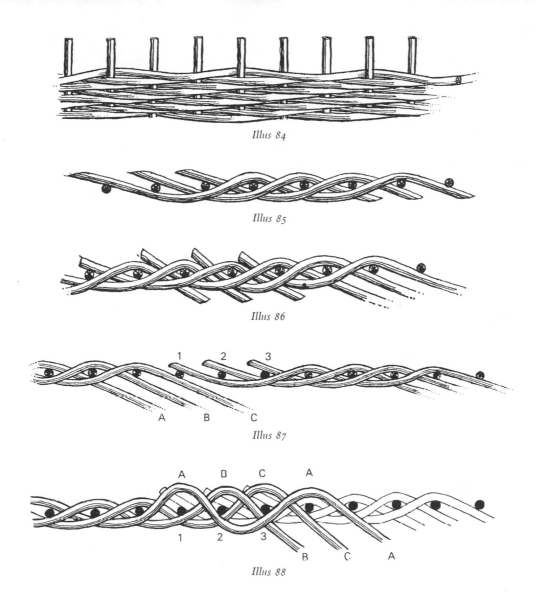

Illus 84

Illus 85

Illus 86

Illus 87

Illus 88

ber of stakes divisible by 4 plus 1. The weaving canes go as usual from left to right but over 2 and under 2. At the start of the next round they will automatically divide the pairs of the last round. (The artist has drawn some of the pairs of stakes single for clarity.)

Rib-randing (Illus 84) must be worked over a number of stakes not divisible by 3. The close weave is useful on lids. Joining is the same as for simple randing.

Three-rod Wale (Illus 85). Three weavers worked in sequence over any number of stakes. Joining-in new weavers or completing a band or single round of waling (Illus 86). In canework the canes are joined in singly as required.

Changing-the-stroke when working from one round of 3-rod wale to another, in canework. The movement is CBAA, as follows: when the leading cane C lies left of stake 1 (Illus 87) it goes in front of two stakes and behind one so that it lies between stakes 3 and 4. Then cane B is worked in front of two stakes and behind one, and then cane A the same. This completes the round. To bring A to the correct position for working the next round, it is worked again (Illus 88). The wale continues as before.

The change-of-stroke or change-over is worked every time a new round of waling is

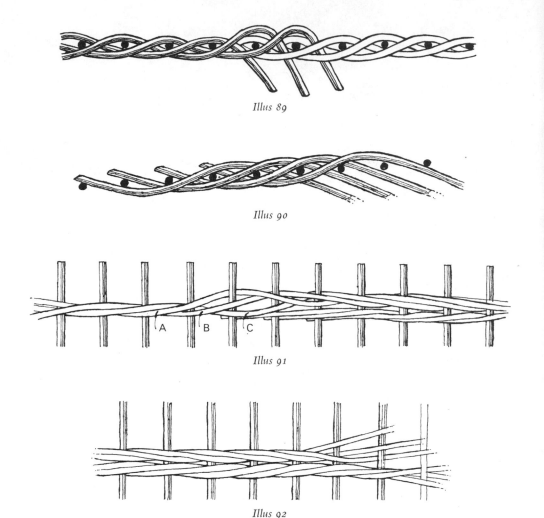

Illus 89

Illus 90

Illus 91

Illus 92

begun. Some workers mark stake 1 until they are able to recognise it.

To complete the wale before going on to another weave, the change-over is *not* worked. A, B and C are worked in normal sequence when stake 1 is reached and are either left at the back of the work or brought through to the front so that the movement is uninterrupted (Illus 89).

To change-over from a 4-rod to a 3-rod wale, work the back weaver A in front of three and cut behind one when the start is reached; it will then lie on top of weaver 1. Cut off. With the remaining three weavers work D, C, B in front of three and behind one and they will be in position to work a 3-rod wale and can be called A, B and C.

4-rod Wale (Illus 90). If four weavers are worked in front of two and behind two the weave looks like a 3-rod wale on both sides. This is useful in working strong bands of colour or on a bowl-shape where both sides are clearly visible, and is also a good weave for a base.

4-, 5- and 6-rod Wales are usually worked with four, five and six weavers, going in front of three, four and five and behind one, respectively, though it is possible to vary the stroke to serve a particular purpose.

A change-of-stroke may be used with any number of waling canes remembering that it will always begin with the leading weaver and at the first stake. The formula for a 5-rod change-over would be EDCBAA.

Chain Wale (Illus 91) consists of two rounds, one of waling and one of reversed waling.

Reversed waling is worked the same as ordinary waling except that each weaver passes under the others instead of over them.

Double Chain Wale is worked with pairs instead of single weavers, care being taken not to twist the weavers over each other.

Changing-the-Stroke from the first round to the second, in a chain wale (Illus 92). This is not difficult if one remembers that CBA belong to the first round and so are not reversed. The second A is reversed and others thereafter.

The reverse round of a chain wale is completed by taking the weavers to the inside so that they come together with those of the first round and complete the movement, ie A under B and C to the back; B under C and one and C under two.

Pairing (Illus 93) is usually begun by doubling a weaver round a stake. The join is shown.

Chain Pairing (Illus 94). Like chain waling (Illus 91), it consists of one round of pairing followed by one of reverse pairing, when the weavers are taken under and over each other instead of over and under.

Packing (Illus 95) builds up any part of a basket or base by a change in the normal line of the weaving, with one or more short turns.

Decorative Weaves

When dyed cane is used the following decorative weaves may be worked.

Pairing. One plain and one coloured weaver over an even number of stakes produces stripes. One plain and one coloured weaver over an uneven number of stakes produces a spiral.

3-rod Waling:

(1) With three weavers of different colours worked over a number of stakes divisible by the number of weavers (three), each colour will produce a vertical stripe.

(2) When the number of stakes is divisible by the number of weavers plus one, one coloured and two natural weavers will pro-

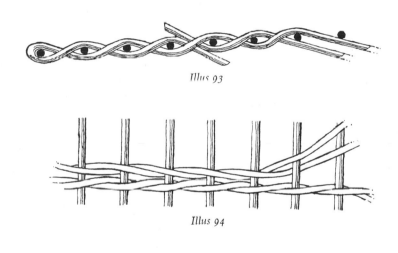

Illus 93

Illus 94

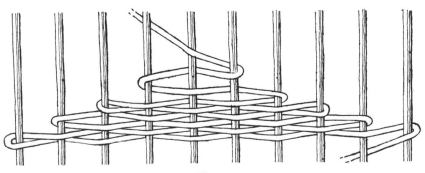

Illus 95

duce a variegated effect outside and a spiral inside the basket.

(3) When the number of stakes is divisible by the number of weavers plus two, the spiral will be outside (going to the right) and the variegation inside.

(4) To reverse the spiral at (3) and make it go to the left, cut off all three weavers, and reinsert them and wale from right to left. The coloured weaver comes out of a space where there is already a coloured one.

(5) A spiral of coloured dots is made with one coloured and two natural weavers and the stakes divisible by three. Work three rounds of wale, then let the coloured weaver and a natural one change places and work three rounds. Continue these six rounds.

N.B. The change-of-stroke would not be used in these decorative wales.

Illus 96

Bases

Round Base (Illus 96). A given number of sticks are pierced at their centres with knife or bodkin and others are put through them. If an uneven number is used, the greater goes through the lesser. These interwoven sticks are call a *slath*.

A decorative beginning to the tying of the slath (Illus 97.) A single weaver is bent at the centre.

Tying the slath with pairing (Illus 98). This is usually done twice or three times round.

Illus 97

Opening out (Illus 99). After the slath has been tied in its four parts these are divided; in the case of 4 through 4, first in twos for one round of pairing and then singly, opening the sticks out like a wheel. The base is then paired until the right size. (No decorative cross has been made as in Illus 97.)

Another decoration of the slath worked with lapping, chair cane or willow skein (Illus 100). Begin with a large cross as shown in Illus 97. Work with both ends until the interlacing looks like the diagram. It is not necessary to make diagonal crossings at the back, and the two canes will come out next to each other. Finish by tying the blocks of 4 with one round of pairing.

Another decorative slath (Illus 101) is made with a number of sticks divisible by four such

Illus 98

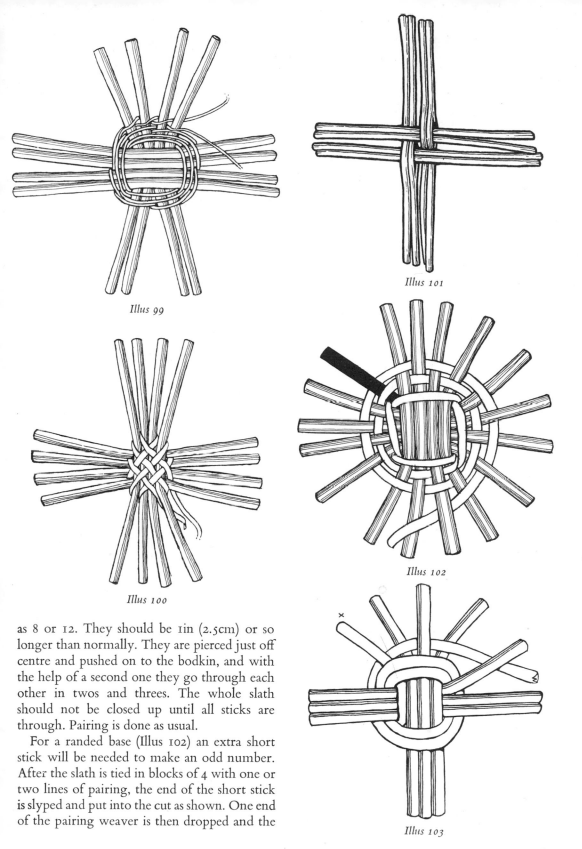

Illus 99

Illus 101

Illus 100

Illus 102

Illus 103

as 8 or 12. They should be 1in (2.5cm) or so longer than normally. They are pierced just off centre and pushed on to the bodkin, and with the help of a second one they go through each other in twos and threes. The whole slath should not be closed up until all sticks are through. Pairing is done as usual.

For a randed base (Illus 102) an extra short stick will be needed to make an odd number. After the slath is tied in blocks of 4 with one or two lines of pairing, the end of the short stick is slyped and put into the cut as shown. One end of the pairing weaver is then dropped and the

67

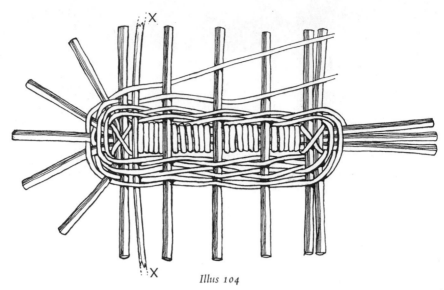

other is used to rand the slath open. The weaving cane in this case is not doubled but bent a few inches from one end.

If the bottom sticks are of fine material, do not pierce them but just lay them across each other. This shows a base where sticks and weaver are the same thickness and which will either be randed or needs an odd number of sticks (Illus 103). The unshaded stick X is the end of the weaver which is looped over to make the extra stick. This is a convenient beginning to a round basket where sticks and stakes are cut in one.

Oval Base (Illus 104). The short sticks are pierced with a knife or bodkin and the long ones put through them. The slath is then tied with a round or flat weaver, the short end being put down the slit in two canes at one end and the cross made. From this proceed to wind, crossing each stick at the back and making a cross at the other end. Here add another weaver and pair the slath twice round. Then open out the ends. This may be done by pairing or by randing with two canes, as shown in the drawing. The whole base may be paired or randed but a paired base has an inherent tendency to twist, overcome in part by reverse or fitch pairing. A randed base will not twist.

The stake X in the drawing is not essential to an oval basket. It is a *league*, ie a stake which passes right round the basket, taking the weight. To cut a league make it the same thick-

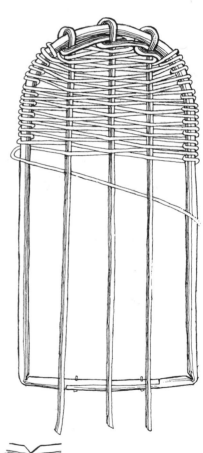

Illus 105

ness as the stakes and twice the length of the stakes plus the width of the base. It may be put through the base after weaving, using a bodkin, but is easier if added after the first round of opening out. Two leagues are usually used. It is worked into the upsetting at either side exactly like a stake.

Base or Lid on a Shaped Frame (Illus 105). The sticks are scallomed, ie thinned down to a long, flat point and taken round the frame as shown. The randed weave begins at the centre and is worked the same way as in the rectangular base. When about 1½in (4cm) away from the other end, the ends of the sticks are scallomed as before and the weaving finished. Scalloming is easier to work with willow than with cane because the rods kink and stay rigid when dry. The cutting of a right-angled corner is shown in the small drawing.

A Shaping Board (Illus 106) is an aid to making a frame. The willow rod or heavy cane is tied to it when damp and allowed to dry. The slyped overlap, as shown in Illus 105, is lightly nailed to the edge of the board. Any shape of frame may be made in this way, but the board should be slightly smaller than the finished base.

The professional worker will not need such an aid but it will be helpful to the amateur in making an exact shape.

Another method of setting cane to a given shape is to draw the outline on a plank or board and knock in small nails at intervals along it. Damp cane may then be bent round the outside of the nails and left to dry there. Damp cane wound round a broom handle will set in a spiral and keep its shape when dry.

Thicker cane, whether glossy or matt, is best bent into shape over a gas flame. It must be kept on the move or it will burn. The frames of cane furniture are made in this way but the amateur needs skill, care and practice.

For the use of a wooden base with holes, see p 78 and Illus 138.

Insertion of Stakes in Round or Oval Base. Illus 107 shows this process in a simple round or oval base, usually one stake on either side of the bottom sticks, which are first cut off closely. The stakes are then pricked-up and held together with a twisted hoop until the upsett is put on.

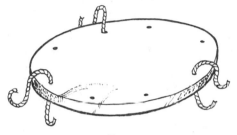

Illus 106

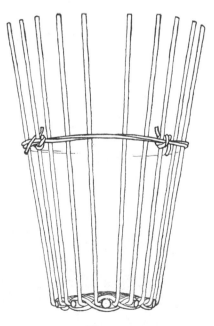

Illus 107

69

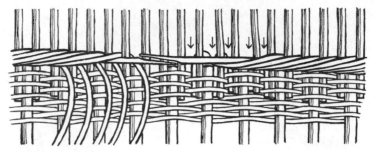

Illus 108

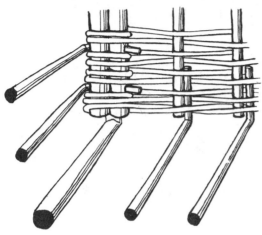

Illus 109

Upsetting. This is the most important part of any basket and determines the final shape. The first round is worked on the bottom to cover up the angles of the bent stakes and the ends of the bottom sticks, and to give the basket a firm rim to stand on. It may be a 4-, 5- or 6-rod wale. Illus 108 shows a 5-rod wale worked over a core of a slightly thicker cane which is slyped at both ends so that they will lie together. When worked on an oval base it is best to start the wale at one end so that the core joins on the curve.

The start of an upsett must be very firm. In canework the weavers should be put down into the base on the left-hand side of consecutive stakes and brought round behind them to the right. (The bottom is facing the worker.) They will then be tightly locked. This is shown by

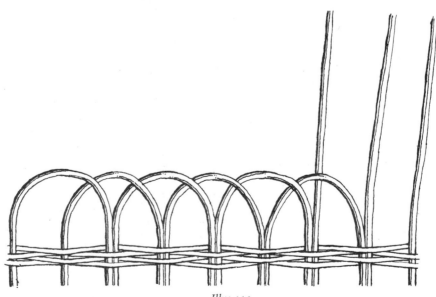

Illus 110

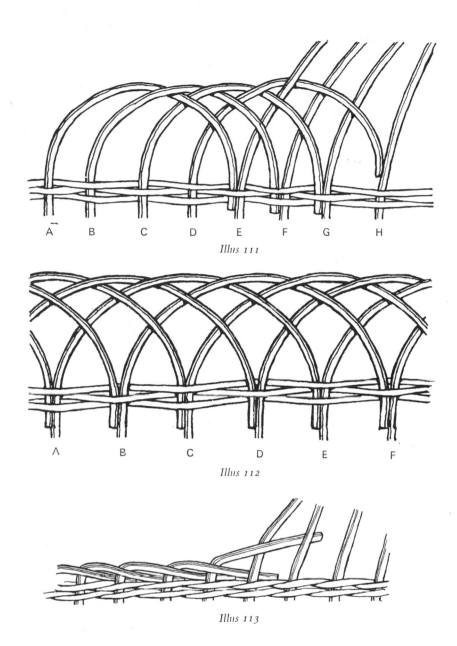

Illus 111

Illus 112

Illus 113

arrows in Illus 108. After the first round the base is set up on the table or workboard and the subsequent rounds of upsetting are worked bringing the stakes into the right position (see p 174).

Stakes into a Rectangular Woven or Frame Base. Illus 109 shows the detail of a corner post which has been slyped and the point put down by the end cane inside the weaving. A bodkin is driven at intervals into the side sticks of the base at a slight upward angle to make holes for slyped stakes.

Borders

Simple Scallop (Illus 110). The length of standing stakes required depends on the distance between them and can easily be measured with an odd piece. The ends should go well down into the weave.

Scallop (Illus 111 and 112), where A goes behind B, over C and D and down by the left of E. For length of standing stakes see last border.

Simple Trac Border (Illus 113) requires only a couple of inches of standing stake

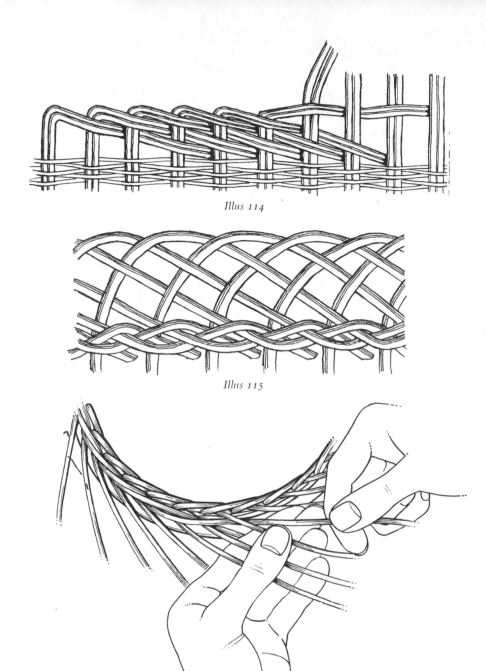

Illus 114

Illus 115

Illus 116

Trac Border Worked with Pairs of Stakes (Illus 114). In front of one, behind one, in front of one, behind one. To work this type of border hold each pair of canes at the bend with the finger and thumb of the left hand and bring them down with the right hand. This border should be tight and upright.

Composite Trac Border worked in three movements (Illus 115).

(1) Take each stake behind one, in front of one, behind one and in front. All stakes now lie on the front of the work.

(2) Take each stake behind the next all the way round. Stakes will now be pointing up-

wards to the right.

(3) Take each stake behind the next all round. Stakes will now point down and to the right. Length of standing stake is about 9in (23cm) when stakes are 1in (2.5cm) apart.

The border looks well worked in pairs and has the advantage of having the ends hidden.

There are many tracs. These are only three. Length of standing stakes will vary according to the distance they travel.

Roll Border (Illus 116). Excellent for a round or oval tray. The stakes above the wale should be 12in (30cm) long, damp but not squeezed. The first round of behind two brings the stakes down to a horizontal position and is completed. The following three rounds are tracs of over two and under one, with each round completed and held tightly against the last one in working. Note the position of the hands. The ends of the last round are hidden. If more than three tracs are required an extra 3in (7.5cm) should be allowed.

3-rod Plain Border (Illus 117–20)

Take 1 behind 2, 2 behind 3, 3 behind 4 (Illus 117).

Take 1 in front of 3 and 4, behind 5 and to the front between 5 and 6. Take 4 down with and behind it (Illus 118).

Take 2 in front of 4 and 5, behind 6 and to the front between 6 and 7. Take 5 down with and behind it. Do the same movement with 3 and 4. Continue, always taking the front cane of the left-hand pair. Short ends will be left to be cut off (Illus 119).

The finish of the border (Illus 120). After the last upright stake and its fellow have been brought down and put round and under stake 1, three pairs of stakes will be pointing to the right, and the longer ones should be called ABC. Thread them through one by one as shown, thus completing the pattern. It will be seen that they always *pass in front* of the stakes 2, 3 and 4. Help them through with the bodkin.

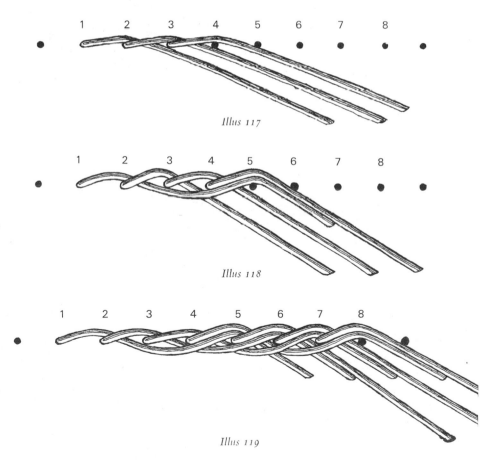

Illus 117

Illus 118

Illus 119

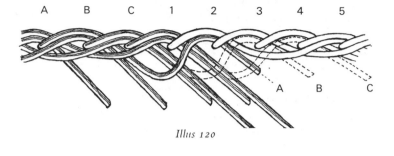

Illus 120

Illus 121

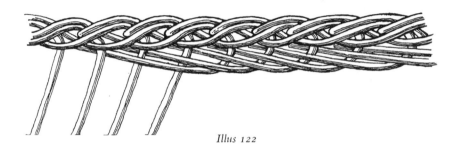

Illus 122

Illus 123

Length of standing stake when stakes are ⅝in (1.6cm) apart, as on a wooden tray base, is 5in (13cm); but when 1in (2.5cm) apart 9in (23cm).

3-rod Plain Border with Follow-on Trac (Illus 121). After the last border has been completed the ends should be 3–4in (8–10cm) long; slype them and pass each one under the next two and through to the inside between the border and the weaving, so that it rests against the third upright to the right. Standing stake length is

2–3in (5–8cm) longer than for the 3-rod border.

3-rod Plain Border with Back-Trac (Illus 122). The back-trac is worked after the border in Illus 117–20 has been completed. The ends are pointing outwards and to the right. The back-trac is worked on the far side of the basket and goes from right to left. Each stake goes over the next two and under the third. Pull tight. Standing stake length is 4–5in (10–12cm) longer than for the 3-rod plain border.

4-rod Plain Border (Illus 123). This is worked the same way as the 3-rod plain border in Illus 117–20 but the first, second, third and fourth canes are brought down and the first cane passes in front of the fifth and behind the sixth. The fifth cane is brought down with it. It needs about 12in (30.5cm) of standing stake when stakes are 1in (2.5cm) apart.

3-pair Plait (Illus 124–9). Standing stake length above the weaving when stakes are ⅝in (1.6cm) apart, as on a wooden tray base, is 6in (15cm). Three extra stakes 6in (15cm) long are required the same thickness as the stakes and a 'guide' stick about 4in (10cm) long. The 'guide'

is shown as a hairpin shape and the extra stakes unshaded.

The finish of the border is shown in Illus 128. The last two pairs are taken up and through where the 'guide' now is and the 'guide' removed. The first pair has been completed in the drawing. The last two extra stakes are in position and the long stakes have only to be brought down and through.

N.B. Many caneworkers do not use the extra stakes at all and it is perfectly possible to work the border without them, but they are essential in willow work. Illus 129 shows how the extra canes may be removed and the pairs taken

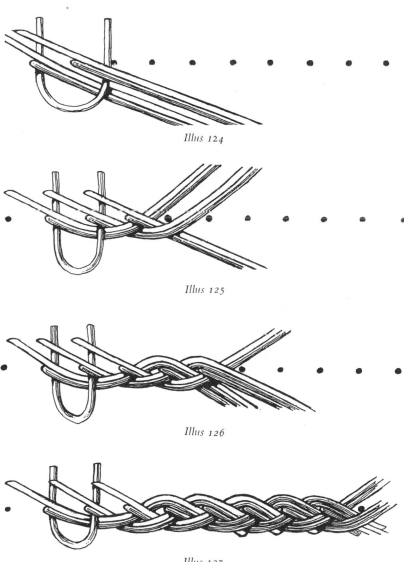

Illus 124

Illus 125

Illus 126

Illus 127

Illus 128

Illus 129

through in their places. This has been done with the first pair. The last two extra stakes are shown black and the second is in process of being removed.

5-pair Plait (Illus 130–5). Standing stakes length when stakes are ⅝in (1.6cm) apart is 9in (23cm), but a large plait on a shopping basket may take double this length or more. Five extra stakes 9in (23cm) long are needed and a 'guide' 7 or 8in (18–20cm) long, longer if the plait is larger.

Sec 3-pair plait (p 75) for the method. Illus 135 gives the alternative finish.

Plait on side of basket. For this the standing stakes should be 2 or 3in (5–8cm) longer, and are squeezed or pricked and brought down behind two all the way round. They will then be at right angles to the basket and the plait is worked with the basket held on its side.

4-pair Plait. This is worked like the other two but with four extra stakes. It begins as in Illus 130 and continues as in Illus 131 except that, instead of laying in the fifth extra, the first pair are brought down to make the first three-down. The border proceeds with three working pairs at the bottom and one at the top.

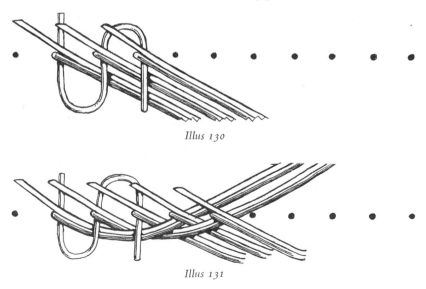

Illus 130

Illus 131

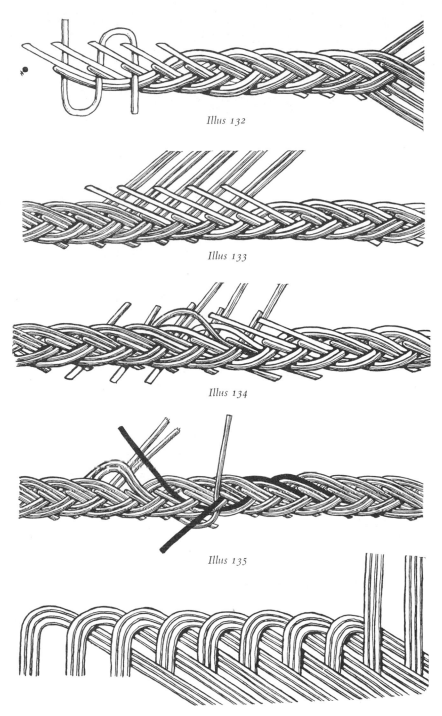

Illus 132

Illus 133

Illus 134

Illus 135

Illus 136

Madeira-type Border. This needs 9in (23cm) of standing stake when the triple stakes have ⅝in (1.6cm) between them.

The threes are taken down behind two threes all the way round (Illus 136).

The threes are taken over two and through to the back. They are then taken over one and brought to the front again underneath and cut off (Illus 137).

This border is effective if worked in three

77

Illus 137

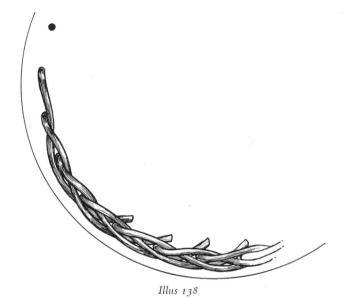

Illus 138

colours. Two coloured stakes can be added to a natural stake when the basket is ready to border and will not show if a deep band of 4-rod waling (Illus 90) has been worked before the border. This will hide the additional ends on both sides of the basket. It is seldom worked in willow but used to be in wicker chairs.

Foot-border (Illus 138). This is a trac border used for securing stakes to a wooden base with holes in it. The movement is behind one, in front of two, behind one, and takes about 3in (7.5cm) of stake. Other tracs may also be used.

Handles

Roped Handles in Cane Basketry. The average number of turns around the bow of a shopping basket is five (Illus 139). It may be less on a shorter handle. The winding cane should be as long as possible, but if a second has to be used, the end of the first piece is woven away into the wale, and the second is introduced in the same way and carries on the movement. The

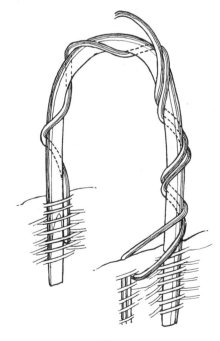

Illus 139

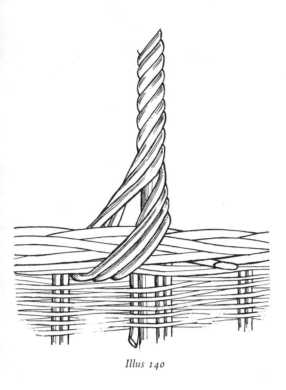

Illus 140

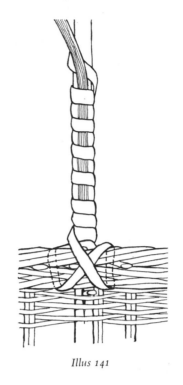

Illus 141

first loop through the basket is held well over to the stake to the left of the bow, so that subsequent ones lie to the right of it and fill the space between it and the bow (Illus 140).

On the lid (Illus 179) do the same, inserting the bow or bows during weaving, and taking the winding cane down into the weaving in front and to the left of the bow, but bringing it out again at the left, a couple of rows of weaving further back. In subsequent turns-round the cane goes down to the right of the last one and comes up again behind the last one.

Lapped Handle in Cane or Willow Skein with Interweaving (Illus 141). This is not so strong as a roped handle and the cross-over is more for ornament than strength. Bows should always be pegged. Pegging with a short peg is done by driving a bodkin through the bow from front to back, obliquely, below the wale. A slyped and soaped inch long peg of No 8 cane or willow is tapped through with iron or hammer. Ends are cut off. A long peg is 6 or 8in (15–20cm) and has the ends woven into the wale.

Illus 146 and 147 show other decorations used with the lapped method. Simple interweaving may be done with more than one cane and patterns and checks made.

Lapping (Illus 142 and 143). At the beginning of any area of lapping the right side of the lapping cane is laid to the cane to be lapped with the short end pointing to the right. The long end is then turned sharply over and covers

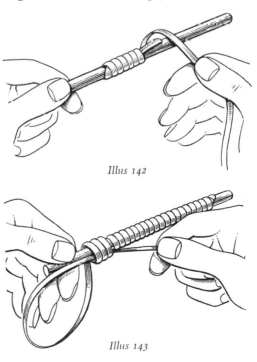

Illus 142

Illus 143

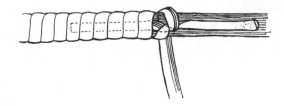

Illus 144

it by binding. Well-damped cane will tighten as it dries. When finishing, continue to bind to the end. Hold tightly above the last three or four turns and loosen these, then turn the end so that the right side again lies against the lapped cane and push the end through the loose turns and out. Tighten these loose turns again with a screwing movement and, when they are firm, pull the end sharply through and cut it off about $\frac{1}{8}$in (0.3cm) long.

When joining-in (Illus 144), if possible a handle should be lapped without a join but if this is inevitable it should be at one side and not in the middle of the bow and on the underside. The right side of the lapping cane must lie against the bow. Afterwards the join is hammered flat.

Herringbone Listing (Illus 145 and 146)
Materials:
A 2- or 3-bow handle nailed together at the top
1 very long and 2 shorter lengths of lapping cane
3 lengths of chair cane No 6 or 4, $3\frac{1}{2}$ times the length of the part of the bow to be listed
1 length of No 6 cane (X in Illus 145)
2 lengths No 8 cane (Y and Z).

Method:
Lap one 'leg' at each side, securing the ends to lie under the listed part. Lap a third 'leg' to the join, working two rounds of twisting over the three bows, as shown in the drawing. Lay in X. Y and Z simply lie in the grooves made by the joins of the three bows. Bind over all three or four times. Then bind in the three chair canes as shown in Illus 145, wrong sides upwards, centres beneath X. Follow Illus 146, taking the chair canes up, pair by pair, twisting them round X to lie out flat as before, and lapping once over X in between each.

To finish, judge the distance carefully, and hold the pairs forward after twisting instead of

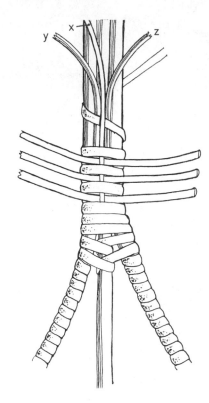

Illus 145

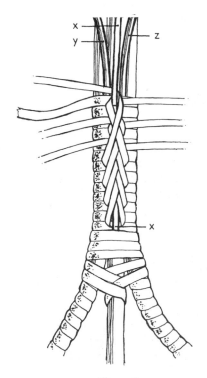

Illus 146

bringing them out at right angles, so that they are bound in with subsequent lapping. All ends are cut off so that they are hidden, and the last 'leg' is finished. The central 'legs' are not lapped. Peg all three bows.

This stroke is used for 'wickering' the handles of silver coffee and teapots, omitting Y and Z and beginning with several plain laps before putting in X.

Crossed Listing (Illus 147)

Materials:

A single bow

1 long piece lapping cane

1 long piece No 4 chair cane

1 piece No 3 or 4 centre cane the length of the bow

Method:

Illus 141 shows interweaving. Listing is worked over the interwoven No 3 or 4 cane. Start by laying the centre of the length of chair cane under this, with the wrong side upwards. To finish bind the ends down under the last few laps.

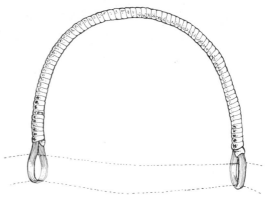

Illus 148

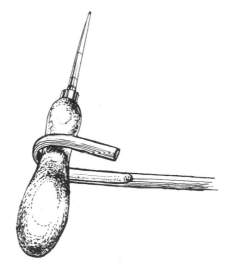

Illus 149

Drop Handles (Illus 148). These may be fastened over the border or made first and fastened to the sides with a loop of flat cane or skein. Illus 149 shows the mellow bow being bent round the bodkin. This may also be done by heating over the cane lamp, but practice is needed. To lap the handle, lay the right side of one end of the lapping cane or skein to the bow, pointing upwards, and turn the cane over it and round it and the bow. To finish: bind to the end, then allow the last three or four rounds to slacken, holding firmly above them. Turn the end and put it up between the slackened rounds and the bow with the right side to the bow. Tighten again with a screwing movement and pull the end up so that all is tight and cut it off close.

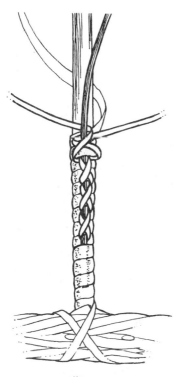

Illus 147

Dropped Ring (Illus 150). Tie a length of a cane into a ring as in tying the first part of a reef or granny-knot, leaving one long and one short end. With the long end turn over the ring four times, returning to the start. Go round again letting these turns lie neatly beside the first ones. Cut off the ends and sew to the basket with a criss-cross of finer cane.

Turk's Head as a handle or button.

With a length of cane make two circles the size of the required ring or button with long end finishing at the top (Illus 151).

Cross the left-hand ring over the right-hand one (X) and put the long end to the left between them, over the right-hand and under the left-hand one (Illus 152).

Separate the two rings at the second cross (Y), which was made at the same time as X, and put the long end to the right between them (Illus 153).

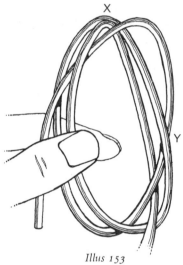

Illus 152

Illus 150

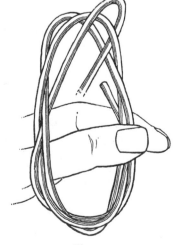

Illus 153

Illus 151

Illus 154

Now (Illus 154) turn the rings by taking hold of them with the right finger and thumb at the same place as they have been held until now. Turn the rings towards you until the last movement faces you and change hands again.

Cross the left-hand ring over the right-hand one and put the long end between them to the left, as in Illus 152. Complete by putting the long end through and down by the short end.

N.B. The long end always goes over and down as in any plait.

The completed ring is doubled, trebled or quadrupled by simply following the short end round and round, always letting the new movement lie to the left of the old one (Illus 155).

This is a knot worked on a sailor's or scout's lanyard, and may be made of many sizes and used as a button or napkin ring, a drop handle or a trimming.

Illus 155

Bow Marks. When a handle-bow goes down into the fabric of the basket it is usual to make room for it by inserting a bow mark by the side of the appropriate stake during the weaving, and working over it. This is a short piece of handle cane or willow the same size or a little smaller than the bow, slyped.

Where two or more bows will go in *together*, work two stakes as one with the bow-marks between them, beginning after the upsett.

Lids and Ledges
Round Lid. This is usually made on the same principle as a round base (Illus 96 and 99). It may be woven in any way that agrees with the weave of its basket, but rib-randing (Illus 84) is particularly suitable.

Sticks should be thicker than weavers. When a large lid is to be made add further sticks after opening out, as soon as the weaving will accommodate them. They are slyped and laid in as shown at Y in Illus 156, then all are paired for one or two rounds before beginning any other weave.

The border on a lid may be worked with the sticks themselves or the sticks may be cut off and stakes inserted, one or two to each stick. With these a border is worked or, as in the case of the lid of the recipe on p 91, when the stakes are upsett before bordering.

When a lid drops into a basket, a *ledge* must be worked into the basket. Illus 157 shows a simple ledge, seen from inside the basket.

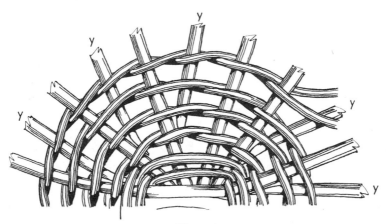

Illus 156

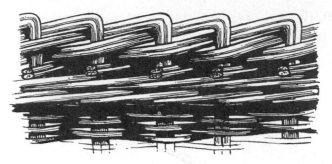

Illus 157

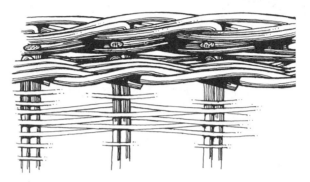

Illus 158

Two rounds of 5-rod wale (see p 64) are worked on the inside of the basket, just below a trac border. Worked from the outside, five rods are used, each one going in front of one and behind four.

The ledge shown at Illus 158 is worked with the bye-stakes or liners of a basket which should be cut about 3in (7.5cm) longer than normally. The border illustrated is the 3-rod plain with the follow-on trac and it was worked before the ledge. At a height of about 1in (2.5cm) below the finished height the bye-stakes were squeezed and bent inwards; two rounds of waling were then worked over the stakes which were then bordered down. Two rounds of pairing were worked on the bye-stakes holding them at right angles to the basket, and then a simple trac border kept very tight. If this ledge is worked with a double trac border, the bye-stakes would be cut longer but would naturally not be bent inwards until after the border was completed. This ledge has the advantage of hiding the unsightly ends of a trac border.

A *ledge outside* a basket to hold a trunk cover generally consists of single round of 4- or 5-rod wale about 1in (2.5cm) below the top of the basket, which is held in a little above it.

N.B. Cane workers will find a jam jar a great convenience in working rib-randing on a lid. After pairing is completed, place the lid on the upturned jar and put the flat of the left hand on it allowing it to revolve, while weaving with the right hand.

Colour Plate 7
Twined workbaskets from China. Many of these little baskets are exported in sets of four or five made to fit inside each other. They are beautifully made of dyed straw (see another pair in colour illustration on p 52) (*Jerome Dessain*)

Illus 159

Notches

Open notch in a Wine Cradle or Dog Basket.

To make this opening or notch first mark the outside stakes of the opening, A and B in Illus 159. Then work a single round of 3-rod wale starting at the next stake to the right of B. When A is reached 1 and 2 stakes are brought down as in a 3-rod border and are used to complete the wale. More or less stakes may be brought down according to the size of notch required. The rods or canes for this round of 3-rod wale should be the same thickness as the stakes. Put in two stout corner posts at A and B.

N.B. Blind turns round A and B are not made with willow.

After the basket has been worked to the desired height and the top wale put on, a 3-rod plain border is worked. Cut two rods X and Y (about 8in (20cm) long for a wine cradle) the same size as the stakes and lay them in as shown at Illus 160 with about half the length protruding beyond the post. Bring X round in front of the post and its stake, behind A, in front of B, and bring down the post-stake with it. Then bring Y round the post (below X) in front of A, behind B, in front of C, and bring A down with it. Take Y1 in front of B and behind C and bring B down with it (Illus 161). This gives the three pairs necessary to work the 3-rod plain border (Illus 117).

Illus 162 shows how the 3-rod plain border is completed at the left side of the notch. It will be seen that stake 7, by the left-hand corner post, is cut off before the border is worked.

The border is usually tied down at the posts in canework with an over-and-over of flat lapping such as chair cane (Illus 177).

Closed Notch (Illus 163). This is suitable as a

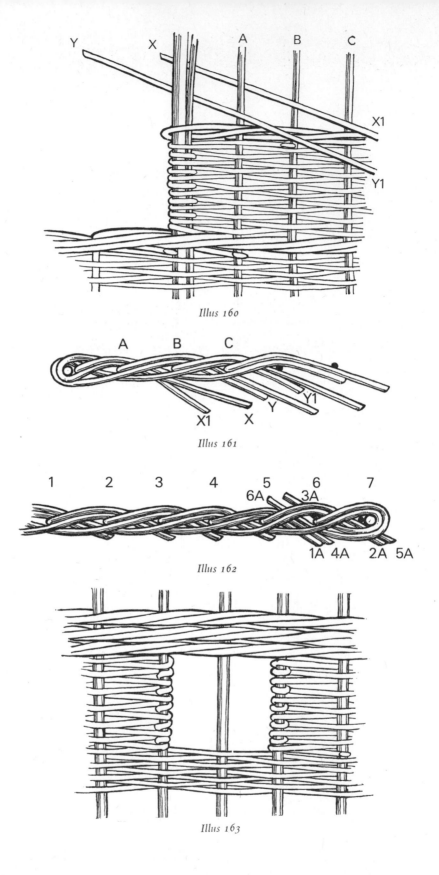

Illus 160

Illus 161

Illus 162

Illus 163

strap-hole on a bicycle basket or finger-hole on a log basket. The central stake may be cut out after the border has been worked, leaving the ends protruding slightly, if a larger hole is needed.

Ties and Trimmings

The simplest fastening for a lid which rests on the edge of a basket is made of a single looped cane or willow, twisted, taken back into the weaving, tied and the ends threaded away (Illus 164). A smaller loop is made on the basket. A peg of handle cane or thick willow can secure this. Tying this peg to the basket may be done by cutting a neat groove round the peg to hold a string, or making a small hole in it with a red-hot nail, heated on a gas flame and held with pliers.

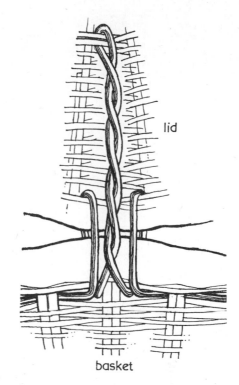

Illus 165

Illus 164

This *tie* or *noose* for a lid is used on fruit baskets and has the advantage of holding the weaving of the lid (Illus 165). It may also be hinged with twists as in Illus 164 going over the borders only.

A plait of 3 or 5 may be used instead of a twist. A 5-plait (Illus 166) is not difficult and is strong enough for small handles also. Two long pieces of fine cane or willow and one half the length marked X are required. The first two are looped round a stake, one below the other and X goes in singly. The movement of the plait is that the outside canes always come across over two canes. In a 3-plait they come across over one cane.

Illus 166

Recipes

WASTEPAPER BASKET (Illus 167)
(Centre Cane on a Wooden Base using
Dyed Cane)

Materials:
7in (18cm) round wooden base with holes
3oz (90g) No 5 centre cane for stakes cut 17in
(43cm) long and liners 14in (36cm) long
$\frac{1}{4}$lb (120g) No 4 natural
1oz (30g) No 4 in colour A
1oz (30g) No 4 in colour B
$\frac{1}{2}$oz (15g) No 4 in colour C
The model has Chinese pink for colour A
Deep blue for colour B
Bright yellow for colour C
Sides:
Cut stakes and liners to the number of holes.
Foot border (Illus 138).
Upsett with 4 canes in colour B, 4 rounds
(Illus 90).
Insert liners.
1 round with colour C (Illus 90).
3 rounds with colour A (Illus 90).
Rand with natural cane until 6in (15cm) high
from the base (Illus 80).
1 round waling (Illus 90) in colour C.
4 rounds waling in colour B.
1 round waling in colour C.
3 rounds waling in colour A.
With natural cane work 1 round of pairing
(Illus 93) taking stakes and bye-stakes separately
Border:
Border with 3-rod plain (Illus 117–20) and a
back-trac (Illus 122).
Measurements:
Height 8in (20cm)
Across top, inside: 9in (23cm); outside: 10$\frac{1}{2}$in
(27cm)

Illus 167 Wastepaper basket (see recipe)

Illus 168 Simple round workbasket, cane (see recipe)

SIMPLE ROUND WORKBASKET (Illus 168)
(Centre Cane)

This basket was made by a student. It has its faults, but the shape is so good that one can forgive them all

Materials:
½oz (15g) No 12 for bottom and lid sticks
3oz (90g) No 5 for stakes and liners
6oz (180g) No 3 for weaving

Base:
7in (18cm) diameter, paired (Illus 93).
8 sticks 8½in (22cm) long (Illus 96 and 99).

Side:
33 stakes No 5, 14in (36cm) long.
33 liners No 5, 12in (31cm) long.
Upsett with 1 round of 5-rod wale and 4 rounds of 3-rod (Illus 85–9).
Put in liners and rand (Illus 80) until 4½in (11cm) high and 9in (23cm) across.
Work 1 round of 3-rod wale, add 2 more weaving canes and work a ledge (Illus 157).
Border with a trac, using the pairs (Illus 114). (The ledge given in Illus 158 may be used. This is worked after the border.)

Lid:
8 sticks of No 12 measuring 1½in (4cm) more than the diameter of the top of the basket, 16 extra sticks half the length (Illus 156).
If diameter is less than 9in (23cm), extra sticks are not needed.
Pair for 5 rounds.
Cut off 1 cane and rib-rand (Illus 84) with right side of lid towards you.
The diameter before bordering must be 1in (2.5cm) less than the diameter of the basket inside, above the ledge.

Border: (Underside towards you)
Insert a pair of No 5 stakes 5in (13cm) long on either side of each stick and extra stick, and work a trac in front of 1, behind 1, in front of 1.

Handles: (Illus 150)

Final Measurements:
6in (15cm) high
11in (28cm) across top
7½in (19cm) across base
  A smaller basket can be made on a 6in (15cm) base; 5½in (14cm) high; 9in (23cm) across top.

ROUND WORKBASKET (Illus 169)
(Centre Cane and Buff Willow)

For texture, colour and shape
Materials:
2oz (60g) No 5 for stakes
3oz (90g) No 3 for weaving
¼lb (120g) 2ft–2½ft (61–76cm) fine buff willows for sticks and liners

Base:
7 buff willow sticks 7in (18cm) long (thickness of No 8 cane) (see pp 14, 15 for treatment of willow).
Paired. Diameter 5in (13cm) (Illus 93 and 99).

Sides:
29 stakes No 5 10½in (27cm) long.
29 buff willow liners, same thickness, 6½in (17cm) long.
Upsett with 1 round of 5-rod wale and 3 rounds of 3-rod (Illus 85–9).
Insert liners and slew (Illus 82) with 2 canes to a height of 4¾in (12cm) following the shape in the illustration. The stakes and liners must be wetted and mellowed for a short time before the inward curve is made.

Illus 169 Round workbasket, cane and willow (see recipe)

91

Work 1 round of 5-rod wale.

Then 3 more rounds of slewing, still curving inwards.

Cut off willows and work a trac border, behind 1, in front of 1, behind 1 (see Illus 113).

Lid: (a trunk cover)

8 willow sticks 1½in (4cm) longer than the diameter of the top and 1 stick half the length, slyped at one end (Illus 102).

Pair 3 rounds to divide the sticks after tying the slath and slew the lid until it is the same size as the top of the basket.

Insert a 7in (18cm) stake of No 5 on either side of each lid stick and work 1 round of 3-rod wale taking in each block of 2 canes and 1 willow.

Cut off willows, turn stakes at right angles.

With the right side towards you work 5 rounds of 3-rod wale, testing the lid to see that it fits over the basket (see p 83).

Border with a 3-rod plain border (Illus 117–20), leaving the ends on the outside.

Handle:

A loop of natural calf leather 1in (2.5cm) wide and 8in (20cm) long, with the ends tapered and taken through and tied inside the lid.

Final Measurements:

Height to top of 5-rod ledge: 5in (13cm)

Height to top of basket: 5½in (14cm)

Total height of basket to top of lid: 7½in (19cm)

Across base: 5¼in (13.5cm)

Across basket at widest part of curve when 3¼in (8cm) high: 7¾in (20cm)

Across top of basket inside: 7in (18cm)

Across lid inside: 7½in (19cm)

TALL OVAL SHOPPING BASKET (Illus 170)
(Centre Cane and Buff Willow)

This basket could be made in all cane, but the buff willow gives colour and strength

Materials: From 3ft (90cm) buff willows:

4 bottom sticks, 11½in (29cm), cut from the butts

11 bottom sticks, 6½in (16.5cm), cut from the butts

46 liners, 11in (28cm), cut from the rods giving a thickness of No 4 to No 7 cane

3oz (90g) No 5 cane cut into 42 stakes 20in (51cm) long and 2 leagues 45in (114.5cm) long

Illus 170 Tall oval shopping basket (see recipe)

7–8oz (230g) No 3 for weaving

1 length No 8 cane for core of upsett

2 pieces No 16 cane 28½in (72.5cm) long

2 lengths No 6 chair cane

2 lengths No 4 chair cane

Base: (see p 68 and pp 14 and 15 for treatment of willow)

Make the slath 5½in (13.5cm) long (Illus 104 and 171) and weave the base, putting in 2 leagues. Base measures 10in × 5in (25.5 × 12.5cm).

Sides:

Double-stake 6 sticks at each end and single-stake the rest (Illus 19 and 107).

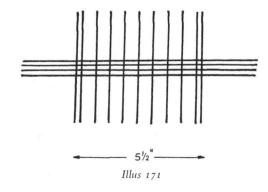

5½"

Illus 171

Upsett as Illus 108 and then with 3 rounds of 3-rod wale (Illus 85–9).

Put in the liners with the belly of the willows to the inside of the basket.

Slew with 2 canes (Illus 81 and 82) using a second pair because of the even number of stakes.

When 9in (23cm) high the basket measures 12in × 8in (30.5 × 20.5cm) on the inside.

Work 3 rounds of 3-rod wale.

Border: (Illus 113, 117–20 and 121).

The trac of in front of 1, behind 1, is worked on the inside after the follow-on trac.

Handles: (Illus 147–9).

Final Measurements:

Height: 10½in (26.5cm)

Top inside: 12in × 8in (30.5 × 20.5cm)

Illus 172 Large shopping basket (see recipe)

LARGE SHOPPING BASKET (Illus 172)
Cane reinforced with White Willow)

This basket could be made in all cane, but is stronger with willow. The design is traditional
Materials: From 3ft (90cm) white willows:

4 bottom sticks, 13½in (34.5cm) cut from the butts

11 bottom sticks, 9in (23cm), cut from the butts

46 liners, 7in (18cm) long, cut from the rods giving a thickness of No 6 to 8 cane

3oz (90g) No 8 cane, cut into 46 17in (43cm) stakes

2oz (60g) No 5 for the wales

6oz (180g) No 3 for randing

3 pieces 8mm handle cane, approx 33in (85cm) long

2 or 3 lengths glossy lapping cane

1 length No 6 chair for listing

Base: (see p 68).

Make the slath 5in (12.5cm) long (Illus 104 and 173) tying and randing (Illus 81) with No 3 cane until base measures 12in × 7½in (30.5 × 19cm).

Sides:

Double-stake the end sticks and single-stake the 7 middle sticks on either side (Illus 19 and 107).

Upsett with No 5 cane as in Illus 108 (or with a simple 5-rod wale) and a single chain wale (Illus 91 and 92) using 4 weavers in front of 3 and behind 1.

Insert liners.

Rand (Illus 81) with No 3 until basket is 5in (12.5cm) high. After 1in (2.5cm) insert 6 bow marks (see p 83) at central stakes and at the third stake away from these, on either side.

Finish with 2 rounds of chain waling as before.

Cut off liners and work a 4-rod plain border (Illus 123).

Handle:

Remove bow marks and insert handle canes, nailing together at centre and sides.

Follow Illus 145 and 146.

Peg all 3 bows (see p 79).

Measurements:

Height of basket: 6in (15cm)

Height to top of handle: 12½in (32cm)

Length of basket outside border: 16in (40.5cm)

Breadth of basket outside border: 12in (30.5cm)

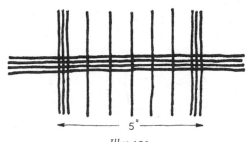

Illus 173

ALL-PURPOSE PLATE (Illus 174)
A small Centre Cane version of a
Buff Willow tray)

Materials:
10 pieces No 12 cane, 9½in (24cm) long, for bottom sticks
½oz (15g) No 2 cane
1½oz (45g) No 4 cane
2oz (60g) No 5 – cut 40 stakes 9½in (24cm) long
1 short length No 4 chair cane for decoration of slath
Base: (Illus 96, 99 and 100).
Begin weaving with No 2 cane. After dividing all canes singly, pair for 1 more round.
Rib-rand (Illus 84) for 8 rounds with No 2.
Change to No 4 for 12 rounds.
And to No 5 until base measures 8½in (21.5cm) across.
Sides:
Insert 2 stakes to each bottom stick.
Upsett with No 4 (p 70), 1 round of 4-rod wale in front of 3 and behind 1, and 4 rounds 3-rod wale (Illus 85–9 and p 64).
Border: (Illus 117–121).
Measurement:
8½in (21.5cm) across inside
1in (2.5cm) high

Illus 174 All-purpose plate (see recipe)

SWEDISH PLATE (Illus 175)
(Cane and Buff Willow)

This basket is a direct copy of a Swedish one but is an object lesson in good design
Materials:
No 12 cane cut into 8 bottom sticks 7in (18cm) long, and 1 of 4in (10cm) long
1oz (30g) No 5 cane cut into 33 stakes 9in (23cm) long
1oz (30g) No 3 cane
1oz (30g) Matt lapping cane
18in–2ft (45–60cm) buff willows. Cut 33 stakes 9in (23cm) long, roughly the thickness of No 5, from the rods
Base: (Illus 102).
Tie and rand (Illus 80) for 10 rounds with lapping cane.
Side:
Before cutting off bottom sticks insert stakes in pairs of 1 cane, 1 willow – the willow always

Illus 175 Swedish plate (see recipe)

to the right, with the right side of the base facing – 2 pairs per stick except for 1 single pair to give the odd number. Push stakes in for 1½in (4cm).
With No 3 cane pair (Illus 93) twice round over the blocks of 2 pairs and 1 bottom stick. Cut off the bottom sticks, closely.
Rand the pairs with lapping cane for 9 rounds, first securing the end with a spring clothes peg

and kinking the willows to get the sett-up from the base.

Border:

A trac with the pairs of in front of 1, behind 1, in front of 1, behind 1 (Illus 114). The willows should be pricked to bend at $\frac{7}{8}$in (2.2cm) above the weaving, and slightly twisted at the finish of the border to prevent cracking.

Measurement:

9$\frac{3}{4}$in (25cm) across

N.B. Willows must be kept mellow all the time, particularly when the border is worked (see pp 14 and 15).

LIDDED PICNIC BASKET (Illus 176)
(Centre Cane)

This basket and its lid are made on a scallomed base. It is not for beginners

Materials:

6$\frac{1}{2}$mm handle cane

1oz (30g) No 12 cane

5oz (150g) No 6 for stakes and liners

1lb (450g) No 3 for all weaving

1 piece of lapping cane

Leather for harness

Base:

Make a shaping board (Illus 106) 15in × 3$\frac{1}{2}$in (38 × 9cm) with rounded ends.

On this make a hoop with 6$\frac{1}{2}$mm cane (see pp 68 and 69) allowing an overlap of 4in (10cm); 5 scallops of No 12 cane run from end to end.

Rand with No 3 (Illus 80).

Sides:

49 stakes No 6, 15in (38cm) long.

49 liners No 6, 10in (25.5cm) long.

Stakes are slyped and driven into the frame using a bodkin (Illus 109 shows this when a rectangular base is made).

Upsett with 6 rounds 3-rod wale (Illus 85–9).

16 rounds randing.

2 rounds 3-rod wale.

3$\frac{1}{2}$in (9cm) slewing, 2 canes (Illus 81 and 82).

2 rounds 3-rod wale.

23 rounds randing.

4 rounds 3-rod wale.

Cut off liners.

*1 round 4-rod wale (see *Measurements*).

Illus 176 Lidded picnic basket (see recipe)

4 rounds pairing (Illus 93) setting the work inwards.

Border with a trac of behind 1, in front of 1, behind 1 (Illus 113).

Thermos partitions (optional):

2 pieces of 6$\frac{1}{2}$mm are nailed 4$\frac{1}{2}$in (11.5cm) in from the ends of the basket, just below the 4-rod wale, from side to side, and are lapped with flat cane; the end is first passed to the outside of the basket, over the nail and inside again.

Measurements (outside):

10in (25.5cm) high

Bottom: 16in × 5in (40.5 × 12.5cm)

*At 4-rod wale: 16in × 6$\frac{1}{2}$in (40.5 × 16.5cm)

Top: 14$\frac{1}{2}$in × 5$\frac{1}{2}$in (37 × 14cm)

Lid:

Tack a piece of No 12 cane to either side of the shaping board to make it wider. Make a base like the basket.

Sides:

56 stakes No 6, 6in (15cm) long.

Work 7 rounds of 3-rod wale.

Border with 3-rod plain (Illus 117–20).

Measurements (outside):

1$\frac{1}{2}$in (4cm) deep

16$\frac{1}{4}$in × 6$\frac{3}{4}$in (41.5 × 17cm)

Harness:

The basket illustrated has a harness of scarlet

kip leather, $\frac{7}{8}$in (2.2cm) wide. The handles are double, hand-stitched, and a single strap with a buckle holds the lid on. The brass studs have split pins and the 4 at the base of the handles are put through the basket and hold the harness firmly to it.

Alternatively:

The basket could have drop handles of cane (Illus 148) and fastenings of various types (Illus 164, 165 and 166).

WINE CRADLE (Illus 177)
(A variation on a familiar design)

May be made on a wooden or a frame base (Illus 178 and 105). If the latter is used the shaping board should be made from the same diagram as the wooden one (Illus 178) but $\frac{1}{4}$in (0.6cm) smaller all round. The same number of stakes and the same method will be used for the rest of the cradle. The scalloms should be of No 8 cane and the base woven with No 3.

Materials:

A wooden base as in Illus 178 with 31 holes, to take No 5 cane and 2 larger corner holes

$1\frac{1}{2}$oz (45g) No 5, cut into 31 stakes $13\frac{1}{2}$in (34.5cm) long

2oz (60g) No 3 cane ($2\frac{1}{2}$oz (75g) for the cane-based cradle).

2 corner posts of white willow or No 12 cane, 4 in (10cm) long and 2 for the front, 6in (15cm) long

$6\frac{1}{2}$mm handle cane

No 6 chair cane 2 long pieces

Sides:

Work a foot border behind 1, in front of 1, behind 1 (Illus 138).

Insert the corner posts.

Upsett. Double chain wale (Illus 91 and 92 and text) setting the front stakes forward and bringing stake A to the centre (Illus 178).

Rand (Illus 80) for 8 rounds.

Then pack either side (Illus 95) beginning at the third stake forward from the corner post and working a clear round each time between the short turns. There should be 5 short turns to each side.

8 more rounds of randing.

The cradle should then *measure* $1\frac{3}{4}$in (4.5cm) at the back and $2\frac{3}{4}$in (7cm) at the front.

Illus 177 Wine cradle (see recipe)

Insert a bow mark of $6\frac{1}{2}$mm cane at the centre-back stake (see p 83).

The Notch: (see Illus 159).

1 stake only is brought down: stake A in Illus 178.

Upper Side:

Insert a corner post by the side of the stake on either side of the notch (Illus 159).

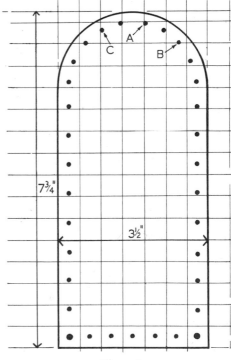

Illus 178

Insert a bye-stake of No 5 8½in (21.5cm) long to the front of stakes B and C.

Rand for 10 rounds using the bye-stakes as stakes and making a round turn at the front corner posts at every round.

After 1 or 2 rounds put in a bow mark of 6½mm cane at the eighth stake forward from the back corner at either side.

Pack the sides 5 times giving 2 clear rounds between each short turn.

Double chain wale, beginning at the front right-hand post by doubling 1 pair of canes round it to make 2 pairs and laying in the third between the second and third stake. On reaching the left-hand front post, when the leading pair has gone behind it, begin the second row thus; working from right to left:

(1) Take the second pair round the post from front to back and forward again between post and stake to its left.

(2) Then take the leading pair round in front of the post and the stake to its left, behind the third stake and forward again.

(3) Cut off the third pair as it lies to the front and reinsert it between the second and third stakes in the new row.

Three pairs are now in sequence and the reverse movement is made automatically by working an ordinary wale from right to left.

To complete the chain wale at the right-hand post take the leading pair round it from back to front and to the inside and cut off.

Cut off the other 2 pairs on the outside.

Border:

3-rod plain (Illus 117–20) first cutting off the back corner posts.

Handle: (made in 2 pieces)

The one from side to side is lapped first (Illus 141) without interlacing.

Second has a long slype folded over the first and nailed (Illus 149).

It is lapped from front to back with single piece of No 3 interlaced.

Peg all 3 handles (see p 79).

Bind each side of the notch with chair cane before cutting off the posts and trim the front with a ring (Illus 150) of No 5, sewn on with chair cane.

Final Measurements:

Height at front from base: 5¼in (13.5cm)
Height at back from base: 4in (10cm)
Height of side-to-side handle: 9½in (24cm)
Length from back to front at the border: 9½in (24cm)
Width at border at widest part: 5in (12.5cm)

ROUND LINEN BASKET (Illus 179)
(Centre Cane and Wooden Base)

The design is based on the oil jars of the Mediterranean countries

Materials:

12in (30.5cm) round wooden base with holes 1in–1¼in (approx. 3cm) apart. (Every other hole on a ready-made base.) An uneven number of holes is preferable.

½lb (230g) No 10 cane cut into 26in (66cm) stakes, and liners the same length less the amount needed for the foot border.

2lb (900g) No 8 for weaving
1oz (30g) No 3 for weaving lid
1oz (30g) No 5 for weaving lid
No 12 cane for lid sticks
2 lengths No 14 for handle, 9in (23cm) long

Illus 179 Round linen basket (see recipe)

Base:

Work foot-border (Illus 138).

Sides:

Upsett with 2 rounds single chain wale (4 rows) (Illus 91 and 92) setting out slightly. Add liners and rand (Illus 80) until basket is 10in (25.5cm) high and 15in (38cm) across.

Shape in. At 12in (30.5cm) high the neck is 12in (30.5cm) across.

Neck:

Squeeze stakes all round.

Work 1 round of chain wale, holding stakes vertical in the first row; squeeze again and work second row holding stakes well out.

Work 5 rounds of 3-rod wale (Illus 85–89) working on the inside of the basket and keeping the neck at a wide angle.

Using No 5 cane, work 1 round of pairing (Illus 93) to divide stakes and liners.

Work a 3-rod plain border on the edge, and then a back-trac, in front of 1, behind 1, mellowing the cane well first (Illus 117–20 and 122).

Lid:

Cut 8 sticks of No 12 cane, 1in (2.5cm) longer than the diameter of the lid when finished.

Begin as for a base (Illus 96 and 99) weaving with No 3 cane.

Pair twice more round after dividing sticks.

Cut 1 bye-stake to each stick and insert (Illus 156).

Work 2 more rounds over the pairs and then another to divide all singly.

Lid will have 32 sticks.

Rib-rand (Illus 84) for 5 rounds with No 5 cane. Slype the ends of the handle canes and slip them into the last 2 rounds of weaving so that they lie by 2 adjoining stakes on either side, and continue to work over them.

Rib-rand with No 8 cane until lid is ¾in (2cm) less than the required diameter.

Cut and insert an 8½in (21.5cm) stake of No 8 cane to each stick and work a 3-rod plain border (Illus 117–20) working on the inside.

Handle:

Complete as described on pages 78 and 79, with Illus 139 and 140.

Lining:

Line the basket with plastic material.

Measurements:

Height to top of handle 16in (40.5cm)
Height of basket to rim 14½in (37cm)
Width at widest part when 10in (25.5cm) high 15in (28cm)
Width at rim edge 15½in (39.5cm)

STRONG SHOPPING BASKET WITH ROPE HANDLE (Illus 180) (Centre Cane, split Palembang and White Willow)

If willow is hard to get it may be replaced by Palembang or centre cane

Materials:

¼lb (120g) No 8 cane cut into 38 stakes 23in (59cm) long

3oz (90g) No 6 cane for upsett and top wale.

½lb (240g) Palembang size 5–8, split (see p 17) and used for weaving base and sides, but used whole as a core in all wales.

From 3–4ft (90–120cm) white willows cut:

9 bottom sticks 8½in (21.5cm) from the butts
3 bottom sticks 14in (35.5cm) from the butts
38 liners about the thickness of No 8 cane 9½in (24cm) long

2½yd (2.30m) 3-strand hemp rope about ⅝in (1.6cm) diameter thick or two pieces 8mm handle cane.

Illus 180 Strong shopping basket (see recipe)

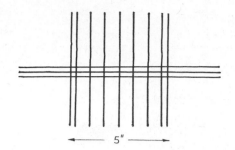

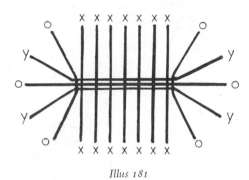

Illus 181

Base: (see p 68, pp 14 and 15 for the treatment of willow)

Make the slath as in Illus 181.

Bind it with split Palembang making a cross at each stake but no binds between.

Rand the base.

Base measures $10\frac{1}{2}$in × $6\frac{1}{2}$in (26.5 × 16.5cm).

Sides:

For staking up follow the second diagram of Illus 181; Xs = single stakes, Os = double stakes, Ys = treble stakes.

Upsett as Illus 108, with 5 canes of No 6 over a core of Palembang, then with 3 rounds of 4-rod chain wale each worked over a core of Palembang (Illus 91). Put in liners with the belly of the willows to the outside of the basket.

Rand with split Palembang using 2 pieces beginning at opposite sides because of the even number of stakes.

When 8in (20cm) high the basket measures 14in × 10in (35.5 × 25.5cm) on the inside.

Work 3 rounds of chain wale as for the upsett.

Border: (Illus 123).

Finish with a follow-on trac (Illus 121).

Handle:

Cut $2\frac{1}{2}$yd (2.3m) of rope in half. Join again to make a circle with 2 shroud knots with the ends marled and served with hemp twine. The ropes

should measure 31in (79cm) between the 2 knots and must be exact. To make this consult:

>*Knots, Splices and Fancy Work* by Charles L. Spencer or
>*Rope Splicing* by P. W. Blandford, both published by Brown, Son & Ferguson, or *The Ashley Book of Knots.*

When completed sew the handle to the basket with No 8 cane following Illus 180 and giving a tight stitch between the 2 halves of the knot itself.

Finally lap the centres of the 2 ropes together to make a hand hold, using split Palembang, for 5in (13cm) with short pieces of Palembang interwoven under 2 over 2 (Illus 141), at the same time laying a piece of Palembang in the gap between the two ropes to fill it.

Final Measurements:

Height of basket to rim: $8\frac{3}{4}$in (22cm)

Height to top of handle: 16in (40.4cm)

Top inside rim $10\frac{1}{2}$in × $14\frac{1}{2}$in (26.5 × 37cm)

N.B. This basket may have a rigid cane handle lapped with Palembang.

MINIATURE CRADLE (Illus 182)

Materials:

A few lengths No 1 cane

A few lengths No 0 cane

2 short pieces of No 8 for rockers

A short length of No 2 chair cane

Base and Sides: (these are made in one)

3 pieces No 1, 15in (38cm) long, and 6 pieces 12in (30.5cm) long.

(Illus 183) Set outside stakes $1\frac{3}{4}$in (4.5cm) apart. The end stakes should be 1in (2.5cm) longer at the hood end.

Pair this, taking the 3 long stakes together at the ends, for 1 round.

Open out and reverse pair (Illus 94) until base measures $3\frac{1}{4}$in × $1\frac{1}{2}$in (8 × 4cm).

Add 4 extra stakes at each end making them the same length as the rest.

Upsett with 4 rounds of 3-rod wale.

Add $2\frac{1}{4}$in (6cm) liners at one end and $3\frac{1}{2}$in (9cm) ones at the other (hood) end.

Rand with 2 canes for 8 rounds (Illus 81).

Then pack the hood end for 5 turns each side (Illus 95) beginning at the side stake next to the centre one.

99

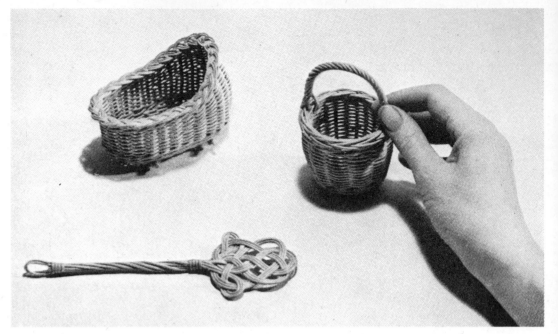

Illus 182 Miniatures (see recipes)

Rand for 6 rounds, curving the hood.
Pack again 4 times beginning at one stake nearer the end than the last time.
Work 2 rounds of 3-rod wale.
Border:
3-pair plait (Illus 124–9).
Rockers:
Damp 2 short pieces of No 8 and curve.
Sew with a cross of chair cane to the upsett at either end.

MINIATURE ROUND SHOPPING BASKET
(Illus 182)

Miniatures are good practice in handling the material
Materials:
A few lengths of No 1 and No 0 cane
A short piece of No 6

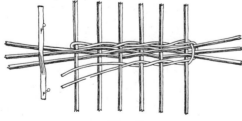

Illus 183

Base and Sides:
6 pieces No 1, 18in (46cm) long, for bottom sticks and stakes in one (Illus 103).
Pair or rand until 1in (2.5cm) across.
Upsett (Illus 85–9) with 4 rounds 3-rod wale.
Add liners, 2¾in (7cm) long, No 1.
Rand (Illus 80) until 2in (5cm) high.
Work 2 rounds 3-rod wale.
Border: (Illus 117–21).
Handle:
Bow of No 6 and weaver of No 0 (Illus 139 and 140).
Measurements:
Height: 2¼in (6cm)
Across top, outside: 2½in (6.5cm)
Height to top of handle: 3¾in (9.5cm)

CARPET BEATER (Illus 182)
Full size

Materials:
3 lengths of No 12 cane or Palembang the same thickness about 12ft (3.6m) long
1 length of the same 3ft 6in (107cm) long
1 length of 6½mm or 8mm handle cane or kubu 2ft 6in (76cm) long
Lapping cane
Wire

S

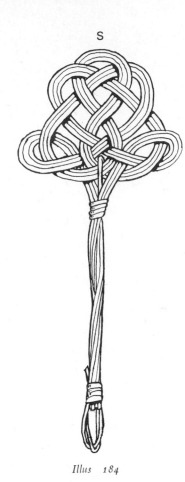

Illus 184

Method:
Take the centre of 1 long piece of cane and follow Illus 184, starting at S and working with both ends. When the pattern is complete, work in the other 2 long pieces separately, one above and one below the first.

Handle:
Slype one end of the short No 12, and when wet and mellow bend it over the crossing as shown. Lap it to the handle cane with wire for about 1in (2.5cm). Lap all canes together with lapping cane and twist them round the handle cane. Turn up the end of the short No 12 to make a loop and lap all together with lapping cane.

Miniature

Illus 182 is made of No 1 cane. The head is $2\frac{1}{4}$in (6cm) long and the whole beater 7in (18cm) long.

BREAD OR FRUIT BOWL (Illus 185)
(Centre Cane, Fine)

Materials:
8 pieces No 12 cane, 5in. (13cm) long
1oz (30g) No 3 cane cut into 33 stakes $10\frac{1}{2}$in (26.5cm) long
$1\frac{1}{2}$oz (45g) No 1 cane for weaving

Illus 185 Bread or fruit bowl and cane rattle (see recipe)

Base: (Illus 96–9).
3½in (9cm) across.
Sides:
Stake up (Illus 107).
Upsett with 1 round 5-rod wale and 3 rounds
3-rod (Illus 85–9 and Illus 90).
Rand (Illus 80) until 1¼in (3cm) high and 6in
(15cm) across.
Work 1 round double chain wale (Illus 91 and
92).
Rand until 2¼in (8cm) high and 6in (15cm)
across.
Complete with 1 round of 3-rod wale.

Border:
Worked in 3 separate rounds:
(1) A 3-rod plain border (Illus 117–20) which
    brings all stakes to the outside.
(2) A back-trac of in front of 2, behind 1
    (Illus 122).
(3) Still going from right to left (as for the
    back-trac) take the ends under 2 through to
    the inside of the basket under the border.
    Pull tight.

Measurements:
Across the top on the outside of the border:
6¼in (16cm)
Across the top on the inside of the border:
5⅜in (13.5cm)
Height: 2½in (6.5cm)

CANE RATTLE (Illus 185)

Materials:
6 pieces No 5 cane, 22in (56cm) long
1 piece No 5 cane, 14in (35.5cm) long
No 2 cane for weaving
No 6 chair cane
Construction:
Put 3 through 3 as for a base (Illus 96).
Tie together with chair cane and add the short
stake. Pair open (Illus 102).
Rib-rand the ball (Illus 84) finishing with a
round of pairing.
Insert a bell or 2 folded pieces of tin.
Bring stakes together and lap with chair cane,
turning up the long end for a handle.
Trim with 2 single Turk's Head rings of chair
cane (Illus 151–5).

Colour Plate 10
Bamboo work basket. The finest Chinese split bamboo
work makes this round workbasket. Much of the sides
and the lid are actually double with a decoration of
tapered flat bystakes laid over the stakes and then a
figure-of-eight pattern worked over them. Much of
the waling is 4-rod to hold both sets of stakes. There
is a deep foot.
  The technique is stake-and-strand but it is very far
removed from most baskets made in the West.
Measurements:
Diameter at top: 9in (23cm)
Diameter at bottom: 5in (13cm)
Height of basket: 3½in (9cm), overall 5in (13cm)
              (*Collected by C. B. Dix, Rangoon, 1937;*
                                     Jerome Dessain)

For texture, colour and shape
Materials:
½lb (225g) 2½ft (76cm) fine buff willows for all sticks and liners
6oz (180g) No 8 for the stakes
1lb (450g) No 5 for weaving sides and base
3oz (90g) No 3 for weaving the lid
Base:
10 sticks 12½in (30.5cm) from willow butts the thickness of No 8 cane (see pp 14 and 15 for treatment of willow). Make slath (Illus 99) paired and well-domed. Put in 2 leagues (see p 68) of No 8, 52in (132cm) long, after 10 rounds pairing (Illus 93). The leagues will cross over each other on the outside of the slath. Diameter 10in (25.5cm).
Sides:
37 stakes No 8, 26in (66cm) long.
37 buff willow liners 18in (46cm) long.
Upsett with 1 round of 5-rod wale and 5 rounds 3-rod (Illus 86–9).
Insert liners and slew with 2 No 5 canes (Illus 82) keeping a slight outward flow. Aim for 13in (33cm) across at 9in (23cm) high. At this height soak and mellow the stakes.
Curve in. When 11in (28cm) across and 11½in (29cm) high work 3 rounds of 3-rod wale and then slew for another inch (2.5cm). Diameter 9in (23cm).
Work 1 round of 5-rod wale and draw off.
Work 2 rounds pairing with No 3 cane.
Border:
Work a trac border behind 1, in front of 1, behind 1 (Illus 113).
Lid: (a trunk cover).
8 willow sticks 9in (23cm) long and 1 stick half the length, slyped at one end. (Sticks should be 1½in (4cm) longer than the diameter of the top) (Illus 99).
Make the slath and pair twice round to tie it using No 3 cane. Then twice round taking the sticks in twos and twice singly. Insert the half-stick at a suitable place and slew with 2 canes for 8 rounds making a slight dome. Add 6 extra willow sticks, slyped, into the slewing arranging them at even intervals (Illus 156).

Colour Plate 11
Round linen storage basket

Colour Plate 12
African coiled baskets. These are all modern baskets made for sale and not just for domestic use, but the technique is age-old. Probably they are all made by women because this sort of sewn basket is, by tradition, woman's work.

The large plate on the left is from Cameroun in Central Africa and is made of palm leaves, natural and dyed, sewn over the hard central ribs of the leaves which make the coil. The centre is worked first quite lightly and then the long coloured stitches are worked over it as a decoration. The only tool would be an awl, perhaps metal but quite likely of sharpened bone. The design is worked by eye and is satisfactory and dramatic though the worker did not count her stitches or make any measurements. The dyes are probably natural.

The rest all come from the coastal area of Kenya. The small mat is also made of one of the many palms, the colours being worked into the coil by laying them over and sewing them down at intervals. The effect is of fine work but it was quickly done – the back is quite rough.

The small two-colour basket is finely made of raffia and the simple pattern is nicely worked.

The bowl on the right is of palm fibre and, though the coil is heavy, the actual stitching is quite fine. The final effect is quite different from the other palm basketry, and more sophisticated. All the dyes used in the Kenya baskets are synthetic (*Jerome Dessain*)

Work 2 rounds of 3-rod wale and slew again until the lid is the right size, approximately 8½in (22cm).

Work 1 round of pairing and cut off the sticks. Cut 33 stakes of No 5 cane 9in (23cm) long and insert them by the side of the sticks. Roughly every other stick will have a stake either side. Turn the lid so that it is standing on the top of the dome.

Squeeze the stakes and set up at a right angle with 1 round of 5-rod wale in No 3 and 6 rounds of 3-rod wale.

Border:
3-rod plain leaving the ends on the outside (Illus 117–20).

Handle:
A loop of 5-plait in No 3 (Illus 166) about 4in (10cm) long, worked diagonally across the slath.

Measurements:
Height to top of basket: 13in (33cm)
Total height to top of lid: 15½in (39cm)
Across base: 10in (25.5cm)
Across basket at widest part inside: 13in (33cm)
Across top opening: 7in (18cm)
Across lid inside: 8¼in (21cm)

Rush

The use of rushes in basketmaking can hardly be called a technique in itself, drawing as it does on several of the others – on plaiting, on twining, and on stake-and-strand. The material may be used to weave frame baskets or to make a coil foundation. But it is so distinctive, particularly in its youth when the colours have an unrivalled subtlety and delicacy, that it has become a favourite among amateurs, especially women. It does not require the strength of hand and arm needed for willow and is easier to work well than cane. Rush does not appear to be widely used for baskets in other temperate zones, perhaps because the techniques we use in the United Kingdom are not traditional to them.

Tools
The only essential tool besides a pair of scissors is a football lacer or a packing needle with a flat eye set in a wooden handle (Illus 186). Soft string is needed for sewing plaits and for tying stakes to the mould, also a ruler, a wooden mallet, old towels and cloths and thin polythene sheet. Most baskets are made over moulds, such as flower pots, rustproof tins and made-up wooden or hardboard blocks.

The design of woven rush baskets depends greatly on the moulds over which they are made. One must be sure that the shape of the mould is good before beginning to use it. Perhaps a cooking-pot appeals to the eye, or part-way up the side of a jar promises a good shape. Stick some tape round it at this point and study it. Most clay flower pots have good proportions but many plastic ones do not. Remember that you will not harm a fine piece of pottery by using it as a mould, and the old shape in the new material can be a source of real pleasure.

The sorting and grading of rushes can be as important to good design as they are to good craftsmanship. Knowing how many you want at one time comes with practice.

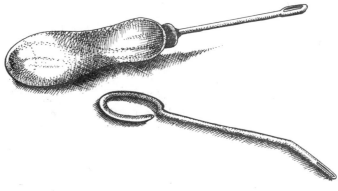

Illus 186

Rush plait used for shopping baskets can be attractive to look at but tends to be rather heavy and plaiting rush into hats and sandals is not usually very successful. Given adequate strength, particularly in the latter, the result will appear lumpy unless you have very small feet and slim ankles.

Notes on Working

Rushes, as mentioned above, must be carefully sorted into thicknesses before use and thin tips discarded. Bottom sticks and stakes are cut in one and are always cut from the butts, so are measured to include diameter of the base, twice the height of the side and twice the length needed for the border. When sorting for a checkered base the general rule is that 3 stakes, flattened, should measure 1in (2.5cm) for small baskets; bigger ones to carry any weight should have 2 stakes to 1in (2.5cm). It is an advantage to cut rushes on the slant, which makes it easier to thread the needle or lacer.

If a stake breaks, a new one is pulled down over the broken end for about 2in (5cm) into the weaving, using the lacer or needle.

Additional stakes will be needed if sides have an outward movement or if a large round base is made. A single one is threaded in beside an existing stake, the threaded end being trimmed later; two may be added at once by doubling a rush and pairing in the bend (Illus 188).

If an unfinished basket has to be left on its block overnight it should be wrapped in a damp cloth covered with polythene. A finished basket must dry thoroughly in the air before being taken off the block, never in the sun or by the fire. A damp sponge is useful while working. Pressing is done by gentle hammering with a mallet while the rush is still damp.

Weaves

Weaves used in rush working are: pairing (Illus 93 and 188), chain pairing (Illus 94 and 192), sometimes waling (Illus 85) and randing (Illus 80), also known as check, worked over an odd number of stakes. It should look like a base weave in Illus 188. In pairing and waling the weavers must be thinner than the stakes, and in check weaving they should be the same thickness.

Joins. For pairing and waling take a new weaver, bend it about 6in (15cm) from the tip and loop it over the next stake to be woven round. Use the new long end with the old short end and the new short end with the old long end.

For check weave lay a new rush over the old one with a 2in (5cm) overlap.

Bases

A round or square base is the foundation of most work (Illus 187), and both are begun in

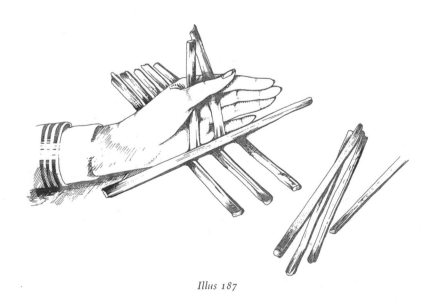

Illus 187

the same way. Cut an even number of butt stakes, say 10. Lay half the stakes, 5, side by side on a damp cloth on the table, alternating butt and tip. Hold them down with the side of your left hand, 2in (5cm) left of centre. Pick up the second and fourth under your left thumb: lay the first of the other 5 across and drop the second and fourth over it. Pick up the first, third and fifth and lay in the second of the other 5. Lay in the other 3 in the same way. This check square should measure about 3in (7.5cm) either way.

Now (Illus 188) bend a fine rush in the middle, loop it over the corner stake on the far left and pair tightly all round the square, turning as you work so that the pull is to the right. Continue pairing, arranging the stakes so that they are even distances apart. To make a round mat or basket, pair rather more tightly at the corners to round them off.

Round Base – the Spider (see Illus 198). For this, 7 or 8 butt stakes the right length for the basket, ie diameter + twice the height + twice the length needed for the border, are tied tightly with string in a bunch at their centres. Every end is paired and when the diameter is about 2in (5cm) every other stake has another threaded down beside it and all are again paired singly. Further stakes may be added later to suit the size of the basket. All joins and ends should be on the under side, and the weaving rushes should be graded so that the finest are at the centre.

Rectangular Bases (Illus 189). These are begun on the block – usually and most suitably wood – which is to mould the basket. A square block has the same number of stakes each way; an oblong block needs longer stakes for the length and a larger number of shorter stakes for the width. In both cases the check base will come up to the edges of the block. One can use drawing pins or staples to pin the stakes to the block or, better, a strip of thin wood can be tacked over the end with the nails between the stakes. After completing the rectangular base, tie it to the block with strings which run right round and tie the stakes round the middle of the side (Illus 190). When the weaving of the side is firm, and the block held tightly, these strings should be removed.

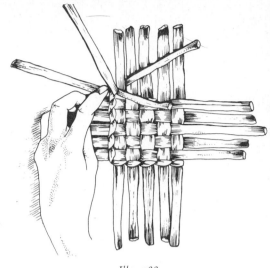

Illus 188

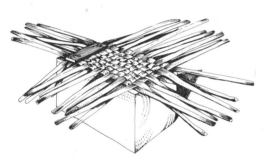

Illus 189

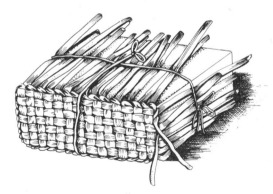

Illus 190

108

A small foot may be made by taking each stake below the next two stakes to its right and bringing it upright again between the third and fourth. Stakes must be 3in (7.5cm) longer to do this.

The upsett may be pairing or a wale. Extra stakes should be added if the sides are to be flown.

Oval Bases. Oval baskets must be made on oval blocks, never easy to find. Oven-glass dishes do well and it is helpful to stick paper-tape on the sides and to mark the centres on this, particularly if the ends are to be raised. The bases are begun like rectangular ones, but with more pairing before setting them up. A round or oval base is put under its mould and the stakes are tied up in the same way as the rectangular one.

If check weave is introduced into the side it should always be followed by a few rounds of pairing or wale before bordering.

N.B. Waling tends to pull the stakes over to the right, pairing pulls to the left. Both must be watched for and corrected, otherwise the basket may go out of shape when it is off the mould.

Any one of these bases will make a table mat if finished off with a simple border (Illus 191).

Borders

In working a border the stakes are always twisted. The simplest border is made by taking each stake down behind the next one to its right. Using the needle, each end is pulled down under two or three rounds of pairing (Illus 191). This takes 1½in (4cm) of standing stake.

The 3-rod border (Illus 117–20) with standing stakes 6in (15cm) long, and the trac (Illus 113) are both used, also the Madeira border (Illus 136 and 137) which will look quite different in rush (Illus 192) worked with single stakes, 8in (20cm) long.

Handles

These are always soft. For carrying, the most useful is the rope or twist (Illus 192). It is worked on a finished basket with a firm, thick border.

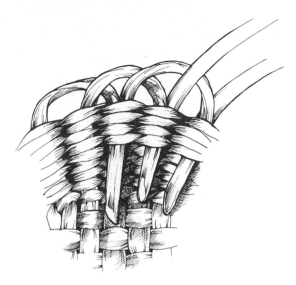

Illus 191

Illus 192

Take two or more good rushes four times the length of the finished handle and arrange them together with butts and tips alternating. Using the needle, pull them through the side below the border and two or three rounds of the weaving, leaving an equal length inside and out. With the outside set in the right hand and the inside set in the left hand, twist both sets to the right and lay the right-hand set to the left over the left-hand set. Do this continuously keeping the twist even and tight. When the rope is long enough the two sets of ends are pulled through the basket from back to front and from front to back, and are threaded away into the fabric.

Such handles may either go across a basket or along the sides.

Another handle or pair of handles for a rectangular basket is a continuous plait or braid of five rushes, which may be sewn on the outside going down one side, under the bottom and up the other side to make one handle, and down and round again to make the other. The spliced join should be at the bottom. In more advanced work, the plait is made first and is tied in position on the block with the stakes. It is worked over up the side and comes out inside the border.

See also Lids.

Lids

A straight-sided basket which is to have a lid fitted over it must always have the simplest border (see Illus 191). The lid is made over the bottom of the basket which is up-ended with the block still inside it. The cover should fit as tightly as possible and, when finished, is left where it is to dry thoroughly.

Handles on Lids. These may be twisted or braided or made of a covered rush ring.

To make this ring: tie the centre of a long strong rush, well mellowed, in a single knot, making a ring of the required size to suit the lid. Take both ends round again to give a ring of three strands, then twist one end tightly on itself and bind the ring round and round halfway. Do the same with the other end. Where they meet bind in one end with the other, and and then pull the loose end through the binding with a needle. Make all tight and neat and cut off both ends. Sew the ring to the lid with another small twisted rush.

A rush will also make a pleasing Turk's Head (Illus 151–5).

Plaiting or Braiding

Besides matting for covering floors, table mats and baskets may be made of plaited rushes. The easiest is the 3-strand plait and this will vary in thickness according to the number and size of the rushes used for each strand. It is essential to keep the look of the strands even. A rough guide may be:

Table mat	2 rushes per strand
Floor mat	6 rushes per strand
Log basket	9 rushes per strand

The finished braid may either be coiled on its edge or laid flat. For the former each coil is sewn to the next through the centre with string and a packing needle. The type of fine hemp or linen string used for a rug-weaver's weft is suitable. For the latter the edges are sewn together, and in both cases the sewing must not show. Table mats are generally made with the plait on its edge and larger baskets with the plait flat. Floor mats may be made by either method, larger ones are usually made with the plait flat. It is advisable to let the braid dry partially before sewing, because of shrinkage.

Many plants besides rushes may be used for plaited mats and baskets. The garden irises *sibirica* and *germanica*, the wild flag *pseudacorus* are suitable; gladioli, Montbretias, red hot pokers, the day lily (*Hemerocallis fulva*), are among braidable garden plants. Leaves should

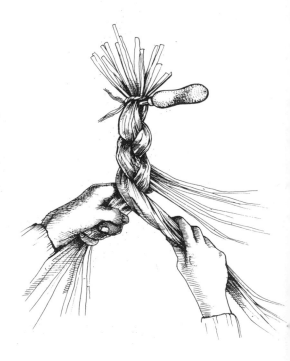

Illus 193

be cut in autumn and hung up in bunches to dry. They are prepared for use the same way as rushes except that they should be kept in water for forty-five minutes or longer before mellowing.

Plaiting. All plaiting is done at a tension like netting; the strands may be tied together and pinned down with a bodkin (Illus 193) when the plait is thick or, if thin, tied with a loop of string to a wall hook or even over one's foot. The hitched loop may be moved up the plait as it lengthens.

A 3-plait with three rushes may be started by laying two together and doubling the third over them at their centres. In this way there are no ends. New rushes are joined by plaiting-in butt to tip or tip to butt and dropping the old end, which is cut off afterwards.

A 6in (15cm) table mat takes about 5yd (4.5m) of plait.

A log basket with the plait on edge takes about 18yd (16.5m), and with the plait flat 50–60yd (46–55m).

A round 5-plait is shown in Illus 166.

Flat Plaits. A flat 5-plait (Illus 194) should be made with five rushes of even width tied together at the butts which are laid on the table under a weight until the plait is going well and can be tensioned. Hold them flat with the left hand and, with the right hand, take the outside right-hand rush and turn it to the left at an angle of 45° over 1, under 1, over 1, under 1. Now bring the four back again to the right in sequence and in the same way. All plaits with an odd number of strands turn over 1 on both edges.

Illus 195 shows the reverse side of a plait of 7, strands at both sides turning under.

Illus 196 shows the plaiting of 4 strands. Here they turn over on the right side and under on the left. All even numbers do the same when going over and under 1, and are reversible.

Flat plaits may be made with any number of odd or even rushes though the odd numbers are the most usual because the turn-over is easier. To try them out, cut ½in (1.3cm) strips of firm paper and stick the top ends to the table with Sellotape.

Joins are made by laying new rushes over the old ones and arranging them so that the ends

Illus 194

Illus 195

are hidden by strands coming over.

N.B. The more strands the more difficult it is to keep the width constant.

Lengths of these plaits, with several rushes to each strand, are made into matting by sewing the edges together with fine string, hiding the stitches in the turns.

Illus 197 is an excellent example of the use of flat plait, in this case of both 7 and 5.

Illus 196

Illus 197 Frail or flail. This rush basket comes from Essex, England, and was made in the late 1920s. It consists of lengths of 7-plait spliced and sewn together. The handles are from a continuous plait of 5, flat down the sides and bottom but becoming round for the handles. Height 12in (30cm), width 15½in (39cm), breadth 5in (13cm), it was used by a farm worker to carry his mid-day meal to the fields.

Such baskets can be dated from the twelfth century with certainty. They were also used by workmen to carry tools. There were other sizes following the above proportions and sometimes a single broad plait was used to make the main part and the handles were covered with leather and ran through holes in the lid.

Another old name for this type is flag basket, perhaps because it could be made from the leaves of the wild iris or flag (*Museum of English Rural Life*)

Recipes

SMALL OVAL BASKET
(See colour illustration on p 34)
(Rush)

We like to gather strawberries and raspberries into little country baskets for the table. A leaf or two at the bottom prevents fruit stains and looks pretty.

Mould:
An old jelly mould with an oval of card stuck on the bottom with Sellotape because it was recessed. Centres at ends and sides were marked on tape. Any oval bowl with approximately 6in × 4in (15 × 10cm) base would do.

Materials:
A handful of rushes prepared for use.

6 stakes 16in (41cm) ⎱ width when flat-
9 stakes 14in (36cm) ⎰ tended, 3 to 1in
4 extra stakes 7in (18cm) ⎰ (2.5cm)

Base:
Make an oblong checker base (Illus 189).
Pair round it 3 times, flat on the table (Illus 188) being careful to keep 1 long stake central at either end.
Tie with fine string to the mould, endwise and crosswise.

Sides:
Work 1 round of 3-rod wale. Drop 1 weaver and pair with the remaining 2 once round.
Insert an extra stake into the wale and the pairing at each corner, using needle or lacer. The ends will be cut close as soon as woven in firmly.
Work 6 more rounds of pairing and then 1 more line over the 8 stakes at each end (Illus 95). Thread ends away.

Border:
8 stakes at each end are flattened and bent over to the outside and threaded down through 4 rows. The centre two are ⅞in (2.3cm) high, the rest a little lower to make a nice curved line.
All other stakes are twisted and taken down, each by the front of the next one. Ends are cut slanting and evenly to $\frac{3}{16}$–$\frac{1}{4}$in (5–6mm).
If it is necessary to remove the basket from its block while bordering, put it back again for pressing and drying.

Measurements:
Base: 4in × 5½in (10 × 14cm)
Inside top: 4¾in × 6½in (12 × 16.5cm)
Height ends inside: 2¾in (7cm)
Height sides inside: 1⅝in (4cm)

ROUND EARED BASKET
(See colour illustration on p 34)
(Rush)

For small quantities of soft fruit and berries on the table

Mould:
A plastic peanut-butter pot. The recessed bottom is covered with a circle of card stuck on with sticky tape.

Materials:
A handful of medium fine rushes prepared for use.

10 stakes, 16in (41cm)
Width when flattened: 3 to 1in (2.5cm)

Base:
Make a square checker (Illus 188).
Pair round it until it fits the base of the mould.
Tie to the mould with 2 pieces of soft string.

Sides:
Work 2 rounds of 3-rod wale. Drop one and pair with the others until 1in (2.5cm) below the top of the mould. Work 1 round of 4-rod wale and complete. Work 2 more rounds of pairing, and draw off.

Border:
Flatten all stakes carefully and with the lacer draw them down one by one through the top 2 rounds of pairing and the 4-rod wale. The bend should be just above the rim of the mould. This must be done carefully to keep the stakes of even height.
The ends are cut evenly about ⅛in (3mm) below the wale.
Leave the basket on the mould until dry, then remove and trim ends inside.

Measurements:
Diameter of top: 3½in (9cm)
Diameter of bottom: 3⅛in (8cm)
Height inside: 2⅛in (5.5cm)

COVER FOR A FLOWER POT
(See colour illustration on p 34)
(Rush)

The pot used as a mould has no holes in the bottom so it could be used for cut flowers as it is. If a border such as the Madeira (Illus 136 and 137) were worked, the pot could not be taken out and would form a lining for the basket. Made this way it would be suitable for growing spring bulbs indoors.

Materials:
Medium fine rushes prepared for use.

Mould:
A plastic flower pot $4\frac{1}{2}$in (11cm) across the bottom and $5\frac{1}{2}$in (14cm) across the top. Depth inside $3\frac{1}{2}$in (9cm).

Base:
Make a checker square base (Illus 188). Pair round until it fits the bottom of the mould. Tie to the mould twice across the bottom and right round.

Sides:
Work 2 rounds of 3-rod wale to set up the sides.

Insert the bye-stakes between the stakes by pulling them through the wale with the lacer (1 between each stake may be too many, 17 is about right).

Pair the side until $\frac{1}{2}$in (1.3cm) below the rim of the mould. Work 1 round of 4-rod wale and draw the ends down into the pairing to finish. Cut off the ends of the bye-stakes level with the base.

Border:
Work a 3-rod plain border (Illus 117–20).
Press and dry the basket on the mould and then cut off the ends of the border at an even slant so that they form a decoration.

WORKBASKET WITH LID (Illus 198)
(Rush)

A simple classic basket large enough to hold sewing as well as needles and cottons.

Mould:
An 8in (20cm) cake tin, round with straight sides, 3in (7.5cm) deep.

Materials:
Medium sized rushes, some smaller for centre weaving, prepared

For the basket: 7 stakes 18in (46cm) long
  14 extra stakes 8in (20cm) long
  7 stakes 7in (18cm) and 7 stakes 6in (15cm)
For the lid: exactly the same as for the basket

Base: (the 'Spider' see p 108)
With fine string tie the 7 long stakes exactly and tightly at their centres. Bend half of each over like a hairpin. If done carefully the string will be hidden and the weaving will make a 7-point centre.

With a fine rush bent in the middle, pair evenly over all 14 ends. After 4 more rounds add an 8in (20cm) stake to each. Pair once over both together. Pair all for 5 rounds.

Add 7 more stakes (one every fourth).

Pair as in the last sequence and add 7 more where it will make for an even fabric.

There will now be 42 stakes. Pair until the base fits the mould.

Tie it to the mould and work a 4-rod wale (p 64) on the bottom and draw the ends off.

Sides:
Set the base on the table. Double a rush round a stake and pair until the basket is the right height, being careful to keep the stakes vertical.

Border:
Twist each stake and take it down behind and with the next one to the right, pulling it through 5 rounds of pairing with the lacer.

Illus 198 Workbasket with lid (see recipe)

Illus 199 Unsewn plaited table mats (see recipe)

When dry cut off closely.

Lid:

This is made over the bottom of the basket when it is fairly dry and still on the mould. It will dry in this position.

It is made exactly like the basket but without the wale. Work about 5 rounds of pairing after the turn. The border is the simple one in Illus 191. It should be about 1½in (4cm) deep.

Handle:

See p 110.

Smaller sizes of this basket may be made over smaller cake tins. For these, stakes may be cut a little shorter and the last set of extra stakes may be omitted. A 3-rod border (Illus 117–20) also looks well on the lid.

UNSEWN PLAITED TABLE MATS
(Illus 199)

This group of half a dozen 6in (15cm) table mats were hand-made by the Deben Weavers in Suffolk, England. They use one or two special aids to quick working but these are not necessary for the amateur worker. They are woven and not sewn together.

Materials:

Medium rush, prepared.

Method:

Begin by laying a rush across the centre of another, with about 10in (25cm) of the butt above A, and the rest below G (Illus 200).

Plait H, F, G, in that order, once each, and

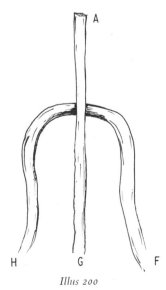

Illus 200

then bring A down behind and up to the front between F and G. Continue to plait with H, F and G 4 times each, and then bring A round behind and up through between F and G again. This will draw the plait together into a circle.

After 2 more plaitings add a second rush to H, leaving 10in (25cm) of the butt projecting. Plait twice more, using the 2 together, and do the same to F, and then to G. Plait twice and bring A through as before. It is advisable to plait this beginning as tightly as possible.

You will now be plaiting with 3 pairs of rushes with 4 equidistant butts; 1 butt will be taken behind and up again after every second plaiting. This movement is repeated throughout.

As the size of the mat increases a new butt will be needed between each of the first 4. It is most convenient to let this new rush take over in the plait.

When the mat is the required size the ends are threaded through into the last round.

This method requires a little practice because the plaiting must be tight and even. The finished mat should be well pressed under a board and a weight until dry.

LOG BASKET (Illus 201)

This is the most traditional of all rush baskets, strong and good to look at. It uses a lot of material but has the advantage of absorbing the rushes which may not have been used for other things, the very thick as well as the thinner.

Material:
Approximately 8lb (3.6kg) of natural rush which must be prepared as usual. About 18yd (16m) of 1½in (4cm) wide plait will be needed for the basket and another 3yd (2.7m) for the handle. One ball of fine brown twine and a medium packing needle.

Method:
Plait (see Illus 193). Tie together the butts of about 36 medium-size rushes and fasten them to a hook or nail (a window latch may be convenient). Divide them into 3 even groups and plait firmly giving each a half-turn as it is brought over. It is easiest to plait with the right

hand, holding with the left one, or vice versa if left-handed. Once the thickness of the plait has been established, thicker and thinner rushes can be used. Joining in is done frequently, sometimes 2 or 3 at a time, to maintain the thickness. Plait the whole length, coiling up the finished part as the work proceeds. Professional plaiters have a wooden bar about chest height to which they tie the plait and over which they loop the finished length.

Let the plait dry out before beginning to sew.

Base:
This is made by coiling the plait on its edge and sewing through the centres, coil to coil, to make a round with a diameter of 15in (38cm).

Side:
Continue the first round of the side, letting it stand on edge on the last 2 rounds of the base. Sew edge to edge from now on. The stitches should show as little as possible, and if it is difficult to get the needle through it may be helpful to rub it on a bar of kitchen soap.

The basket should be upright.

Finishing:
When about 12in (30.5cm) from the end – the end will be immediately above the beginning of the side – cut the plait that distance ahead. Wet and mellow this length, then undo it and replait, reducing its thickness by removing rushes until it is about ½in (1.3cm) thick. Stitch down the end neatly.

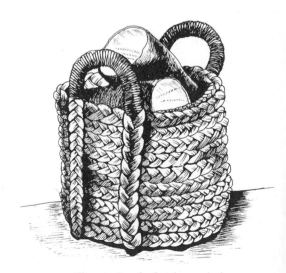

Illus 201 Log basket (see recipe)

Handle:

This is a continuous plait passing twice right round and under the basket. It will measure twice the diameter of the base, plus 4 times the height of the side plus 2 lengths to give a comfortable handle-hold. The join should be on the base and should be spliced or bound flat. After the handle has been sewn on, the loops may be bound with twisted or firmly plaited rush as shown in the drawing. It takes about $3\frac{1}{2}$yd (3.20m) to bind one handle. If the handle is very well-plaited this is not necessary, but will make it stronger.

Measurements:

Diameter of base: 15in (38cm)
Height from floor: $12\frac{1}{2}$in (32cm)
In siding, the plait may be laid flat instead of

Illus 202 'Shoe' basket. A frame or ribbed basket made of white skeined willow in the Hebridean Islands off Scotland. It is for eggs, but for some reason is known as a shoe basket, perhaps because of the shape. These baskets, which are always country-made, became quite popular at craft exhibitions concerned with the Festival of Britain in 1951. The making of the bond over handle and rim is described on page 122 (*Primavera Ltd, Cambridge*)

on its side. This will make a stronger basket but will take twice the length of plait and nearly double the quantity of rushes. Unless the diameter of the base is increased to about $16\frac{1}{2}$in (42cm) the basket will not hold so much, because the sides will be thicker.

Frame or Ribbed

This type of basket (Illus 202) is made quite differently from any other. It is essentially a working basket for agriculture or fishing and seems mostly to have been made by the workers themselves, and by gypsies, and very rarely by professional basketmakers. This does not mean that it cannot be most excellently made, a pleasure to look at as well as to use. Illus 13, 203, 240 and 241 bear this out. Why it should only be 'country-made' is probably a question of tradition, rather than any deliberate policy on anyone's part. The fact that it can be made of a variety of materials, many of them wild and indigenous, does set it aside from European workshop practice. Such materials compared with the cultivated osier-willow are called 'unkind' and could never be worked as quickly,

Illus 203 Jamaican creels or hampers. Jamaica has three types of working baskets, one is European and the other two are African. In the foreground is the European, the sort of willow pannier you would expect to see on a donkey carrying peat or potatoes in the misty landscape of the Orkney or Shetland Isles. But willows do not grow in the tropical climate of Jamaica. To make these creels or hampers as they are called, the country people use a shrub known as rose-apple (*Eugenia jambos*), and a tree of the Philodendron family known as wis. Its aerial roots hang down 30 or 40ft (9 or 12m) and are used for baskets and for wicker furniture making.

The creels in this market scene come on the backs of donkeys and mules bringing produce, and a large basket, in shape like two of them joined together, is also made. Generally it has the square pattern at the junction of handle and frame shown in Illus 211 and 212. The origin of these splendid weight-carriers seems to lie with a large number of Irish farmers who came to settle in Jamaica in the eighteenth century. The Irish lilt is still audible in some Jamaican voices.

At the back of the photograph are some of the African baskets called ground baskets. There are half a dozen shapes, all round, some with lids and handles. This type came with the slaves and so did the *bankra* (an Ashanti word) – soft palm baskets. The ground ones are made of rose-apple and split bamboo and are often carried on the head, again with produce from the owner's ground or garden. Sometimes the edges are bound with the metal strips which come with

imported cardboard cartons. They are to be seen in all the markets, used to display fruit and vegetables as well as for their transport. One can see today how it was in the markets of Europe eighty years or so ago, and for all the years before that – baskets everywhere (*Author's Collection*)

(*Facing page*)

Illus 204 Ose or hen basket. This is one of the most widely known as well as one of the most interesting baskets of the world. Most people believe that its origins are Scottish and there is a body of evidence to support this theory. For instance it went across the Atlantic with the Ulster-Scots immigrants who finally settled in the Appalachian Mountains of Virginia in the eighteenth century. It has been made there of local materials ever since, very well on the whole and with no alterations.

A modern example appeared at the 'Living Traditions' exhibition in Edinburgh in 1951, made by basketmakers at Kilmuir in Skye. It was said to have been made originally to carry a broody hen from one croft to another, but others said that it came from Scandinavia where, incidentally, it is called the Scotch basket.

After the Edinburgh exhibition it immediately became high fashion and was made in tremendous numbers all over Britain, some masters training one man to make it and nothing else, and not only did the craze hit Britain; it was copied in bulk in China, Japan, Poland and Jugoslavia. By the end of the 1950s it fell out of fashion.

Herr Christoph Will, formerly director of the National School of Basketry at Lichtenfels in Germany, tells me that for eight years every girl had to have her *Schiffsswingen* – her rocking boat. The design had been known there for a long time, being only one of a group, made in much the same way, in the basket museum in nearby Michelau. The name was given to it at some time because it looked like an old ship. And certainly it does resemble the ship looking like an heraldic crescent moon in very early manuscripts.

I believe its origins are very old but probably not Scottish, though they may be Celtic. It appears much earlier than the eighteenth century in connection with birds, for I have found it in fourteen illuminated manuscripts dated from the twelfth century onwards, shown as the basket in which St Joachim carried the sacrificial doves at the Presentation of Our Lord in the Temple. It appears in the same rôle on Opus Anglicanum embroideries of 1315 and in a stained-glass window of York Minster. Sometimes the basket is wider and flatter but the unique structure is the same. Another use, when it was probably larger and heavier, was as a builder's basket, hooked to a simple winch to take stones. In this guise I have nine manuscript references also from the twelfth century onwards. It must be stated regretfully that at this time our Scottish neighbours were not much engaged in painting and embroidery and it is very doubtful if a basket of their invention would have come to the knowledge of the artist monks of Canterbury. I would suggest that it was indeed known outside Scotland as a hen basket even in those days.

There seems no trace of it in pictures after the fifteenth century and it was perhaps forgotten in the south of England. But of course it has never been 'lost' and there has always been someone able to make it. The borders between England and Scotland were never closed and at some time it went over – with gypsies, with itinerant basketmakers, who knows?

As we know it now, the standard English or Scottish pattern is made of white willow 15in (38cm) high to the top of the handle and 7in (18cm) across the circular openings; it is 18in (46cm) wide at the widest part and 11in (28cm) across the bottom. It has 5 complete hoops and 14 shorter ribs put in after the weaving of the top is begun (*CoSIRA*)

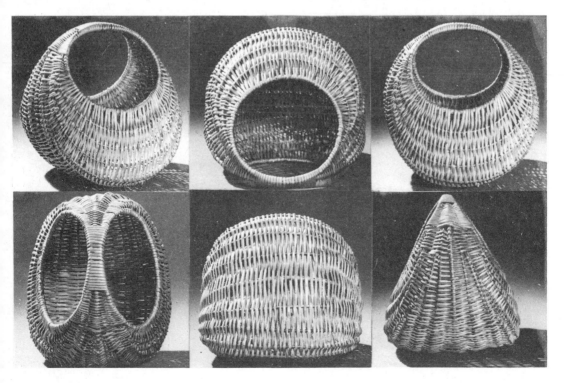

Illus 205 Southport boat. This is one of the few baskets to which we can give date and inventor, but because a basket cannot be patented and the design was first-class, the Southport boat has been copied all over the world. Few people today, however, know that it originally had a lid and a band of ash spale running underneath from end to end.

The basket was designed about 1830 by Mr Cobham of Mawdesley, a few miles from Southport in Lancashire. It was taken partly from the Morecambe Bay cockle basket and from other ribbed baskets made by gypsies in the area. The manufacture was developed by a local basketmaking firm, Thomas Cowley, whose men made it in all sizes. The willows were always buffed and there is a tradition that the famous local osier known as Dicky Meadowes, a variety of *Salix purpurea*, was the only willow that would make it. Since some 'boats' were large enough for a child to sit in (for advertisement) this is not likely, but the little willows must have been excellent for the smaller ones, some so tiny that they had to be finished off with a crochet hook.

The handle and the band were made of ash, boiled and then cut thin with a cleaver or billhook. This made the 'boat' a great weight-carrier, designed originally for taking butter or eggs to market.

Other baskets made in Mawdesley on the 'boat' principle include clothes whiskets, butchers' baskets, satchel boats and round boats for shopping. The principle itself is peculiar neither to Mawdesley nor to Britain, but there is no doubt that it was never better applied than in Lancashire.

The example here was made by the inventor's grandson, Alfred Cobham, and is in the collection of Dryad of Leicester (*Author's Collection*)

therefore the professional basketmaker, working on the system of piecework, would shun such things.

There is no doubt that the method is very old, for such baskets appear frequently in illuminated manuscripts, being used by builders to carry stones by winch to the higher storeys of a building. Its origins seem to be European, and it is thought by some to be Celtic in origin though I have not been able to verify this. It can be both strong and light, depending on the thickness of the frame and ribs and the sort of material used to weave it.

At its most complicated it takes forms like the ose or hen basket and the Southport boat and a splint basket from the Appalachian Mountains of the southern United States of America known as the Kentucky egg basket (Illus 240). As the experts say, in all its forms it is made by hand and eye, not by measurement, and if the first rings are wrong it will never come right.

It is to be hoped that some new designs in this technique may be forthcoming. It needs considerable manual strength to make the frame of rods in the round, and those workers who have access to wood suitable for making splints and can master the use of it, will probably find flat frames are less arduous to bend and join.

I would suggest some study of the examples illustrated. This is a type of basket which could be very satisfactorily made in 'hedge-row' materials and should be tried; but the technique is seldom described and so is not often used except by people lucky enough to find a countryman who can teach them, and such a person is rare nowadays.

Construction

The principle is a rigid horizontal ring of wood which may be round, oval or rectangular. The tapered ribs which form the belly of the basket are not fixed to the rim but are woven in as the making proceeds. If the basket is to have a handle, the construction is made rather easier because the handle is generally a second ring which crosses the first and passes right round underneath (Illus 207). The weaving begins at the rim where the ribs go in. This may also be where the handle crosses.

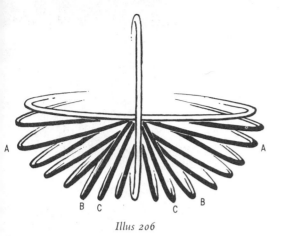

Illus 206

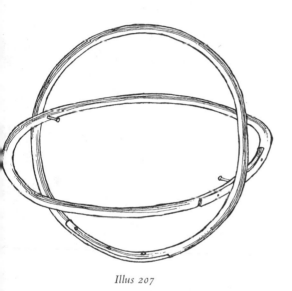

Illus 207

that A, B and C go in very early, though there are no rules and every shape varies. This will be evident from a study of the photographs with this section.

Weaves

One method of starting the weave of a handled basket is to make a tie or lashing of flat material

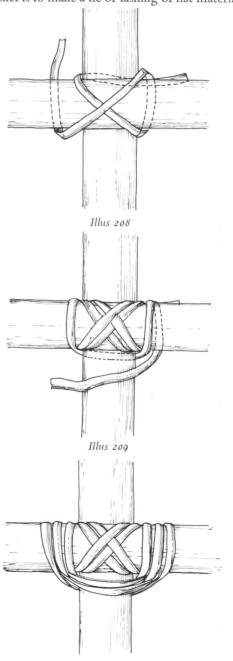

Illus 208

Illus 209

Illus 210   'X' Lashing

The best material for these foundation rings is wood such as hazel, ash, willow, birch or hickory, but Illus 217 shows handle cane or kubu. Cane is somewhat flexible and if it is used the basket must be made with a cross of wood as a mould to hold the horizontal rim in shape. The four ends of this cross are nailed temporarily to the rim, two of them where rim and handle meet. The pieces of this cross-mould will each measure the diameter of the rim.

The placing of the ribs and actual frame construction is shown at Illus 206. The ribs may be made of cane, of willow rods or whittled from wood. They are made in pairs and are introduced as the weaving proceeds. It will be seen at the junction of rim and handle rings. This may be a simple cross made once, twice or more (Illus 208 and 209) followed by square lashing (Illus 210). This appears on some Appalachian splint baskets but is not much seen on European ones. The other tie is shown in Illus 211 and 212, and about this I have some interesting folklore from Mrs Sue Stephenson of Lynchburg, Virginia. As she says, the tie is universal on rib baskets, but she knows it as Four-fold Bond or Christ on the Cross. It is also known as *Ojo de Dios* – Eye of God, refer-

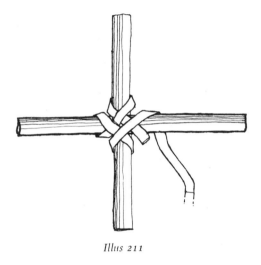

Illus 211

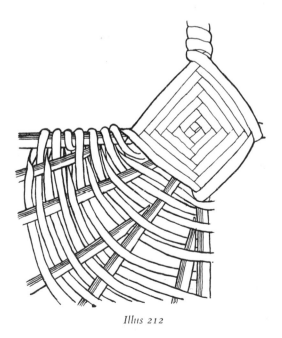

Illus 212

ring to a magical symbol used by the Huichol Indians of north-western Mexico. Small crosses covered with brightly coloured yarns and dyed grasses are made as Christmas ornaments, though they were probably originally pagan good-luck symbols. They are found all over South America and the south-western United States. The same diamond occurs on English corn dollies. In Belgium, among the basket-making Walloons, it is called the Ear.

Double Version of the Eye-of-God or Four-fold Bond (Illus 213). This can be worked on a rib basket with the handle ring inside or outside the frame ring.

Method:

A–C is the handle ring, D–B is the frame ring, X is the start. Follow the arrows until the last one. Then complete the double turn as at B, C and D as follows: go forward over A and back to D underneath; over to A again, round A, over to B and back to A underneath. Then on to B again, round B, and continue. Unless this is done every time round there will be no complete bond at the back. The bond is two strands in the front and one strand at the back. Such ties give the first ribs a resting place on either side, and Illus 212 shows how the weaving is begun, one side of the basket being woven a little way and then the other. The shorter ribs go in as required and the simple randing weave changes to accommodate them. It may be advisable to take a round turn round the frame every now and then though this is not essential. If a flat weaver has a right and a wrong side it must always twist as it comes from below so that the right side is uppermost.

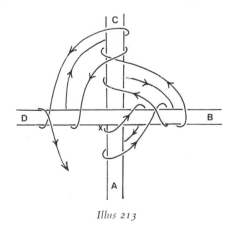

Illus 213

N.B. Illus 212 is not drawn to scale, the two foundation rings are always much thicker than the ribs.

Some packing (Illus 95) will be needed to keep the weaving the same width. The last few inches at the centre, where both sides meet, should be quite straight so that the basket is neat to look into. Joins in the weavers are made by laying the new end over the old end, and never at the rim.

Handles

These may be lapped or left plain. In the 'shoe' basket (Illus 202) the handle ring is made of a twist of three willow rods instead of a single rod. The ends lie flat at the bottom of the basket. This is elegant but rather more difficult to do. Handles must be finished before the basket is made.

N.B. Some makers use small nails in the construction of the rings, others regard this as a heresy. I would say use anything – nails, string, teeth, clothes pegs, and remove them when they have served their purpose.

Other framed baskets are shown in Illus 214, 215 and 216.

Illus 214 Crealagh. This curious basket probably originates from the Isle of Skye, where it was collected by the late Dr Evelyn Baxter. The name is a local one but there are others.

It was used for wool to be carded and was placed at the feet of the carder or spinner, often beside the fire because warmth makes wool easier to card.

The length of this one is 19½in (50cm), the diameter 12in (30cm) and the opening 6½ × 5½in (16.5 × 14cm). There is no record of how it was made but it seems to be a variety of frame or ribbed basket with two frames crossing each other diagonally and held by the lashing called the 'Eye of God' (see p 122) which is here horizontal (see also the basket in Illus 216).

The idea of the crealagh was apparently taken to Canada by Scottish emigrants in the nineteenth century or earlier because two smaller ones called wool- or nut-gathering baskets were collected there. They were made by pushing the end stakes of two funnel-shapes together to make a rough but unmistakable copy of something remembered (*National Museum of Antiquities of Scotland*)

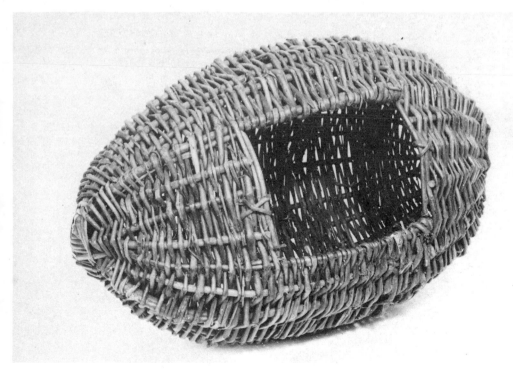

124

Facing page

Illus 215 Worcester scuttle maker. In the Bewdley area and the Wyre Forest this basket was called a scuttle; it could also be called a wisket, a slop or a skip.

No-one is making them today; for the few years when the same type of basket was still obtainable in Cumbria, suppliers on the Welsh borders used to buy them there (see Illus 10). Making methods were different. In Worcestershire and Shropshire, only a billhook was used, cutting hazel for the rim and split oak saplings – known as spale – for the rest.
(Photograph by Miss Wight of Hereford)

Illus 216 This basket was given to the Museum of English Rural Life by someone who believed it to be native to the Channel Island of Sark, but it is exactly illustrated in Augustus Egg's painting 'The Travelling Companions' *c* 1860 in Manchester Art Gallery. Two pretty girls in huge crinolines are sitting in a railway carriage looking out at Naples; the basket holds oranges.

The one illustrated is expertly made on two elongated oval hazel frames crossing diagonally and tied by a horizontal version of the 'Eye of God' (see p 122). The weaving is skeined buff willow, varnished. It is quite possibly Italian (*Museum of English Rural Life*)

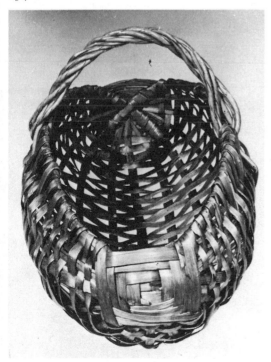

Recipes

LIGHT FRAME SHOPPING BASKET (Illus 217)
(Cane)

Materials:

2 lengths of Kubu (shiny handle cane) 8mm thick, 40in (102cm) and 39in (99cm) long
No 16 centre cane for 4 pairs of stakes
¼lb (120g) shiny lapping cane

A cross frame 11in × 11in (28 × 28cm) is needed. If this is not lap-jointed but made of one piece of wood nailed on another, the lower piece (going from side to side, ie handle to handle) must be rather over ¼in (6mm) longer either side, because it will be fastened there to the handle ring, which is outside the horizontal one, and not to the horizontal ring at all four points. A lap-jointed frame is preferable.

Method:

Make 2 circles, one 11in (28cm) diameter and the other 11½in (29cm) diameter and follow Illus 206, 207, 211 and 212, and explanatory notes on pp 120–123.

OVAL FRAME-TYPE DISH (Illus 217)

An introduction to frame-making and the construction of this type of basket.

Materials:

1 piece of Kubu or 8mm handle cane about 30in (76cm) long for the frame
No 12 cane for sticks
1oz (30g) flat lapping cane for weaving
(The whole could be made in willow with skeins for weaving)

Construction:

Make a slightly squared oval frame 9¾in × 5½in (25 × 14cm) with an overlapping join about 4in (10cm) at one side. It is not necessary to use a shaping board, but the frame can be kept in shape during weaving with a temporary twist across the centre.

Nail a centre stake of No 12 on the under side from end to end, allowing for the curve. Bind it in, working from the centres first at one end and then at the other. After about 6 turns set another stake on either side of the centre one and weave that in. Finally add 2 more stakes. Continue to weave from each end alternately, taking a round turn over the frame after each

crossing. It may be necessary to pack once or twice (see Illus 95). Join the flat cane by laying the new end over the old one.

For a larger dish more stakes are needed.

For the method of weaving see Illus 105. In this illustration the stakes are scallomed and not nailed or laid in.

DEVON FRAME BASKET (Illus 218)
(White and Brown Willow)

This 40 year old Devon basket was made for a fly fisherman to take a couple of peel or sea trout to a neighbour. Lined with ferns there could be no more delightful present. It is used now for picking flowers for the house.

Materials:

About 60in (1.5m) cut from the butt end of a stout 14ft (4.25m) white willow rod or hazel wand

8 white willow rods 3–4ft (90cm–120cm) long for the ribs

A handle bow cut from the butt of a willow the same thickness as the frame, measuring 22in (56cm)

4 white rods 6ft (1.83m) long for the twist

For weaving, 3ft (90cm) brown willows and a few small white rods

Frame:

Slype each end of the long rod for about 4½in

Illus 217 Light frame shopping basket and dish (see recipe)

(11.5cm) so that they will overlap and fit together. Tie temporarily, this is preferable to nailing.

Shape the frame into an oval measuring on the inside 19½in × 11in (49.5 × 28cm). The join is at the middle of one side. Tie the frame across the centre with a small rod bent in half and twisted. This will keep it in shape while the basket is being made.

Ribs:

Scallom (p 36) the butts of 6 ribs to one end of the frame, working from right to left, setting them 1in (2.5cm) apart and cutting the scalloms long enough for each one to be held under the next two. The end of the last one should be brought back to the right, over itself to lie against the next rib on the inside.

Starting at the centre of this end, rand across with small white rods and back again for about 1in (2.5cm) at the same time laying in the slyped butts of the last 2 ribs against the frame at either side, and kinking them where they leave the frame to go down in line with the others.

Slew (p 40) with 2 brown rods until nearly halfway down the basket, making a good dish-shape. (There are no round turns made over the frame itself.) All ends lie inside and never at the edges. Join butt to tip.

Handle Bow:

Slype either end of the handle bow on the inside of its curve for about 2½in (6cm). Push one end down between the overlaps of the frame and make it rest inside against the first rib. Tie up the overlap again until the other end is worked.

With the bodkin open a slit in the frame on the opposite side and push the other end of the bow through to rest on the first rib on that side.

Ribs:

Now attach the other ends of the ribs to the frame. This is done in such a way that they can be adjusted before the basket is entirely finished. It is never easy to get the curve of the bottom exactly the same at both ends, and the weaving is much slower in the second half.

Twist each rib on itself (p 36) holding it

firmly at the place you estimate it should begin to go round the frame from the outside – as a scallom does. Then position all 6 in the same way as the scalloms at the first end, but leaving the tips several inches longer.

Kink the two unscallomed ribs in the right places and weave the tip of one right across the basket, and the other above it, to and fro, until it nearly fills the space. Do not finish off entirely until the rest is worked.

Slew the rest towards the centre, adjusting the length of the ribs if necessary.

Finally finish the twisted rib tips by weaving them away and cutting them off.

Handle:

This is the second twisted or rope handle on p 46. It uses pairs of white willows going across and back once.

Measurements:

Finished basket outside centres: 20in × 7½in (51 × 19cm)

Approximate depth at the centre: 3in (7.5cm)

From base to top of handle: 10in (25cm)

Illus 218 Devon frame basket (see recipe)

Coiled

History

Little coiled work is done now in Europe except for small straw baskets for the table and those large Ali Baba ones sold for laundry. But in the United Kingdom there is a very old tradition of lip or lepe-work, a seedlepe being a kidney-shaped coiled straw basket for sowing corn. Beehives were made this way, and cradles and capacious armchairs at a time when our ancestors usually sat on wooden stools or benches. The chairs had flat arms wide enough to take a cup or a plate, and hoods against draughts, and were used by sick or infirm people or 'such women as have been lately brought to bed'. Some were made of coiled willow twigs but the makers were still called lip-workers. The chairs themselves seem to have had several names such as 'Growneing' or 'childbed chairs'. Twiggen or beehive chairs is a happier name. They lasted a very long time and there are still a few in museums. Ben Johnson, who was a contemporary and friend of Shakespeare, had one, and John Donne wrote of one in a poem.

Chairs with wooden frames and high curved coiled straw backs are still made on the islands north of Scotland and are known as Orkney chairs.

Design

The making of fine coiled baskets is the most laborious method of all, unless we include Indian and African twine weave which may have as many or more stitches to the inch.

Illus 219 Straw Kishie. This basket of coiled straw finely sewn with twine was made by Bruce Lawrenson of Shetland. In the Orkney Islands the high-centred backs of chairs are made in this way. The frames are factory-made these days and the chairs are popular, being good in draughty places. Such straw work lasts a long time (*Studio Swain, Glasgow*)

Variations of shape are generally of subtle curves since most of such baskets are round, that is if conventional materials are used. Design with unconventional materials such as wool and manmade fibres is being pursued with vigour in some parts of the world, though not among professional or what one might call natural basketmakers, so I cannot comment upon it.

Design in colour is generally geometric, and among the great coil cultures, such as the North American Indians and some of the African countries, it is endlessly variable and often most striking and beautiful (see colour illustration on p 104.) Before attempting to introduce pattern into a basket or mat it is best to study baskets or illustrations of them. The makers generally worked by eye, with no drawings in front of them, but it is very much easier to divide a circular base into equal sections, marking them temporarily with thread. The beginning of each new round must be carefully marked all the way across the bottom and up the side, and should show as little as possible at the end.

Construction

The basic principle of making coiled baskets is simple. It is in fact the same as coiled pottery: a long rope or a bundle or single strip of material called the *core* is coiled round and round. Each coil is sewn to the one beneath. The core may be sewn lightly so that the foundation shows (Illus 219) or it may be completely covered by the *sewing material*, which may be wide or narrow.

The Core. Many materials are possible, see Chapter 2. Centre cane is the easiest to handle; raffia in a bundle; rush in a bundle and straw the same, if the stalk is long and it has not been combine harvested – rye or oat straw give shine and colour; splints cut fine, and rope. Many of the garden plants given on p 22 can also be used with success.

Sewing Materials. Raffia, flat lapping or chair cane are the easiest. Bramble, particularly the thin green kind that grows in the shade of woods. This has few if any prickles. Wild clematis; willow skein; twine or string; fine splint or skein made from various woods.

Naturally the longer the fibres the easier it is to use.

A soft core such as raffia will be easier to work if it has a strand of something firm, such as thin cane, in the middle of the bundle. This will help, especially in the making of an oval base which is inclined to twist to begin with.

Beginning with a Core of a Single Cane. Taper the end of the cane with a knife. Damp well and curve between finger and thumb (Illus 220).

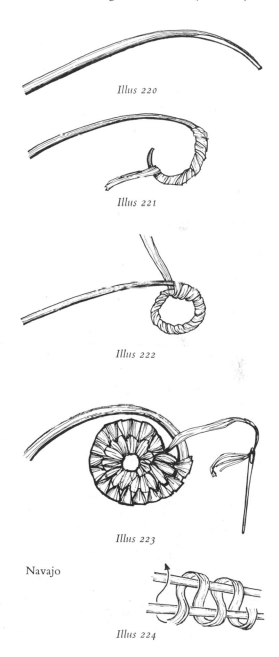

Illus 220

Illus 221

Illus 222

Illus 223

Navajo

Illus 224

Thread the rough end of a piece of damp raffia in a chenille or raffia needle. Lay the other end along the core towards the tapered end and wind over it, going away from you, until the point is reached (Illus 221).

Roll the bound point on itself as tightly as you can and then sew over the join, into the hole, away from you, three times to secure it (Illus 222).

This is the beginning of nearly all coil patterns. If using two or three canes, taper and then set them one shorter than another by about $\frac{1}{4}$in (0.7cm). Native people do not use a needle but an awl, usually of bone, to make a hole for the point of the thread to go through.

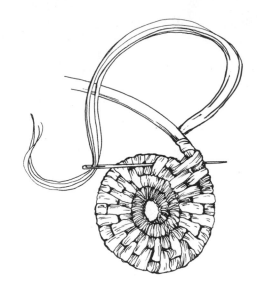

Illus 225

Stitches

Figure-of-Eight or Navajo stitch (Illus 223) may be begun by oversewing the first round; in other words, continuing the three stitches all round the first coil.

The stitch follows by taking the thread over and under the free end of the core and the last coil, passing between them. It goes over the top to the back, comes forward between, over the lower coil and through below it to the back, forward between and up and over to the back again, making a figure-of-eight (Illus 224).

Sometimes a single wrap round the free end is made between the figures-of-eight. This makes the work a little less dense.

Oversew. With this stitch there is no figure-of-eight twist. Two coils are oversewn together and as the free end is sewn so the stitch comes between those of the last coil. When a bundled core is used the stitches may go through the lower coil. This is the stitch used on the kishie on p 128. The sewing is open and most carefully spaced.

Another straight oversew stitch is taken through the stitching of the lower coil only and not through the coil itself. This is generally done with a strong material such as flat cane.

Lazy Squaw (Illus 225) is begun as in Illus 220–2 and the first coil is oversewn plain.

For the second round: wrap once round the free end of the core towards you, and then over and down, stitching between the last two coils and then back, up and round the free end again. A more open fabric may be made by wrapping

two or three times round the free end of the core. The stitches of further rounds will go into the wrapped spaces of those below.

To increase the diameter it will be necessary to stitch twice into the same space at intervals, and as one becomes more expert these will be spaced out evenly, helped out by more than one wrap round.

Other Stitches. There are other ways of stitching the coils together, found particularly in Indian baskets. For a study of these consult the Bibliography; the literature is considerable. But the introduction of colour may be done effectively in the three stitches given above, and round and oval baskets made; though it is not easy to make an oval basket of any size by the coil techniques. Oval mats are quite satisfactory.

To Make an Oval Mat or Base

Do not taper the end of the core but wrap several inches, going away from the tip, according to the length of the oval shape you wish to make. Bend the core along the wrapped end, wrap the free end several times and then wrap both together once. Wrap and wind until both are covered. Continue coiling using the stitch of your choice.

Coiling and stitching may be clockwise or anti-clockwise. This is a matter of personal preference.

Hints on Working

Shaping the Sides. This comes with practice. It is easier to begin with a small straight-sided basket which could be a coaster, or if taken higher, have a lid. Such a lid can be flat or slightly curved, and have a coil sewn on the underside to fit into the basket. With a hole in the centre it could hold a ball of string or, with a handle, serve to hold sewing oddments. Having mastered a straight side a curved one may be attempted.

Joining the Core. One tries to join the core as seldom as possible except when using a bundle of straw or other material when new pieces are added all the time. When they were making large straw objects such as beehives, the workers used to 'size' the core with a hollow bone or a bottle neck, which was put over the core at the beginning and stayed on it until the end (Illus 226).

Illus 226

The joining of cane cores is done by splicing, cutting old and new ends to fit together.

Joining the Sewing Material, either Plain or Coloured. This is done by binding in the new piece with the core a short distance before it is needed and then binding away the old end. Colour is introduced in the same way. If a whole band of colour is to go right round the basket, the plain end would be cut off and bound in, but when colour is used in dots of one or two stitches only, the plain end is bound in with these and then is brought out

again and the coloured one is bound in. In this way two or more colours can be used together, but on the whole the use of two with a neutral background is as much as the eye will take in, and many of the most effective patterns are worked with one colour only.

Finishing. This is done by tapering the end of the core, whether hard or soft, and oversewing it to the last coil, ending at the end of a round. If the core is completely covered elsewhere, care should be taken to cover the last coil with both sewing and wrapping. If it should not be covered, a good finish can be made by sewing round the top a second time in the opposite direction.

Plaited

History and Design

The history of plaiting has still to be written; it will embrace many things in which these multitudinous patterns are to be found: fish traps, fans, snow shoes, mats, hats, hair ornaments, chair seats as well as baskets. Could you design a new plait? Somewhere in the world, now or in the past, it surely has been made already. Forty plaits are illustrated in a book from America *The Techniques of Basketry*, by Virginia I. Harvey. Many of these are found in textile weaving too.

Perhaps the most productive designing may be done by trying different plant materials in different patterns, and then seeing if they can be worked into something useful as well as interesting or decorative. Practice is cheap, using flattened drinking straws or even strips of paper. It is fun to learn how to do these things, as it is to learn to knot rope or to do cats' cradle. Its significance beyond that is probably personal and limited, unless you are trying to trace ethnological patterns, a very serious study.

The first covering or matting made by man was an interlacing of vegetable fibres. Evidence of this work, of the simple type where two elements run at right angles to each other and parallel to the edges, has been found in Swiss lake dwellings of the Stone Age. Most of the weaving is plain 'tabby', though some twill

131

weave of the same age has been found in Jugoslavia. Diagonal plaiting appears to have been very rare at this time and there is no evidence of containers being made.

But since those far off times plaits have grown in complexity and variety. They should properly be considered a branch of textile weaving, though seldom using tools. Plaited baskets and mats are made over a great part of the world, particularly in hot and humid climates where the maximum of air circulation is important. Manual dexterity being no prerogative of high civilisation, the most complex are often made by the simplest people who are paid a pittance for exquisite hand work which nowadays may be roughly machined into cheap hats and bags for tourists.

Old patterns survive by being passed from one woman to another – much basketry is women's work – and quite little girls may be seen plaiting straw and grasses after school hours beside their mothers and grandmothers. Partly no doubt it is to help the family finances, partly it is a way of growing up and one still sees it, especially on islands, in the Mediterranean, in the Far East and the West Indies – places where the tourists go.

Some of the most beautiful versions of plaited basketry come from Indonesia; the workmanship and finish of the baskets is superb (see colour illustration on p 34). But so is the plaiting of the Arawak and Amerindians of Guyana, which is remarkably like it in both design and finish although the materials are different. In Sarawak and Indonesia, it is bemban, pandanus, bamboo and rattan; in Guyana split *mamuri* and *meuru* – a local type of cane – another called *nibi* and a plant much like raffia known as *tibisiri*. The technique of the baskets in the colour illustration is a very similar type of twill plaiting though the shape is typically Malaysian.

Almost every traveller over fifty will remember the 'pilgrim basket', made in the Far East, which was cheap hand-luggage before the suitcase and the zip fastener were invented. A shiny, yellowish oblong box made of twill plaiting of almost any local material, it came in many sizes and qualities. The strongest were of cane, and the most expensive canvas-covered.

Their characteristic was a deep lid, fitting closely over the base, and the basket could expand simply by being over-filled. Those for sale in Europe generally had two leather straps and a handle between them; for indigenous use a single cord sufficed. The airborne pannier in Illus 1 was based on these wonderful things, which held the worldly goods of so many emigrants. Old attics must hold them still, a home for memories or mice.

Some Arawak plaits of Jamaica have survived in the countryside to be taken up by the descendants of African slaves, though the Arawak people were wiped out by the Spaniards in the sixteenth century. Larger mat patterns do not seem to have survived.

Mats are a subject on their own but the same patterns that are woven into their baskets are used for the beautiful sleeping mats of Sarawak. Simpler pandanus mats are used everywhere in Polynesia, the islands of the Pacific Ocean. Very fine and elaborate ones have been used for barter from the earliest times and have found their way so far over the southern seas that it is impossible to know the dates, makers or islands of origin of many that are now in museums. Much research has still to be done.

Plaiting is not an outstanding west-European technique. Rush matting for floors seems to have come to the west at some time in the fifteenth and sixteenth centuries. It was made in long simple plaits about 3in (7.5cm) wide, sewn together at the edges – and is still. Yet in the Middle East mats of palm, not rush, had been made for centuries without sewing at all, using an ingenious method of plaiting in a cord at the edges.

In 1961 I was approached by Professor Yigael Yadin, Israeli archaeologist of Masada fame, and asked to analyse the making of the palm baskets and mats found in the Cave of Letters near the Dead Sea. These were the containers in which so many wonderful finds of the Bar Kokhba period (AD 132–5) were wrapped (see Bibliography). The technique of these baskets and mats is identical, and soft palm baskets from the Near East, on sale still in many parts of the world, are made by exactly the same method. More astonishing still was a now-famous find made in another cave by

Bar Adom and his team, part of the same great exploration. This was a cache of 429 copper objects – mace and axe heads, chisels, crowns, spiral ornaments and other things wrapped in a mat. It was the carbon dating of this mat which first confirmed to the archaeologists that their find was of the Chalcolithic period, between Bronze Age and Stone Age, and about 3,000 BC. Preserved in the desert cave for nearly 5,000 years it was made in exactly the same way, as follows.

Construction

Unsewn Plaited Baskets and Mats. These, with their at least 5,000 years old technique, are made of one plait, usually of nine weavers but sometimes of thirteen, winding from the centre or base outwards to the rim (Illus 227). Each round is joined to the next by a cord which is enclosed in the outside edge of the plait; the inner edge of the next plait is woven round the cord of the last. The cord is invisible except for a ridge running between the plaits, and if the cord is withdrawn the whole basket unwinds in one long plait.

To *start* twist the 9 ends together, put the loop of the cord over them and tie them to a weight or over your foot so that they are plaited at a tension. All plaiting is over 2 and under 2. Drawing A shows the plait and it will be seen that the cord runs down both edges for the first 8 folds, after which it passes down the outside fold only.

The first weaver on the left is passed to the right, over the cord and over 2, then under 2 and out to the right. The first weaver on the right is then passed to the left, again over the cord and over 2 and under 2 and out to the left. The second weaver on the left is then passed right over 2 and under 2 and out to the right; thus we have 4 weavers on the left and 5 on the right. The second weaver on the right is then passed over 2 and under 2, and so forth. When there have been 8 folds on either side, and 5 weavers are lying over to the left, the next fold from the right is made over the cord and over 2 and under 1.

Drawing B shows that the *whole plait is now turned 180°*, so that the twisted ends of the weavers are nearest to the worker. There will

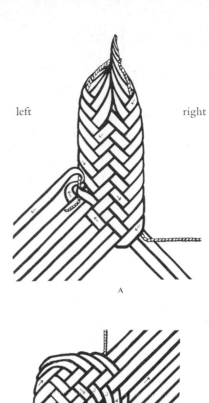

left right

A

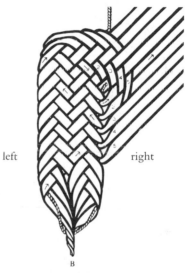

left right

B

C

Illus 227

now be 6 ends on the right and 3 on the left. The next weaver in sequence on the left (marked with an arrow in B) is now woven over 2 and under 2, and so on until it reaches the cord; it is then passed between the seventh and eighth on the right side of the plait and comes out over the cord. In B, weavers 2, 3, 4 and 5 are shown after having been woven in this manner. This tight turn of the plait upon itself produces one or two errors in the weave – where the weavers have gone under 1 instead of 2, to stabilise the weave. From now on all actual weaving is done from one side; the right-hand weavers are passed to the left across the plait, up and around the cord and the edge of the previous round (drawing C), and are then folded over to the right again.

As work proceeds, it will become necessary to increase the outer edge of the plait. This is accomplished by taking two weavers through 1 cord-space, ie between 2 folds of the previous round. This is done as the need arises and not by following any set rules.

The *edges* are finished by reducing the size of the plait gradually, by working 2 of the weavers together 4 times and tapering all but the far right one with a knife. This weaver is used to sew down the cord and the tapered ends below the edge of the previous plait.

Sometimes *rims or borders* are strengthened by plaiting in a thicker cord on the last round. Mats often have no cord on the outer edge.

The *handles* may be short loops of various thick round plaits or ropes and, their junction being the weakest part of the basket, they are sometimes taken right round the basket and up the other side to form a handle there, then down again and round to meet their beginning. Another method is to separate the strands of cord used to plait the handle and run them down the sides, under and over the ridges, knotting them underneath the basket. See also Chapter 5 on Care and Repair, p 150.

The Florentine market scene (Illus 261) shows the same type of basket in use in 1760.

Sewn Plaited Baskets. Baskets may also be made by sewing plaits together (Illus 197). Rushes are suitable for this because of their length and flexibility, but other plants may be used when they are damp and mellow (see

Chapter 2 on Materials for rush, raffia, straw and palms). The section in Chapter 3 on the technique of rush (p 111) shows the plaiting of 3, 4, 5 and 7 strands of material. Illus 166 shows a round plait of 5 going over 2.

Straw Plaiting. The plaiting of corn straw has become a craft with a literature of its own. It is by tradition decorative, and has a long history in which ceremonial – pagan in origin and associated with harvest – winds its way through the centuries and cultures of both East and West.

Several excellent books have been written on the plaiting of ancient and modern cult objects known in England as 'corn dollies'. This craft has been revived since the 1951 Festival of Britain when a remarkable sculpture in straw of the Lion and the Unicorn was shown in the exhibition on the south bank of the Thames. The maker, Fred Mizen, came from deep in the corn-growing area of Essex and had learnt the art from his father. Few people had ever seen it, but now corn dollies are extremely popular among women's clubs and appear in churches at harvest festivals, always skilfully made and sometimes most artistically used. It is not basketmaking, but many of the plaits used are universal and may also be found in the palm crosses carried in Easter processions in Catholic countries round the Mediterranean. Corn and palm make lovely ephemeral things which, seen for brief glimpses

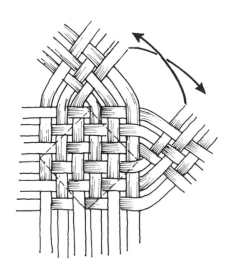

Illus 228

in a passing procession, have the richness of goldsmiths' work.

Woven Plait (Illus 228) shows the beginning of the simplest type of woven plait to make a shallow round basket from flat material such as lapping cane or splint. The pieces should be long enough to go right across and up the sides without joins. If continued in the same way and moulded over a dish or wide bowl it will make a basket. Two rings of handle cane split in half are sewn round the edge, one outside and one inside, using chair cane for sewing, going over both rings twice about every inch, and knotting the ends to each other to finish.

The larger of the two carrying baskets in the colour illustration on p 33 is begun in this way.

———

Illus 229 Cane ball and interlaced dish and mat (see recipes)

Recipes
BALL (Illus 229)

This ball is used in the traditional game of south-east Asia – *chinlon* in Burma and *sepak raga* in Indonesia and Malaysia – where a few players stand in a circle and keep the ball in the air by the use of knee, instep, heel or ankle. A game of great skill and delicacy of touch, but not competitive.

Some balls are woven from 6 strands of split cane in a star pattern.
Materials:
4 long pieces of No 7 cane, 1 natural and the others different colours.
Take 3 canes and make an interlaced triangle at the centres.
With one set of ends form another triangle the same as the first and bring all canes up to the first one again. With the fourth cane, weave under and over the other canes between the 2 triangles. This will form 4 interlocking circles. Go round and round using both ends of the canes until each circle is about 10 rounds wide.

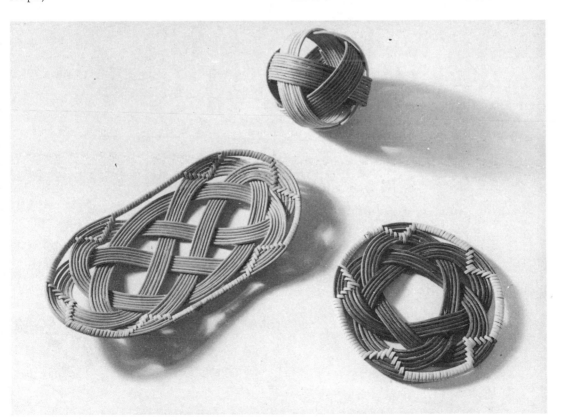

Spring clothes pegs will help to hold the canes in the early stages. A little glue will secure the ends inside and the ball may be varnished.

Diameter:

4in (10cm), but the ball may be a larger size using thicker cane. Thinner or bleached cane is not suitable.

INTERLACED DISH (Illus 229)

The interlaced figure is called an 'Ocean Mat' in seaman's parlance, being usually made in rope. This dish, like the mat in Illus 229, is a central figure of 6 strands with 2 outer rings laced on with chair cane.

Materials:

2 or 3 long pieces of No 5 cane

2 or 3 pieces of No 3 chair cane

Construction: (Illus 230)

Work flat. The centre of a length of No 5 is at B. Lay the left-hand cane D over the right-hand C. Curl D round as shown and hold it down. Thread C over and under D following the dotted line. By taking the arrow end up on the right side of D you complete the figure.

Weave both ends round until it is 6 rounds wide. For lacing method see the next recipe.

Measurements:

8½in × 4in (21.5 × 10cm) before adding the outer rings. (First complete figure measures ½in (1.3cm) less.)

Can be made larger and with thicker material.

INTERLACED MAT (Illus 229)

This is a copy of a mat made in Japan from a type of cane not imported here. It was dark-brown in colour and the lacing was chair cane. It is in fact a flattened Turk's Head (see Illus 151–5).

Materials:

2 long pieces of No 7 cane

1 long piece of No 3 chair cane

Method:

It consists of a 5-sided figure (see Illus 231) with 2 separate circles round the edge. The chair-cane lacing is done from left to right and joins of the circles should come where they are lapped to each other, the inner circle being joined before the outer one. If Illus 229 is studied carefully it will be seen that one side of the V-shaped lacing pattern is worked over 2 canes and the other over 3 canes. When the mat is reversed the opposite is the case. The change from one to the other takes place at the base of the V.

For instruction for lapping see Illus 144 and text p 79.

To complete the circle undo the start and lap in both ends together.

Measurements:

Diameter of inner figure: 5in (12.7cm)

Diameter of finished mat: 5½in (14cm)

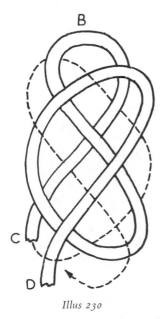

Illus 230

Illus 231

Twined

History

The essential characteristic of a twined basket is that it is flexible, both warp – normally called the stakes or ribs – and weft being of a soft or semi-soft material. Twining is probably the oldest of all techniques, radio-carbon dating of twined-basket fragments found in Danger Cave, Utah, prove them to be at least 9,000 years old.

The work done by Professor Vogt on Stone and Bronze Age basketry and fabrics in Europe (see Bibliography), stresses the strength of twine weave. The finer the material used the stronger it is and, as he says, it can be so tight that the warp threads disappear altogether. He found such fragments from the Stone Age in Switzerland and in the Cueva de los Murciélagos in Spain, where they were made of esparto grass. Late Bronze Age (c 1000 BC) twining was found in Denmark and at La Tène in France. Twining was the technique used to tie in short pieces of fleece to make a pile or nap and, in New Zealand, feathers in the twined cloaks of the Maori – a technique still remembered and handed on for ceremonial use.

Few Europeans will have identified a twined

Illus 232 Kikuyu twined baskets from Kenya. These little bag-like baskets are made from the bark fibre of the shrub *Abutilon usambarense*, not unlike hibiscus, which is common in the Kikuyu country of Kenya, 6,500–8,000ft (2,000–2,500m) in altitude. Such baskets range in size from 6in (15cm) tall, to large ones for carrying garden produce. The twine weave that makes them is so close (15 stitches to 1in; 6 to 1cm) that they will hold water.

The Kikuyu women who make them use somewhat the same method as the Tlingit women of Alaska use when preparing spruce roots, also for twine weaving. In this case they chew the inner bark of Abutilon to separate the fibre, which they then roll on their thighs to twist it. This, and the twining of the basket, they do as they walk along.

The little one is over thirty years old and the big one is a píondo, a market basket. There is no other decoration. Though these baskets are round, the base begins as an oval about ¾in (2cm) long and the new vertical warp threads are added quickly until, by the time the diameter is 3in (7.5cm), it has become almost circular.

The flat handle is woven straight on from one side and, when long enough, it is woven into the opposite side after the border has been worked. The border is unusual, being about ¼in (6mm) deep, sewn over the warp ends which are turned over. I cannot find anything like it among North American Indian baskets.

Anyone who knows the dilly baskets of the Australian aborigines will see a marked resemblance, but dillies have narrow corded handles and are generally small (*By permission of Mr and Mrs Douglas Leakey*)

basket, for today they are rarely made in Europe, but the Chinese and some North American Indians make them still and there are many in museums all over the United States. The colour illustration on p 85 shows twined workbaskets made by the Chinese and Illus 235 shows one made by the Tlingits of Alaska. Illus 232 shows another made by the Kikuyu of Kenya, equally finely woven and very much a part of their living world. The aborigines of Australia also make what are called 'dilly bags' very like these but longer and thinner, varying from 6in × 1in (15 × 2.5cm) to 14in × 6in (35 × 15cm). They are carried by cords and the painted designs on them, in chalky yellow and white, are unique and unmistakable. Twined baskets used to be made in Hawaii from the rootlets of *Freycinetia*, and were much admired. An open form of twining was used in New Zealand in the making of fish traps. The basket in Illus 233 looks entirely different though the actual technique is true twining – it comes from one of the islands to the north of Scotland where plant life clings low to the ground. The warp is made of oat straw and the weft of imported baling twine.

Construction

Technically twining is simple as Illus 234 shows. It is no more than the movement we call pairing (Illus 93) which is a twist of two weavers round the warps. In more elaborate Indian work the 3-rod weave is used and sometimes a horizontal weaver is laid across the warp and woven in, but where it is remarkable is in the closeness and tightness of the weaving, it can be so close and tight that it will hold water.

Materials are most frequently thin or split roots and grasses, strong enough to be pulled tightly. The material used by the Kikuyu is the inner bark of the shrub *Abutilon usambarense* which is exceedingly strong and long-lasting. Unlike the Australian bush their country is lush forest, but this fibre is stronger than anything else growing there, and the industrious women of the Kikuyu have always made their baskets, ropes and cords from it.

The Alaska Tlingit twine their baskets (Illus 235) using the younger and tougher roots

Illus 233 Peat kishie from the Shetland Isles, off the far north of Scotland, made of oaten straw and twine, by the method called twine-weave (see p 137). No trees or shrubs grow in Shetland and other materials used for local agricultural bags or baskets were heather roots, stalks of docks and coarse grass. Carriage on the back was usual and these baskets also served for pony-panniers (*Museum of English Rural Life*)

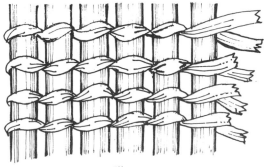

Illus 234

138

Illus 235 Twined Tlingit basket – a berry-gathering basket of southern Alaska. Finely made twined baskets like this were a speciality of the Tlingit Indians, and a few are still made to sell. This one was made by the Koluschan family as part of their household furniture. The softness of the colouring points to considerable age and vegetable dyes. Modern Tlingit basketmakers use commercial dyes and are given to decorating their work with pictures of fish and canoes rather than flowing geometric patterns like these, which never seem to repeat themselves. The material is spruce root and the decoration, which is twisted with and over the main fabric, is dyed grass (*Gunn Memorial Museum, Washington, Conn*)

Illus 236 Fish cassie. This is a true primitive from the Island of Orkney. It is a back creel 16in (41cm) deep and approximately 17in (43cm) across the top, woven of heather roots and stalks, proving that a basket can be made of almost any growing material (*Author's Collection*)

of the sitka spruce. The roots are gathered in spring as soon as the ground is free of frost, and some again in autumn. The length varies from 3–20ft (1–6m) or more. Within a day the bark is peeled from the roots by steaming them and pulling them through a split stick. During the summer they are stored, coiled up, to await the long nights of winter.

When the baskets are to be made the roots are soaked under water until soft, and then split in half. Larger roots may be split into three or four. The root is held taut in the teeth and the splitting done with a thumb nail. A knife is used for trimming and cutting.

Grasses are used for making a pattern called false embroidery. They are bleached in boiling water after being gathered green, and may be dyed, nowadays with commercial dyes. At one time berries and roots were used for colours but neither these nor the commercial dyes have proved fast, and few Tlingit baskets have the bright colours they had at their beginning.

Some openwork is done either by separating the lines of twining or by crossing the warps over each other. Patterns tend to be geometrical and most baskets are round, some with fine lids. Most enchanting are the huge high hats with painted designs of great distinction. A chief's hat could have a high narrow crown trimmed with the skin of an ermine falling down to the brim.

The Kikuyu women also dye their twined baskets and have the same difficulty in getting the dyes to remain fast.

It is not my purpose to suggest that we of the West should make baskets by the twining method. It is too strange for us, and it is never likely to become a fashionable craft except among collectors. It depends more on a lack of materials than on a choice (Illus 236), and on a long tradition. Only the Indians of the far north of America seem to have made it into art form and as that it is already dead and gone.

4

Baskets of the United States of America

The Settlers

In thinking of baskets from the United States of America we must distinguish between those made by the early European settlers and their descendants and those made by the native Indians, the best examples of which were made in the West and so have only been available for general appreciation since towards the end of last century.

European techniques are based on the osier-willow and on some split coppice woods such as oak and sweet chestnut, but Indian techniques are widely varied because the different tribes lived all over the great continent and used vegetation arctic, temperate and tropical, from the spruce root to the agave, with the hardwoods and the grasses in between.

The two cultures did merge to some extent and borrow from each other. In the early days the settlers had neither the time nor the need to make baskets like the Indian ones – fine enough to hold water or hot stones for cooking – and the faith they brought with them needed no baskets for its simple ceremonies.

In New England the Indians traded baskets for cloth and metal goods and made the agricultural baskets the colonists needed. It is also said that they taught them the use of black ash for splint. Ash, both black and white, certainly became the most used and easily available material for New England baskets, but it appears that attempts were made to grow European osiers and also to use the round rods from native willows to make traditional European shapes.

Origins of techniques are always difficult to verify and one can never be dogmatic, for one thing the techniques are nearly always much older than one thinks. It is especially hard to be sure in America, where historic time is short and national pride strong. The making of splint is not the prerogative of the Indians nor, as has been suggested, of the Swedes. Splint, or spale or spelk as it is also known, has been made and used in the British Isles at least since the early Middle Ages. It is very likely that some of the early emigrants from Britain, adept as they had to be with axe and knife, used and refined the methods they already knew.

It was to New England that the religious sect known as Shakers came in 1774. The movement grew from the English Quakers, and their communities were severely practical and self-supporting. The austerity and purity of their way of life found its way into the design and craftsmanship of the many things they made, first for their own use and then to sell to an outside world still short of comforts and of beauty.

Shaker baskets were on sale by 1801, and by mid-century basketmaking had become one of their best-known and desirable crafts. They used splints of hickory, ash, some oak and poplar, some very thin and fine indeed, and made their baskets over moulds, which partly explains the symmetry of their work (Illus 237). There are said to have been seventy-six different baskets in the order book of one community, varying from large agricultural to tiny ones for children. Of all American baskets their appeal to me is deepest and most heartfelt.

The later settlement of the Middle Colonies,

---

whose more liberal approach encouraged settlers from all over Europe, introduced baskets in the European tradition to Pennsylvania, New Jersey and the Delaware river, first to the seaboard and later to the mountains of the hinterland. Here there are memories of itinerant basketmakers, as there used to be in Europe, like tinkers and gypsies. People allowed them to cut native material in return for baskets at half-price. Pennsylvania Germans settled in western Pennsylvania and, later, the Ohio valleys and here, as well as domestic and agricultural ware, they made tiny splint baskets (Illus 238) for Easter eggs and to hang on Christmas trees. Some European osiers were cultivated by the Germans in Pennsylvania.

The early German immigrants made big coiled straw storage baskets and beehives such as used to be found all over Europe; they appear not to have been familiar with the tradition of splintwork, preferring their own techniques and forms in wickerwork which they adapted, not only to the native willow, but also to many other naturally rounded hardwoods.

One area which has remained more isolated than any other in the eastern United States is that section of the Appalachian Mountains, from West Virginia in the north to Alabama in the south, which was settled by English, Ulster-Scots and a few Germans. It is said that these Southern Highlands, cut off by lack of roads and the wishes of the people themselves, were almost isolated for 200 years.

The traditions of basketmaking they brought with them were naturally European, essentially those of farming and fishing baskets which were made in the British Isles by country people. We know from the tithe maps of the 1840s that many farms in Britain had their own small osier beds, and farm hands and their families made and repaired baskets and panniers on winter evenings as part of their normal work. It seems most likely that these baskets were of frame or ribbed construction like those in Illus 13, 14, 242, generally with hazel hoops and willow for all other parts, and that these are the ancestral baskets of the Appalachian people. It is fascinating to see how closely they are connected to their European ancestry, though the settlers had no pliant hazels or gentle osiers to work with. Nearly all the mountain baskets are made of white oak splint with some ash and a little hickory (see p 22). There were also coiled straw 'lipwork' baskets for raising dough, and beehives.

Allen H. Eaton in his book *Handicrafts of the Southern Highlands* tells how the early settlers had to make almost everything they owned, from log cabins and furniture to pottery and cloth and musical instruments, and at first they made only what they needed. By 1890 many of the original handicrafts were disappearing but a gradual revival began as the outside world learnt to appreciate the skills of the mountain people. Cottage industries were set up, hand-spinning and weaving on their hand-made looms being of particular importance. Craft schools were founded which taught more than the use of hands. Many altruistic people worked with and for the people of the Southern

Illus 238 These little splint tidies from the United States of America date from the nineteenth century (*left to right*) fancy 'half-moon' basket of ash splint and grass, 6½in (16cm) diameter; ash-splint wall pocket with pointed top and fancy loop band; fancy 'half-moon' basket of ash splint and grass, 7½in (19cm) in size; splint wall pocket with a fancy looped band and a ring at the top for hanging, probably on the dressing-table for hair combings (*Division of Textiles, Smithsonian Institution, Washington, DC*)

Facing page (above)

Illus 239 Baskets from the Appalachian Mountains (*left*) potato basket. Except for the material this could be one of the baskets being made in Illus 10 or Illus 215. Thousands were made in what is now called Cumbria and sent over the border to the farmers in the Scottish Lowlands. Roughly and quickly made they served their purpose perfectly both there and for the people who took the memory of them to America; (*right*) A service basket. This is a twentieth-century copy of an eighteenth-century basket. Many were made in sets and fitted inside each other. They feel much more American than the other basket illustrated; a little finer than the early New England splint baskets, a little shallower and wider than the Nantucket ones, and having bottom and side stakes in one. They are stake-and-strand made, not ribbed. The bound-on rim is typically eighteenth-century American too, and the finely carved handle (*Sue H. Stephenson*)

(below)

Illus 240 Twin-bottomed egg basket from the Appalachian Mountains. If we compare this with Illus 14, its Scottish ancestry is immediately apparent. The settlers, three-quarters of whom were of Lowland Scots descent, first emigrated to Northern Ireland and then came to Western Pennsylvania between 1707 and 1776, eventually finding a home in the Appalachians, west of the Shenandoah Valley. They had to build their own world from scratch and having no hazel and willow like their forefathers had, they made their baskets from splint cut from white oak, in the frame or ribbed technique, and have continued to do so (*Sue H. Stephenson*)

Illus 241 Mountain key basket. A most elegant piece of Appalachian craftsmanship, c 1900, this again is of white oak splint. Half a basket, but the Ulster-Scot ancestry is there (*Sue H. Stephenson*)

Illus 242 Melon basket. Another wholly satisfactory splint basket, this time made from hickory, a more difficult wood to work than white oak or ash. It was made about 1910 and the material was dyed a dark brown with walnut hulls before making. The 'four-fold bond' is worked at the sides (see p 122), and the whole ribbed shape is a delight to the eye.

Such melon baskets, Mrs Stephenson says, were common up to the late nineteenth century and many had two short thick splints set in the bottom to keep the basket steady. There is a recipe for this in Mrs Stephenson's book (see Bibliography). In a quite different way it is as beautiful and as satisfying to look at as any Shaker basket and speaks for America with just as true a voice (*Sue H. Stephenson*)

Highlands and, by the turn of the century, wider educational opportunities were opening, in line with the development of the crafts.

The oldest basket types are shown in Illus 239 and 240, also 204. All others are variations on these themes or else came in with German settlers from Pennsylvania in the early nineteenth century. Little was owed to the Indians and nothing to African influences.

A further craft revival came in the 1920s and the crafts of the Appalachians are now a widely recognised and appreciated element in the cultural heritage of the United States, collected by museums and valued by private collectors. Meanwhile the life of the mountains goes on and if some craft is being forgotten there is always some devoted person ready to blow on the embers and revive enthusiasm, someone who remembers how to do it and who will pass on the knowledge to the young (Illus 241 and 242).

The determination to stick rigidly to the letter of their traditions seems to have been stronger among the German settlers than any others. The Amana colonies of Iowa, 800 miles to the west of their compatriots in Pennsylvania, were founded by a religious sect of Germans, Swiss and Alsatians who came first to New York State in 1842 and moved west to Iowa in 1855. Like the 'Pennsylvania Dutch' (Deutsch) they also grew osiers and used the stake-and-strand technique. It would be hard, at a quick glance, to tell their baskets from those of their homeland.

The baskets of Nantucket Island off the coast of Massachusetts are regarded by their makers and owners as the aristocrats of the American basket world. I confess to finding them somewhat meretricious today though their beginnings were respectable enough. A lightship was established off the island in the 1850s and tours of duty were sometimes as long as eight months, entailing boredom among a small crew. Some seamen took to making baskets as occupational therapy. The initial construction was almost certainly based on a Scandinavian idea of pushing stakes into a groove in the edge of a turned wooden base and weaving the sides with cane, using a mould, either round or oval. The same principle, more coarsely woven,

seems also to have been followed by the nearby mainlanders, using splint. No border was worked but a rim of wood was sewn on, and swing handles of carved wood were generally attached. Most of the early ones were extremely well and laboriously made and pleasing to look at. Of late, people who have little connection with any lightship have added covers, and even borrowed an Esquimo idea of attaching carved bone animal or bird trimmings. They also take the unprecedented step of signing their work, which in any case seems to contain less actual basketry than most.

Another distinctive type of basket is still being made in the Sea Islands region on the coast of South Carolina. These negro Gullah baskets are made of coiled sweet grass sewn with strips of green palmetto leaves. Some have darker rings of pine needles. They are attractive and well made and entirely African, something not found elsewhere on the American mainland.

I am indebted to Mrs Joleen Gordon for her book telling of an interesting survival of frame baskets almost identical with the Appalachian ones in Nova Scotia, Canada. One remaining professional basketmaker, Mrs Edith Clayton, is working and teaching in Halifax. It appears that one of Mrs Clayton's maternal forebears was among the Black people taken by the British when their ships were blockading Chesapeake Bay and other American harbours in the War of 1812, and was brought to Nova Scotia.

There are no written records of the family's beginnings as basketmakers, but it is known that slaves on the American plantations learnt to make English baskets. Mrs Clayton knows that her mother learnt from her grandmother and their traditions go back further still. They have always sold their baskets – made of swamp maple – in Halifax city market.

The North American Indians

The North American Indian felt himself at one with the natural world, with the animals and all wild life, and for him it was peopled with spirits and supernatural beings. These he portrayed on his baskets, his pottery, weaving and sculpture, in his dances, festivals and ceremonials. Images of birds, particularly the eagle, the bear and the snake, predominate. The geometric patterns which decorate so many Indian baskets nearly all come from the natural world: water, clouds and lightning are there with trees and leaves, deer and fish. Baskets were used in ceremonies of healing the sick, at weddings when they held presents of food and played a part in the actual marriage ceremony, at burials, in prayers for rain and harvest.

This at-oneness of the Indian with his world seems to go back almost to his earliest beginnings, though the first basket remains found so far are too fragmentary for it to be apparent. Parts of twined baskets and sandals, dated c 7000 BC, were found in a cave in Utah known as Danger Cave. Indian basketmakers can feel pride that theirs is the oldest known example of the craft in the world, at least until the archaeologists find another.

Such finds of early baskets are always the result of chance, or chance combined with a suitable climate for preservation. And so small were these Danger Cave pieces that they are not shown in museums, their power to amaze being in their appeal to the imagination. It was also in this area that the ancient culture now known as the Anasazi – a Navajo word meaning the 'Old Ones' – was the source of the second oldest find of baskets, in great numbers and in a wonderful state of preservation.

The Anasazi were very much later in time and were divided by their discoverers into two periods: Basketmaker I (AD 100–400) and Basketmaker II (AD 400–700). The second was the richer. The baskets survived as they did because they also were in caves, in a high dry country with small climatic changes and a very low rainfall. The finds were made in 1880 and from then on until the early years of this century societies and collections were formed, both public and private; studies sometimes based on the most painstaking and minute analysis were undertaken, and learned books followed – a body of literature which has been growing ever since. Enormous prices for those days were paid for baskets, as much as $1,500 being paid for a single one.

The title Basketmaker Indians is misleading because most Indian tribes made baskets. These people were the forerunners of the Pueblo civilisation of a few centuries later. They did not make pottery and some of their baskets were made to hold water, covered outside with resin, and were used for cooking when hot stones were put into a mush of cereal.

Indian baskets all over the western United States show an extraordinary variety, the three basic techniques of plaiting, twining and coiling being used in many different ways. Stake-and-Strand, which is known in America as wickerwork, was little used by the Indians.

Materials came from many plants and shrubs. Grasses and rushes were coiled in bundles; rods from the wild willows and hazels also made cores and were split and pared to make the strands for sewing the coils and for twining. Finer baskets were made from cedar bark, spruce and fern roots. In the south-east wild cane was used; and in the north-east white oak, ash and hickory saplings were soaked, pounded and split by the Algonquin and Iroquois to make plaited splint baskets which may be the ancestors of the New England ones we know. It is impossible to say who borrowed which technique from whom, and this is the same among craftsmen the world over. The Algonquin painted their splint baskets and stamped patterns on them with carved potato. Unique to their region is a pattern of curled splint, and also medicine masks made of plaited corn husks.

The splitting of cane was a method long used by the Choctaw, the Cherokee and the Chitimacha tribes who made fine plaited baskets with zig-zag patterns, not unlike those of Guyana and Sarawak. Sumac, yucca and palms were also used by these people living in the Mississippi basin and Louisiana swamps. Baskets like these are still made today in the Qualla Reservation, North Carolina.

Comparatively few baskets came from the Far North because it was sparsely settled. There were, in fact, few materials for the Eskimo-Indians to use – only straw and thin grass. The 'Sacred Circles' exhibition of Indian Art in London 1976–7 showed a small lidded basket coiled from whale baleen – the fine bones of the jaw – with a pair of ivory heads on top, collected by missionaries at the end of the nineteenth century. But the north-west coastal region is known for its twining, the Tlingit and Aleut baskets being paramount. They were soft (Illus 235), made of split spruce roots and often decorated with false embroidery, overstitching being done with coloured grass in geometric patterns. Some of the Aleutian work of twined grass was almost as fine as coarse silk. The Tlingits are still making some baskets though modern dyes and coarser twining do not match their nineteenth-century work. Workbaskets with rattle-topped lids still find ready buyers.

Further south in British Columbia and Washington there is little twining. Spruce and cedar roots are bundled and coiled. A form of decoration known as 'imbrication' was the speciality of the Klikitat tribe. Strips of grass or cherry bark were folded and stitched in when the coil was being sewn together. Sometimes whole baskets were made this way and beads were also introduced. The famous Potlach hats with their thin high crowns, wide brims and painted designs were also made for ceremonial use, but George Wharton James says the art of

Illus 243 Pomo seed-gathering baskets with pestle and mortar. A group of twined baskets of the nineteenth century, made and used by the Pomo Indians of California in the daily chore of grinding corn. The basket top left holds the grain. The one top right, which has no bottom, is placed over the hollow in the stone mortar and a little seed is poured into it and pounded with the stone pestle. Finally the flour is sifted free of the husks through the open twined tray, centre right, into one of the other two baskets.

All these baskets are soft but strong and so finely twined that no flour would go through the weave – only the one without a bottom has been given some rigidity with a stiff rim to hold. They were made and used by women (*Collection 'The North American Indian' by Edward Sherriff Curtis at the University of Exeter, Devon*)

making them had already been lost when he was making his researches at the beginning of this century.

Many and splendid baskets were made in this area. The people were fishermen, living in a society which had wealth, ancient lineage and complex ceremonials. They lived in wooden houses, and their settled life meant that their arts were full of rich complexities of symbolism and meaningful pattern.

The Coast–Columbia River region was known for fine twined baskets with overlay decoration and fibre bags made by twining. The Nootka and Salish peoples used splint and plaited rush.

The central region of California is richest of all in baskets, twined and coiled. The Pomo tribe are best known, particularly today, for their small feather-and-shell decorated coiled baskets, which were always made as presents. They had no other purpose and were often given cords to hang them up by so that the pendant abalone and mother-of-pearl shells should catch the light. Some, decorated with the feathers of mallard and quail, were for

Illus 244 This coiled basket – a Washo gem – was made by Datsolalee, the most celebrated of all American Indian basketmakers. She lived in Nevada from 1831 to 1926, a member of the Washo tribe, and made many baskets. Forty-six made on this scale of excellence are numbered and registered. One not very much larger than this took eleven months to make, having 32 stitches to 1in (2.5cm).

The materials were wild mountain willow, fern root for black and redbud bark for red. The core was generally made of two fine rods and sewing material was the skin of the willow, which lies under the bark, pared as thin as paper and split, almost certainly with the thumb nail.

The patterns of all her registered baskets have this purity and restraint, and the shapes were always perfectly and generously curved. Her name meant 'Wide Hips' though as a child she was called 'Young Willow'. The baskets are all beautiful and the one illustrated has a truly lyrical quality in its decoration (*Collection 'The North American Indian' by Edward Sherriff Curtis at the University of Exeter, Devon*)

ceremonial purposes. Beads were also used.

The Pomo were also expert with the twining technique (Illus 243). Even the most workaday baskets were patterned with colour and bands of twilled twining. Their great back baskets were cone-shaped and carried in nets. They are now collectors' pieces.

Among neighbouring tribes of this largely peaceful area were the Washo, one of whose members, Datsolalee, has become perhaps the only internationally known artist-basketmaker. One of her restrained and perfectly coiled baskets is shown in Illus 244. Her work was greatly admired by Edward Sherriff Curtis, whose magnificent photographic record, *The North American Indian*, includes pictures of her and many of her finest baskets. One is perhaps led to believe that she had no peers, and indeed in her own very particular feeling for design this is true, but there are other women whose work, though more dramatic, is as fine and may well have a greater appeal. Lucy Tellers of the Mono tribe in the same area is one, and there are others of the small Chemchuevi tribe from the lower Colorado River basin whose work also had great purity of line and decoration and distinctive vase-like shapes.

The whole region was indeed full of wonderful baskets, and was relatively untouched by the white man until the discovery of gold in 1848. By the beginning of the present century the Indian culture was shattered, and now very little is left. Shortly before 1890 collection of their work had begun, but this is not the place to describe what must have been a terrible time for the Indians. There were those scholars who tried to learn and understand before it was too late, and they have left incomparable records behind. But it is only from them that we can learn something of the meaning behind the pattern and decoration of these artifacts.

In the south-western states of New Mexico and Arizona, the Pueblo and Navajo Indians still live in adobe villages much as they have always done and many of the original patterns of their lives remain. It appears that religious belief is still strong and, while it endures, it does seem that they and their way of life may endure too. They are the direct descendants of the Basketmaker Indians whose work we may still, if we are lucky, hold in our hands. It is a humbling thought for those of us who are the descendants of the white men who came over the sea.

5
Care and Repair

Sadly, as has already been mentioned and illustrations bear out, baskets in daily use grow rarer and we have other containers instead. They are still, when you can find them, cheap, and few people without some knowledge or special interest value them. This has always been the case, so baskets have tended to be worked to destruction unless they were small and pretty or had some heirloom value. Times are changing; many baskets, once quite common, are no longer made, and it may well be that no one knows how to make them now or even what they looked like.

If you have an unusual basket, though you may remember its history and provenance and not consider it anything special, it may well achieve museum status. Agricultural baskets in particular should never be thrown away or burnt before making enquiries of a local craft or folk museum to see if they are of interest. They are not likely, in Europe, to have much monetary value. Museums do not have much to spend these days, but a basket which has a special purpose may be gladly received to make up an exhibit, or to round out the reconstruction of a workshop, a farming technique of the past, or a Victorian interior.

This is the way the winnowing fans, cap baskets and reticules, bakers' pouches and herring swills are finding their way into the national museums of the United Kingdom. Things are rather different in the United States of America where there is a great heritage of quality Indian work fetching very high prices; there almost any basket is saleable, collectable by someone.

General Maintenance

The business of caring for baskets past their first youth is not arduous but it does mean careful handling. Once the life has gone out of the material and it has become brittle there is little one can, or should, try to do in the way of actual restoration. If the basket is to be kept and not used it should be washed on a fine day and allowed to dry thoroughly in the open air but not in direct sunlight. Soap is not recommended, nor is it generally needed, sponging and light brushing is usually enough. The very fragile basket may not stand this; the tendle (Illus 245) has been invisibly mended by its owner with black sewing cotton, but it is bound for a museum.

If there is any other material such as lining and trimming involved as there is on old Victorian sewing baskets and tidies, treatment must be very light-handed indeed. Better perhaps to leave even dust alone except for gentle blowing and the provision of a polythene bag and a suitable box until the treasure can go under glass.

The following extract from *Museum Procedure: Conservation*, Institute of Agricultural History and Museum of English Rural Life (1971), p 9, is of interest:

Straw work and Basketry
Items of straw, cane or willow are cleaned with warm water or spirit, and woodworm fluid applied when necessary. The use of the latter means an inevitable alteration in colour and so is only employed when infestation is obvious or suspected.

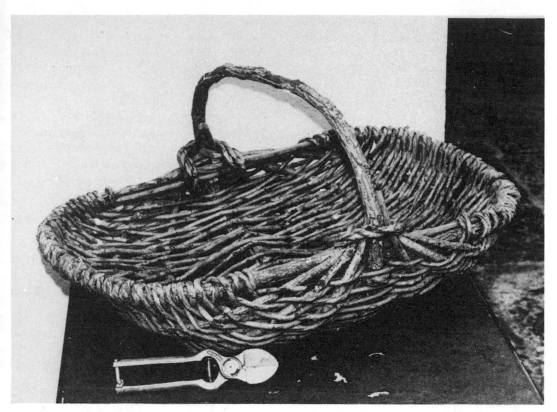

Illus 245 A tendle, an oyster basket from East Mersea, Essex. The tendle is another of the great frame or ribbed primitives, almost certainly unique in construction and to its locality. At one time, when it was the required receptacle for oyster gatherers, it was probably made by quite a few men, now there is one – if you can find him and persuade him to show his skill for posterity's sake.

It is made of green elm saplings 7–8ft (2–2.5m) long with the bark left on, and no nails. The foundation – the basic frame – is two hoops, the horizontal rectangular one being in two pieces meeting and overlapping where the handle hoop crosses it. There are only six ribs and the two nearest to the handle-hoop at the base stand up well above the horizontal hoop sprung against the inside of the handle. The other four do the same but to a lesser degree. The entire framework – 2 hoops and 6 ribs – are tied at either side by an elm-sapling twist which is so constructed that it can be tightened when the weaving of the basket is finished.

All I can say of how it is done is that it begins at the inside with a loop, the ends of which are twisted together and taken round the handle above the frame, through below the frame and across the ribs, and through below the frame again to the loop where they are parted for one to go through the loop to pull tight. This is probably where for the moment the tie is left while the basket is being woven, as all frame baskets are, from the rim downwards, from one side and then the other until they meet in the middle. Finally, one imagines, the tie is pulled tight and twisted away.

This tendle is broken now and is at least sixty years old. Its young owner, valuing it rightly, is sending it to the Museum of English Rural Life. Its measurements are: inside 24 × 15in (61 × 38cm), height 6in (15cm), height to top of handle 13in (33cm).

Tendles were said to last two seasons when in use, but could obviously be repaired to some extent though it was probably quicker, for those who knew how, to make another (*Author's Collection*)

When washing straw work, about one tablespoon of ammonia to two gallons of warm water will lighten the colour and a little borax added to a second washing assists protection. Common salt in the final rinsing provides a measure of strengthening to the straw.

Advice on any special treatment can usually be obtained from the larger museums which have a qualified conservator.

It is always better to keep baskets in a cold place, even if it is a little damp, rather than near a stove or in a centrally heated house. Woodworm, as mentioned in the extract quoted, is another enemy of all basket materials, a fact never to be overlooked by those who import or hold stocks of raw canes and osiers. The world's oldest baskets have been found in conditions where air and light were totally excluded or where the temperature never varied, in dry desert sands, in deep mud, in caves at high altitudes; but these conditions or situations can hardly be artificially arranged. Baskets, like costumes, have to take their chance in most cases.

Baskets of no antique value and in daily use should be kept clean. I give mine, if they appear to need it, a dip and a swirl in clean water once or twice a year and hang them up to dry in an airy garage. It will never harm a willow basket to stand it out in the rain. Garden baskets used for weeds, vegetables and fruit can even have a shower from the hose. Fruit-gathering baskets should be lined with polythene bags so that they do not get stained, raspberry or blackberry stains being impossible to remove – no wonder since blackberry will dye wool. Shopping baskets get the same treatment. Baskets that hang on the wall for decoration get dusty and the small spout of a vacuum cleaner will help here. One should be very careful about putting native baskets with dyed patterns into water; the colours may run and the whole object be ruined. Most of those which leave home today were not made for daily use but to sell to tourists.

The use of varnish is a moot point. In the United Kingdom the majority of professional basketmakers varnish their buff and white willow baskets. They say it is a preservative, which is possible; but more likely it is a tradition and not a very old one at that. It gives a bright new-pin look and whether you like that or not is a matter of taste. It probably does no harm but it wears off unevenly and makes an ageing basket look older than it would if it had not been so treated. It does slightly brighten the colour but if you want to bring out the colours of a basket for photography, wet it, having first tested any but the natural colour with a damp rag.

Nails are obviously undesirable except in hamper-making, where they are used in attaching the metal fastenings and hinges, and in the making of frames of cane furniture. They should not be necessary in making a basket. If they are used in repairing they must be galvanised, iron will react with the tannin in willow and blacken it.

Repairs

Baskets in daily use, with no proud future in a museum show case, should always be repaired if possible. They become old friends and, while they can still be useful, they should be.

Handles are the most common casualties. If it is a willow basket and you can work willow you undo carefully and renew, copying the old, using, if you can get it, the same material. If no longer obtainable you do the nearest you can, cane for willow, darkened with wood dye.

If you cannot do the job yourself take it to a professional basketmaker if one is to be found. His conversation, especially his comments on the making of your basket, will always be worth listening to, if invariably biased, and he will very seldom refuse to help.

I have an affection for those plaited palm-leaf baskets that come from the Near East (p 132 and Illus 261). They are admirable for shopping because when empty they are flat and when full they have no corners. They are also probably as old as any basket and older than any artifact in man's daily use and this is an added attraction. But they do not last. The handles give way first and very soon, and often one over-weights them. One should not grumble, they are very cheap and nice to look

Illus 246 Weighing fleeces in a wool sorter's skep at a Yorkshire woollen mill. Skeps were used in the woollen mills for sorting, combing and spinning. Sorting was done at the top of the building and it is said that skeps were often kicked out of third-floor entrances, this being the quickest way to take them down.

The skips of Lancashire were used in the cotton mills. They also are large wheeled hampers and carried bobbins and caps for the machines. Another, lidded type, rectangular with a beautiful curved flow, was used for transport between mills. All are large open rectangular baskets of willow and cane, standing up to 4ft (1.2m) high and mounted on wheels. Hardboard containers are gradually taking their place but no one seems to want the change.

It is said that every two or three years the skips used to be tied together in long lines and thrown into the 'goit' – the water running by the mill – to soak. This was supposed to keep them supple (*Museum of English Rural Life*)

at, and where they are made they cost little more than a cardboard carrier. But before the handles disintegrate it is a good idea to sew hemp rope – coarse string will do – right round the basket and both handles all in one piece, and shred the ends and sew them flat to the bottom. This hardly alters the look of the basket at all. For a comfortable hand-hold take two strips of leather – the elbow-patching quality will do well – and cover the handles, taking the ends down over the edges for an inch or two and spreading them out and rounding the corners. Either sew them down or fasten them with a couple of split pins. Now the basket will carry on, a comfortable weight carrier until the border gives out and small things start falling through the holes in the bottom. Then, regretfully, I relegate mine to carrying jumble to our village sales and buy another.

Stake-and-Strand Baskets. A more serious repair must be done to willow baskets of the stake-and-strand technique when they begin to show wear on the bottom wale. Here the best expedient is to put on a foot (see p 49 and Illus

57). If there is damage to the stakes the rods can be made longer than usual and run well up the side to replace broken stakes. These can also be given the support of liners (bye-stakes) pushed from above or below, using a bodkin.

A repair which is usually beyond help is a new bottom. Few baskets are worth this, but many were the potato maunds that used to come in for re-bottoming in the heavy lands of Lincolnshire earlier this century. One ingenious basketmaker, Harold Abbey of Selby, Yorkshire, tired of an awkward job, invented and patented a metal bottom with holes round the edge into which the stakes went. There is one of these in the Museum of English Rural Life at Reading.

A broken border, provided it is not due to sheer old age, can also be mended by putting new willow stakes down through the top wale and working the border, cramming down the ends. New twisted handles on the rim can be made of kubu or palembang cane (see pp 47–49).

Broken weavers can sometimes be cut out and replaced by a new rod or cane slipped in when damp. It is a good thing to wet the whole basket if it will stand it when there has to be an extensive repair, this will allow the bodkin to be introduced without breaking the fabric further.

Skeps and Skips. Among the most repaired baskets in the United Kingdom are the huge hampers used in the textile mills of the West Riding of Yorkshire and Lancashire (Illus 246).

They were developed around 1820–30 as part of the whole textile mechanisation process and yet they are almost unknown away from their area of use. At one time hundreds of basket-makers were employed making them but now such firms as survive are mostly on repair work. Some skeps and skips that come in are sixty years old; they need new corner posts, stakes and weavers, new cleats, new wheels.

Frame or Rib Baskets may be repaired too, though only if the frame and handle rings are sound. A liner could support a broken rib part-way along its length and the weaving is easier to renew than in a stake-and-strand basket.

Coil Baskets rarely need repair. They last longer than any others and when they give way, probably due to overwork, decay or insects, that is the end. Straw ones, however, can have their edges mended by oversewing with a material that matches the original as well as possible.

Twine-weave Baskets are so rare these days that even damaged ones may be welcomed by museums. They are, in any case, impossible to repair.

Plaiting of Rush and similar materials may have replacements made using a flat needle, the fabric being made damp first. Mats often come unsewn, but if they actually wear away there is not much to be done unless they give way at an edge when this can be taken off and the whole made smaller. Sometimes it is possible to bind edges with webbing but this alters the look of a mat.

6
Miscellany

The baskets described in this chapter have not been linked to any of the techniques discussed, but have been arranged under headings which show the importance of baskets in the everyday life of those who worked in agriculture and fishing and who sold in the market place. Others, grouped under the heading of Victoriana, illustrate collectable items which may not be familiar to all readers.

Sowing and Winnowing Baskets

Before the mechanisation of sowing, harvesting and winnowing became general in the mid-nineteenth century, baskets were used in these operations in a method of working which remained unaltered throughout the centuries. Sometimes one finds a manuscript portraying such work as in the case of the little medieval figure of about 1280 sowing seed in Illus 247. He shows perfectly the movement described by John Fitzherbert in *The Boke of Husbandrye* of 1523:

> ... set thy left foot before and take a handful of peas; and when thou takes up thy right foot then cast thy peas from thee all abroad; and when thy left foot riseth take another handful, and when thy right riseth cast them from thee. And so at every two paces thou shalt sow a handful of peas and so see that the hand and the foot agree and then shall ye sow even. And in your casting ye must open as well your fingers as your hand, and the higher and farther that you cast your corn the better shall it spread, except it be a great wind.

Broadcast sowing was a crippling occupation since a seedlip would hold up to 2 bushels or 120lb (54kg) of seed corn and was hung round the neck. In medieval times some did it from childhood and became 'happerarsed', that is shrunken or misshapen from carrying it. A

Illus 247 The seedlip, lepe or hopper is seen here slung round the neck of the worker for the broadcast sowing of seed as he walks over a ploughed field (*MS CCC 285 folio 7v, by permission of the President and Fellows of Corpus Christi College, Oxford*)

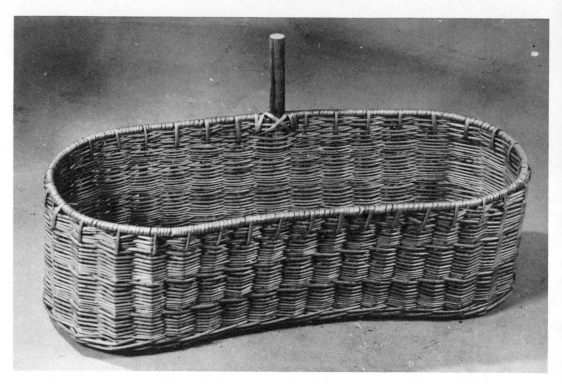

Illus 248 This seedlip was made for the Museum of English Rural Life in 1963 by William Shelley, the last of the old family firm of Leaver Brothers of Salisbury, Wiltshire. It measures 10½in (27cm) by 27½in (70cm) and is 8in (20cm) deep. It is made of white willow, and has a rim of cane bound on with skein (*Museum of English Rural Life*)

---

modern seedlip, made for the Museum of Rural Life, is shown in Illus 248.

As with all other baskets, materials and design of seedlips were adapted to the conditions under which they were used and the materials most readily to hand. Illus 249 shows a sowing basket from the United States of America. It was probably a hill farmer's tool. His fields would be small and he would not have to be burdened by the great containers used by the European lowland farmers.

Such, then, were the baskets used at the start of the farming year. Later, when the corn was safely harvested and gathered in, the basket was again a vital tool, in fact the winnowing fan (Illus 250) is one of the great historic baskets of northern Europe. It was used for 'fanning' away the chaff from the grain after threshing

by hand. A windy day was chosen, and the barn doors were opened for a good draught.

It seems certain that it, or a very similarly made basket, was introduced by the Romans, together with a basket of much the same construction to hold the winnowed grain. The fan is so complicated and laborious that it is most unlikely that there is anyone left in the British Isles who could make it. The French National School of Basketmaking at Fayl-Billot, Haute Marne, include a chapter on it in their manual *La Vannerie*, Vol I, pp 163–5 (see Duchesne in Bibliography), but they do not make it now. To begin with, it measures 40in × 28in (100 × 71cm) and the depth at the back is about 11in (28cm). It is made of a foundation of oak or chestnut or ash slats beginning with two short ones, which cross at the centre. Two willow rods, begun at the tips, pair round these. The ribs are most carefully prepared, each one occupying in its width and length a strictly defined place in the whole structure.

The worker begins by kneeling and holding down the centre with one stockinged foot so that both his hands are free. By the end he is sitting in the middle like a spider, weaving round himself and adding the ribs as he goes.

Illus 249 This neat splint sowing basket comes from the United States of America. The frame is hickory wood, and is of much shallower construction than the seedlips in Illus 247 and 248 (*Department of Textiles, Smithsonian Institution, Washington DC*)

Illus 250 Winnowing fan. Beauty, strength and design superbly fitted to the task for which it is to be used are all combined in this historic basket. Notice the very tight packing of the weaving and the rib construction (*Museum of English Rural Life*)

Illus 251 A putcher. A salmon trap made of brown willow. Assembled, row upon row, in a stout timber framework across the main tidal flow of a river estuary they take fish at ebb or flow of the tide. The swimming salmon enters the putcher's mouth, becomes jammed by the head and is quickly drowned by the flow of water past its gills. Putchers have been used in the river Severn, England, at least since the tenth century, and probably very much earlier. (*Made by I. C. Cadogan, Gloucestershire*)

B Cockle pad for marketing cockles. Made of green willow, it once had a flat lid. Cockles were traditionally collected in coarsely made frame or ribbed baskets, and the women of Penclawydd, in the Gower Peninsular of South Wales, carried one basket on the head and one in the hand, but they use pails now. This example came from Brixham, Devon, but was not made there.

C Cornish cowel. This is a copy of an old pannier carried on the back, made by William Shelley, Wiltshire

D Aberdeen fish landing basket made by Stanley Bird, Norfolk. For general use

E Herring swill, see p 162

F Lobster pot made by the user, A. Hutchings of Beesands, South Devon, from locally grown green willows. The bait 'skippers' are of ash

G Prawn pot made by the user, Edgell of Mudeford, Hampshire from locally grown green willows

H Whelk pot made of cane, from Whitstable, Kent. Now obsolete, and replaced by an iron pot covered with manmade fibre netting

J Hull fish landing basket. A comparatively recent basket developed by Stanley Bird of Great Yarmouth for use on the refrigerated trawlers used by Hull Fisheries Ltd. Made of cane

K Angler's seat

L Fishing creel, see p 162

M Eighth-cran herring basket. Used on shore to show a sample of the catch to customers; not a Government measure. Made by Stanley Bird

N Quarter-cran herring basket, see p 162

P Herring wash basket or wash maund. Used at stage 2 in the kippering industry. The gutted herrings were washed in this basket

Q Oval cobbing basket or cob maund. At stage 1 in the kippering process, the fish were emptied on to a table, split and gutted by hand and thrown into this basket, standing beside the worker

R Cod liver or ice basket to hold cods' livers on long-distance trawlers. They are taken to boilers on board for rendering down for codliver oil. Much used in the North and in Iceland. Made of brown and white willow and cane by Stanley Bird

S Close ice basket. Used on trawlers to carry ice which is mixed with the fish to keep it fresh. Made of cane and wire by Stanley Bird

T Fishing maund. Formerly used for all general handling of fish from trawler to quay to market, but is being replaced by plastic amd metal containers. Made by the Institute for the Blind at Plymouth, Devon, for use by Brixham fishermen

V Miniature quarter-cran herring basket

W Washing basket for herrings. Made of cane, pre-1945, by the Yarmouth Stores, Norfolk

X Open-trawl basket. Used on trawlers for sorting the catch. Made of cane by Stanley Bird

Y Kipper drip maund. A heavy cane basket by Stanley Bird. Used at stage 3 in kippering herring. After washing, the fish are stood in brine and orange dye for an hour in this basket before being hung on 'speats' (wooden racks) to be smoked over an oak fire

---

Illus 252 Identification of Illus 251

A Putcher, Gloucestershire
B Cockle pad
C Cornish cowell
D Aberdeen fish landing basket, Norfolk
E Yarmouth herring swill, Norfolk
F Lobster pot, South Devon
G Prawn pot, Hampshire
H Whelk pot, Kent
J Hull fish landing basket, Norfolk
K Angler's seat, Norfolk

L Fishing creel, Gloucester
M Eighth-cran herring basket, Norfolk
N Quarter-cran herring basket, Norfolk
P Herring wash basket or wash maund, Norfolk
Q Oval cobbing basket, Norfolk
R Liver basket, for cods' livers, or ice, Norfolk
S Close ice basket, Norfolk
T Fishing maund, South Devon
V Miniature quarter-cran herring basket, Norfolk
W Washing basket for herring, Norfolk
X Open-trawl basket, Norfolk
Y Kipper drip, Norfolk

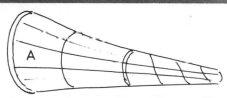

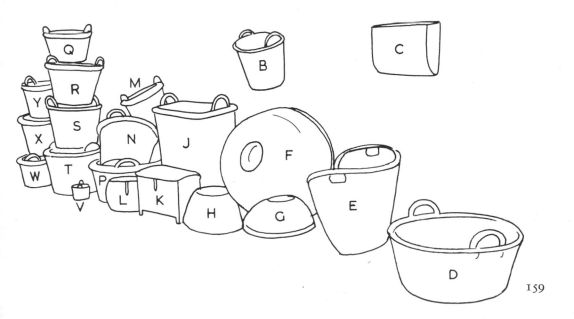

159

The edge is a ring of some pliable wood such as hazel or alder and the ribs, now pared down very thin, are turned over it and taken down into the weaving with the help of a special iron hook, and then hammered down close. The weaving is very tightly packed everywhere and the maker uses the iron all the time. It is no wonder that the fan was always expensive and was one of the things a farmer could never make for himself. It is listed in farm and cattle accounts from the twelfth century onwards. This is also a reason why most museums of rural crafts have one of these fans on view – they outlast most other baskets so it is rarely possible to date them.

Illus 253 Yarmouth herring swill. A unique, primitive basket which for centuries was used in this East Coast town in the herring industry (*Author's Collection*)

Fishing Baskets

In 1969 the Museum of English Rural Life at Reading University held an exhibition of 161 items from its collection of baskets and basket-making tools. These were all English and some-thing of their past was told in prints and photographs. To quote from what I wrote in the catalogue:

Illus 254 A quarter-cran herring basket shown receiving the branded mark of Her Majesty's Inspector of Weights and Measures outside the workshop of Stanley Bird, Great Yarmouth, Norfolk, in November 1963. It was the only English fish basket to be an official measure (*Author's Collection*)

The long history of baskets is something which comes to one only by using one's eyes. There are still many at work in the community, both in town and country. We are so used to them that we hardly notice them and never think of the skill that goes into their making. I hope that as you look at the baskets themselves and at their counterparts in the photographs you may find a new interest in these familiar things, and that their beauty may become apparent and grow.

Although referring to all baskets, the quotation is perhaps particularly relevant to Illus 251 and 252 showing baskets in the fishing industry for, on quays and boats we can still see baskets being used and study them perhaps for the first time.

All the baskets shown in Illus 251 are full of interest but three deserve more detailed mention. The Yarmouth herring swill, for instance (Illus 251 E and Illus 253), was a unique and magnificent primitive made and used only at Great Yarmouth, an East Coast town in Norfolk, England, which has been a centre for herring fishing since Roman times. The exact age of the swill is not known, but it is medieval if not earlier. It is a frame or rib-type construction of hazel and brown willow and was strictly functional. Three swills would carry a cran of herring, each a two-man load.

The system of usage was complicated; three swills were stacked together in a pyramid. Four quarter-crans (Illus 254) filled three swills; one quarter-cran filled the top swill and the other three the bottom swills. This made the top swill lighter to lift down. Empty, they were carried by the central handle and were tied together in bunches. It is said that the long narrow shape developed because of the narrow lanes between the buildings along the quays. They are no longer used except perhaps as log baskets.

The making of swills is an exception to the rule that frame or rib baskets are not made by professionals. The few men who made this archaic object have always been proud of their skill and strength. The top measures 32in × 17in (81 × 43cm) at the widest part, and the depth is 19in (48cm).

The quarter-cran mentioned above and shown in Illus 254 was the most familiar and widely used of British fish baskets and the only one to be an official measure. It has to conform to an exact specification:

17¼in (43.8cm) across the top
14¼in (36.2cm) across the bottom
14¼in (36.2cm) high

The border is 6 behind 2, and the distance between the stakes must be less than the width of a man's thumb, ie the average thickness of a herring. It is made of white willow, wood and kubu cane.

In the nineteenth century there was so much trouble about the weights and measures of herrings that, in 1852, the Commissioners of the Herring Industry fixed the cran (approximately 3½cwt or 180kg) as the official measure for herring, and determined the sizes of baskets and boxes holding 1 and also 1½ cran. The size of the ¼-cran basket was fixed in Scotland in 1889, but not until 1908 did this measure become standard throughout the British Isles. Today herring are sold by weight from metal boxes, and this fine basket is obsolete as a measure.

It was, of course, not only commercial sea fishing which had its interesting baskets and Illus 255 shows a fly fisher's creel made in Somerset, England, of locally grown buff willows, English-randed with the lid made on a hoop of willow. Such a basket is also shown at Illus 251L. Many of these popular baskets came from France at the beginning of this century; they were beautifully made, almost indestructible and are much sought after. The French made them on a three-piece wooden mould, an aid which no British basketmaker would deign to use (see Duchesne, Vol 1, p 273).

Fish traps have a fascination all their own. The putcher shown at Illus 251A is one kind; Illus 256 shows another of the great family of fish traps found all over the world. It is for catching eels in river and marshes, and was made by Stanley Bird of Great Yarmouth. It is a complicated arrangement of a white willow funnel inside a sort of willow bottle, making a non-return valve when the wooden bung is in the narrow end. It is beautifully made and at

Illus 255 The type of fly fisher's creel so popular at the beginning of this century (*CoSIRA*)

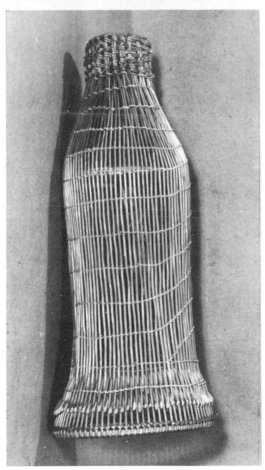

Illus 256 An eel trap showing the arrangement of white willow funnel inside a willow 'bottle'. A similar type of trap was used in the Stone Age (*Museum of English Rural Life*)

one time many men must have known how to make it. Eels as food are not so popular in this country today, but in medieval times they were cultivated and caught in enormous numbers for eating on fast days and were smoked for the winter. In the eleventh century the town of Wisbech in Cambridgeshire, England, a county of fens and waterways, paid the Abbot of nearby Ely an annual rent of 14,000 eels.

A Stone Age version of this trap has been found at Holbaek, Jutland, in Denmark, and we know that people from the same Maglmosian culture visited the east coast of Britain. Early in his history man discovered the non-return principle of trapping fish, not just in Europe, but in many other parts of the world. A book could be written on fish traps alone, so greatly do they vary for the catching of different varieties of fish and so finely made are many of them.

Our illustration of fishing baskets would not

Illus 257 Scottish sculls. Once a familiar sight, they can still be seen in use today on the East Coast of Scotland (*Author's Collection*)

be complete without an example from Scotland with her great fishing traditions. Illus 257 shows two Scottish sculls collected by Dr Baxter and now in the National Museum of Antiquities of Scotland.

The one at the back came from Fife, and that at the front from the Moray Firth. They were once a familiar sight on the fish quays all round the East Coast of Scotland and some are still in use today on the coasts of Angus and Kincardineshire. They are used to carry coiled and baited lines for long-line fishing – normally 500–600 hooks per line, but sometimes, in Arbroath, 1,200–1,400! They are also said to make satisfactory cradles.

A scull is a frame or ribbed basket, with the ribs flat at one end and deeply curved at the other. There are hand-holds where the frame is left bare at either side.

Market Baskets

The selling or 'crying' of strawberries in the streets of our cities must have been a summer business long before there were shops. London strawberries were the best of all they were saying in 1589, the year after the defeat of the Spanish Armada, when they cost as little as 3d a pint and cream 6d a quart. The first strawberry basket we know of was the pottle made of willow spale or chip (Illus 258). In 1843 the girls of Brentford were paid 3s 9d (19p) per gross (144 baskets) for making them. The Francis Wheatley print in Illus 259 from his much loved but highly idealised series 'Itinerant Trades of London' of 1797, shows pottles being carried in a marne. Another print by James Pollard, of a greengrocer's shop c.1820, shows a marne of pottles, some covered with paper and a strawberry leaf, presumably to differentiate between strawberries and raspberries. The Dutch also used pottles though some, if not all, were nearly twice the size of the English ones.

By 1860 the pottle began to go out in favour of the shallow round straight punnet of machined veneer, fastened together with wire staples. These were also carried, full of fruit, in large willow baskets which had false bottoms, allowing two layers without crushing. Later came rectangular 'nesting chips', now overtaken in their turn by cardboard and plastic, but no longer hawked or 'cried' in the streets.

But Wheatley and Pollard were only two of the artists who portrayed the street life of old London. Most people love a market, and George Scharf, an architect of German parentage, fell in love with London's Covent Garden market. He was the last, and the most thorough, of many artists to illustrate that wonderful little world now gone. He tended to sentimentalise over the market people themselves in a way that Paul Sandby, watercolour painter of London Cries in 1749, never did, but he is a good guide. His drawings have never been published and books of them are in the British Museum, Department of Prints and Drawings.

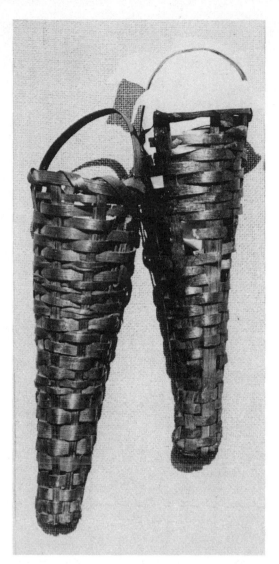

Illus 258 Two pottles made of willow spale or chip (*Museum of English Rural Life*)

Illus 259 Print from Francis Wheatley's series 'Itinerant Trades of London' showing a girl balancing a marne containing pottles on her head, and carrying two more in her other hand (*British Museum, Department of Prints and Drawings*)

He seems to have liked baskets and to have found it interesting that almost every fruit and vegetable had a different one, except for the ubiquitous sieve. Illus 260 shows his drawing of Covent Garden in June, c 1825. As well as the more familiar baskets there are others which even professional basketmakers do not know today.

Since Roman times, weekly markets and yearly or half-yearly fairs have been the means of internal trade in much of Europe. The first, supplying townspeople and country farmers, have sometimes survived: the second, used also by the great estates and religious houses buying and selling on a large scale, have dwindled to entertainments or survive only as street names. For 1,500 or more years at Barnwell, within the present boundaries of the city of Cambridge, was held the greatest fair in England – Stur-bridge or Stourbridge. It ran for three weeks every September and was second only to the fairs of Novgorod and Frankfurt. Not only were most of the goods for these markets carried to and from them in baskets and horse panniers, but basketmakers themselves had stalls in the places assigned to them and these occasions were the most important outlet for their goods. Yearly bulk-buying of agricultural and domestic baskets was still going on during World War I in cities such as Salisbury, Wiltshire, which served a large rural area.

Many country towns still have their pannier market, in name if no longer in reality. This type of market was only for poultry, vegetables, fruit and dairy produce – in fact everything that could be brought in from the farms on a horse or in the hand. Nowadays they are held the same day as cattle and sheep markets; lorries and boxes bring in the produce instead of horses and baskets.

But although baskets are seldom used nowadays in our British markets, this is not so in some other countries. Illus 261, a painting by Johann Zoffany of between 1772 and 1779, now in the Tate Gallery, London, shows baskets which are still being used today in the markets of Tuscany, though they may take some finding.

Other baskets still in use in Italy are shown in Illus 262.

Illus 260 Covent Garden market, London, as George Scharf saw it in June, c 1825. Cabbage crates and strawberry pottles can be seen (*left centre*), a celery load (*over a man's head, centre*). The woman (*bottom left*) is wearing the curious padded hat worn for carrying baskets on the head (*British Museum, Department of Prints and Drawings*)

Illus 261 In this picture by Zoffany, painted in the 1770s, can be seen three white willow baskets, holding grapes and lettuces. They have the twisted borders and handles which are made in Italy, sometimes in France, but never in England.

Behind the old man are two baskets inside each other – the lower one is split sweet chestnut (see p 20). Such baskets come in many different sizes.

The plaited basket on the ground in front, spilling garlic, comes from the Near East and North Africa, and is still seen all over Europe. It has not changed since AD 130, when numbers were hidden in the Dead Sea caves, full of scrolls and other treasures, by refugees fleeing from their Roman oppressors during the Bar Kokhba revolt. Probably it is many centuries older than that (see p 133) (*Tate Gallery, London*)

Illus 262 Baskets still in use in Italy (*left back*) a laundry basket of white willow; (*left front*) a round basket made of chestnut; (*right back*) a flat tray made of reeds and grasses for drying fruit; (*right front*) a table basket made of round and skeined buff willow. For details see pp 120–122 (*Author's Collection*)

Left Back. A large laundry basket of white willow bought in Florence in 1957. Such baskets used to be made in several sizes but are not common today. This one measures 15in (38cm) across the circular bottom and 19in (48cm) across the top. The height is 6in (15cm).

The base is paired but the sides are not woven at all. They are made of the large number of stakes, the butts of 6 willows to each bottom stick. With 12 of these, there are 144 stakes.

A trac side is made in groups of 6, each one of which, at the height of 6in (15cm) above the base, is taken to the left behind 3 groups, down in front of 2 groups, behind 2 groups, in front of 2 groups, behind 1½ groups (9 stakes) and out again. The tips are now down at the base on the outside, and are woven into two rope borders, one above the other, at the base. The lower and thicker one forms a foot for the basket to

stand on. The making of this rope border, which is never made in England, is described in the French manual *La Vannerie*, on pp 249–52 (see Duchesne in Bibliography).

Left Front. In Italian this is a *canestre castagno tonde* – a round basket made of chestnut. It is for general domestic use and one sees many in Tuscany made of this spale or splint, some very much larger and deeper, for marketing vegetables.

Bottom and sides are in one, made of 5 splints 1–1½in (2.5–4cm) wide, and about 21in (54cm) long. These are laid across each other at their centres and paired once with narrower splint. Then 10 shorter splint bye-stakes, sharply pointed, are placed between the bottom ones and the tips, pointing inwards, and randed to hold them in place. These bye-stakes are about 8½in (22cm) long. One wider stake is divided to make an odd number, 21 stakes in all.

The sides are 8 rounds of randing with no upsett. There is no actual border but a cane ring 8¼in (21cm) in diameter is pushed up outside the stakes and these, which are pointed for their last 2in (5cm), are brought over the ring and pushed down through two rounds of randing, the sixth and fourth or fifth and third, which-ever is appropriate.

The basket has been dyed dark brown after making. It measures 6in (15cm) across the base, 8in (20cm) across the top, and stands 3½in (9cm) high.

Right Back. This is a flat tray for drying fruit such as figs and grapes. It is so made that the air can circulate round them.

Such baskets come from Puglia in southern Italy, and Sardinia, and are made in many sizes. This one measures 14½in (37cm) across and stands 2in (5cm) high. It is made of reeds and grasses. Fine lines of fitching run across the base.

Right Front. This table basket was made in Friuli, to the north of Venice, and was being sold in the market in Verona to carry fruit home.

It is made of round and skeined buff willow and was obviously quickly and deftly made, without nails, in the frame or ribbed technique, with good proportions.

The horizontal ring has a diameter of 9in (23cm) and the handle ring is 9in (23cm) high on the inside. It is flattened across the bottom. Two rods have been added to the handle so that it is flat and lapped with skein. The 2 rings are tied with the 'Eye of God' at ·each side (p 122) and there are 8 ribs, the central 2 being kinked below the tie so that the basket is low and flat, standing 2½in (6.5cm) high. It is woven with skein with blind turns taken round the rim between every cross-weave.

Illus 263 Pedlar doll. Such dolls were much loved by mid-nineteenth-century children, though in surviving they have often been parted from their wares. The miniature baskets carried by this doll are skeined and from them and from the pin-papers and boxes we know her to be German. The 16in (41cm) tall pedlar carries ribbon, braid, lace, a pair of gloves ready-made and a pair cut out. Thimbles, pins, beads, hairpins, leather belts, a fan, a wooden dutch-doll, a ball of wool, brass rings, jet, linen and brass buttons complete her stock-in-trade (*Gawthorpe Hall Museum*)

Victoriana

So much is written about the furnishings, the china and silver, the fashions of Victorian times that we tend to forget the basketware. Yet some of it was the work of the highest standard and the minute scale of some of the articles made is an added fascination.

Illus 263–7 all show examples of Victorian basketwork on a domestic level. Such items are getting hard to come by now, but perhaps for that very reason are well worth looking out for.

Modern Rattles

Also on a very domestic level are the rattles shown in Illus 268. Many children's toys are the same the world over but it is interesting to see the different style created from different materials available. These modern examples show how basket traditions can so attractively serve present-day needs.

Illus 264 Made of the finest willow and probably in France, this tiny basket 3in (7.5cm) high was the centre of one of those bead or wool bouquets enclosed in glass domes which decorated mid-nineteenth-century parlours (*Museum of English Rural Life*)

Illus 265 This was probably a reticule or handbag imported from Germany to London and not intended to be used by the well-to-do. The whole fine and simple design, perfectly made of willow skein and black enamelled cane, speaks of the *Jugendstil*, a style which was in revolt against the over-elaborate fashion of late-nineteenth century Europe in decoration and furnishing. It was probably made over a wooden mould (*Author's Collection*)

Illus 266 The cap basket had a higher social status than the reticule (Illus 265). The older married lady who expected to pay more than a brief call took her house cap – a small white linen bonnet sometimes most finely tucked and frilled – to change into. This basket is made of willow skein and straw plait and was probably made over a mould. For this reason it is unlikely to be English (*Museum of English Rural Life*)

Illus 267 This willow workbasket threaded with ribbon was probably imported from Germany. Elaborate fitched work like this was much admired but is seldom to be seen outside museums today because of its fragility (*Gawthorpe Hall Museum*)

Illus 268 Rattles for a baby. The white one (*centre*) is made by Ellison of Evesham, Worcestershire, from specially grown Black Maul osiers. It is only just over 5in (13cm) long, but it is made of seven 3ft (91cm) rods, as near as possible the same thickness all the way down, and very mellow and damp. The butts are tied together 2½in (6.5cm) up, one projecting an inch (2.5cm). Each rod is twisted over two to the right, in the same movement as for a corn dolly. The bell is put in before the top is closed by tying and pushing the tips to the inside. The handle is lapped with a skein, and the longer rod is turned up with the rest to make a loop.

The buff rattle (*right*) is Dutch, and made the same way except for the plaited handle.

The third rattle comes from Indonesia and is made of bamboo in the 'Pigeon's Eye' weave which appears all over the world (*Author's Collection*)

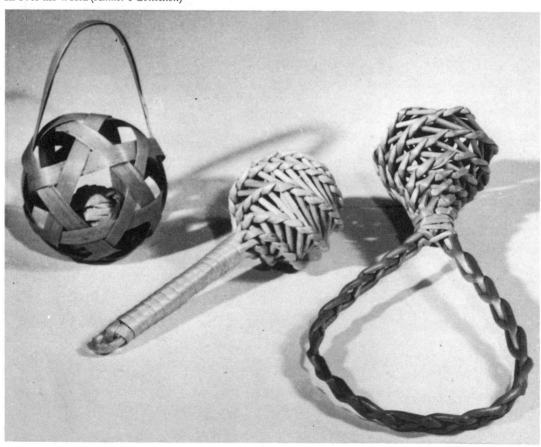

7
Design

Essentials of Good Design

The design of modern basketware in the United Kingdom is, in general, poor. When it is not it has often originated in Scandinavia. There is a real need for trained designers to come into the field of basket design, both of furniture and domestic ware.

Many people going abroad will have been struck by the imaginative use of other materials with basketwork for fashion baskets. The Italians in particular are alive to the possibilities of using traditional spale and willow shapes in new ways. These are interesting, but much of their strawwork has a meretricious charm and much more is downright horrid, which does not prevent it being bought by tourists in huge quantities.

There is no need for us in Britain to borrow ideas from other countries; we have well-trained young designers with fertile brains and our traditional baskets are magnificent. But one must have some knowledge of technique before one can design basketwork and this is seldom taught in art schools. It is obvious that to be economically worthwhile, handmade objects involving any craft techniques, when designed by trained designers, must come into the prestige class. The time may come when we shall insist on paying high prices for handmade domestic basketware and there would seem to be little point in wasting a craftsman's skill making the ugly and cheap as we do today. The value of well-designed handmade things is recognised in this country by a few people but not yet by the many. Yet an industrial country which allows its crafts to die out will lose some-thing vital and precious which once gone will never return. From time to time there must be renewals of interest and enthusiasm if the crafts and craftsmen are not to become crusted and anachronistic.

At present, if you ask the British journeyman working on his plank what basket in his reper-toire he most admires he will probably tell you the florist's basket which was high fashion in 1900. So when the trade sets out to design a piece of modern basketware its standard is not the great traditional baskets of everyday but a Victorian fernholder or basket chair. To that is grafted on the style known as 'contemporary' which in basketry means plywood, coloured plastic and bleached centre cane.

An offshoot of this is that recipes for such things are sold in pamphlet form in shops selling craft materials. They tempt amateurs to buy materials without teaching them anything worth knowing or providing them with any-thing worth possessing. The 'Do-It Yourself' movement is a lucrative business to men with-out an artistic conscience and the public un-fortunately seldom stops to ask if what it is doing itself is worthwhile.

Yet there is no reason why the amateur should not make good baskets. Basketry is being taught in many schools and recreational institutes. But is it being well taught? Some-times, yes, from a technical point of view, sometimes no. Basketry design is rarely taught at all; the same old baskets are turned out and the 'homecraft' magazines and pamphlets are copied.

What should one look for in a good basket

design? Usefulness, strength, shape, texture and colour, right use of material and craftsmanship.

Usefulness. Turn to the photographs of professionally made baskets (Illus 1, 11, 12, 14, 56, 30, 62, 63) and see how many jobs baskets do, and then turn to Illus 167–70, 172, 174–7, 179–80, 182, 185. To employ oneself there is no need to make rubbish.

Strength. A beginner need not make a weak flabby cane wastepaper basket with a scalloped border; it is just as easy to make a strong one with a 3-rod plain border that will not come undone with constant lifting to empty. Strength is not only a matter of the thickness of the material, it comes from a sound knowledge of technique.

The amateur has generally to use centre cane for his baskets because of the difficulties in preparing willow and also because willow requires greater strength of hand and arm as well as greater skill. For lightness, strength and resilience willow is incomparable. It is also beautiful and full of life. On the other hand centre cane has elasticity and is easier to manipulate. With it an amateur can do things which only the finest willow worker can do with willow.

Where willow has the advantage over cane in fine basketware is in strength for weight. This is something the public is inclined to forget. Centre cane shopping baskets and picnic baskets are often asked to carry far too much and break down. No cane shopper should be expected to carry 6lb (3kg) of vegetables and 3 pints (2l) of milk every day. If it is, its life will be short. We have a long willow tradition in Britain, so we tend to work cane like willow, also perhaps to use cane baskets with the carelessness accorded to willow ones. For the same reason we blame foreign maize and palm baskets when they give way, forgetting that in their countries of origin they are treated like paper carrier bags.

A roped or drop handle is stronger than a lapped one because it is worked into or over the side of the basket. A lapped handle depends on pegs and ties. But a handle which is part of the construction, as in a round frame basket (see Illus 13, 14 and 204), is strongest of all. A domed base adds strength, so do leagues and, in

a cane basket, willow sticks and stakes.

Shape. Taste is a difficult thing to argue about because the good taste of one half-century is the bad taste of the next, but a sense of a good shape is different. It is not inborn, but can only be cultivated by looking, if possible by drawing and, when one is learning to be a craftsman, by touch. The best way to learn about the good

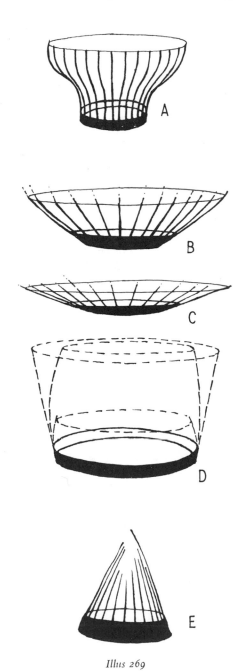

Illus 269

174

shapes of baskets is to look at them and also at pottery. There are many good pots to be seen in museums and exhibitions and a visit to a local pottery will teach one a lot. The relationship between baskets and pots may be seen by looking at Illus 11, 30, 168, 169, 179. All these are pot shapes. Having learnt to recognise a good simple shape one has to learn to make it.

The shape of a basket is determined by its upsett, ie the first inch of weaving that setts the stakes up after they leave the base (Illus 269).

An upsett such as A could never become a bowl-shape however hard one pulls out the stakes above it. B will make a wide bowl, C will make a plate or a very wide bowl, but D will make a narrow bowl, a barrel shape or a wide-mouthed basket. E, an upsett that slants inwards, will never make anything and must be undone.

In France, Italy and the Far East much cane-work is done over wooden moulds. The most complicated bulges and curves can be made by this method. Amateur basketmakers often wish to make these forms and wonder why English craft books are of no use to them. This is not our way of working; our tradition is different. It may surprise some people to know that English baskets are greatly admired in Italy and some of the finest are exported there.

Texture. By texture, we mean the appearance of the surface of a basket. Good texture can only be achieved by practice because first and foremost it depends on smooth even weaving and finish. Variations in texture are achieved by the use of varying thicknesses of material and in the use of different strokes. It is a general rule that a basket should have a wale to upsett and another to finish the side before bordering. Besides its decorative value a wale is a great strengthener and orders the stakes better than a rand or slew.

Flat cane or willow skeins give interesting effects, though large areas will not be so strong as round cane or rods. It is sometimes possible to buy skeins from a craftsman and to work them over cane stakes. True skeinwork is very beautiful and intricate, and is being done again in Western Germany. There are still one or two craftsmen who can make the woven skeined chair-seats in damask patterns. Some of this work is being done on modern Italian chairs and it would be pleasing to see it revived in this country. Plaited rush used to be used with willow on linen baskets and can be used with cane, so can plaited raffia. Straw plait has a lively sheen but has little strength or wearing quality. Buff willow goes admirably with cane and presents no difficulty in class work if it is used for bottom sticks and liners only, since it can be cut up before soaking (see Recipes on pp 91, 92, 94, 105).

Colour. The use of colour in willow basketry in this country is limited to its natural range of brown, white and buff.

Centre cane well worked is an attractive material. Like some people it gains character with age, but it has not the lively natural quality of willow. Varnish gives it a nasty texture and paint makes it more artificial than it is already. The introduction of plastic and enamelled cane has not helped towards good design, it is not a living material and has not the same tensile qualities, thus it is usually employed in bits and bobs and the effects are irritating. After a year or two it appears to perish, and breaks or unwinds.

The use of buff or brown willow with cane will give warmth and life. Palembang also is a pleasant reddish brown and glossy lapping cane gives a pale gold. Many people dye centre cane with fabric dyes. A new field of design is open here and we can now rival the eye-catching colours of foreign baskets and perhaps revive the trade in coloured and gilded baskets which went on in the first and second centuries between Britain and Rome!

Right Use of Material. Bernard Leach, the potter, once said that the craftsman should honour his material. This is not only a poetic statement but a practical one. Material can be used for right and wrong purposes and only a knowledge of it can tell one what they are. You cannot make a silk purse out of a sow's ear but good sows win prizes. New synthetic materials are being produced all the time and it is not easy to decide whether and on what grounds they should be used with natural materials. Often the questions are not asked; cheapness, speed in working and mere eye-catching appeal alone influence the worker. It is possible to use some canework techniques with wire and plastic threads and in general this is more successful than attempts to mix them with cane and willow.

Craftsmanship. Craftsmanship is knowing how to do something, refusing to do it less well than one can, knowing one's material and giving to everything made what may be called finish.

Where the amateur has an advantage over the professional is in the time he has to spend. He can do more elaborate work because his time is not money (see Recipe on p 95). But in common with the professional he must have practice. There is an intoxication in having made something, but like most intoxications it is a dangerous feeling blinding the maker to self-criticism. A basket may do good service but it may still be a bad basket. Cane is a misleading material and it appears easy to handle, as indeed it is compared with willow; but perfectly even weaving, straight stakes and perfect finish require long practice. The old workshop saying that 'there is no such thing as a pair of baskets' is a fair comment on the matter of shape. Every amateur should know the dimensions of his basket before he begins to make it and work with the ruler at his elbow. A basket which turns out much larger by the time the border is reached may have to have a poor mean border because the length of stakes allowed has been used up in the spread of the sides.

The master craftsman can make anything from a laundry hamper to an eel trap, though he will usually have his speciality. The amateur, especially the female one, has limitations and they may be simply of physical strength. Not all of us have strong hands and forearms. It is useless to try to make big baskets with thin material, it is better to buy them.

Finish gives an inevitability to any piece of craftwork whether pot, basket, leather bag, knitted sock, piece of embroidery or papering a room. What is finish? It is the difference between the handmade and the homemade, clean endings and beginnings, the beauty of order which is only achieved by competence, by craftsmanship. Those who cannot see it have not achieved it yet.

Current Trends

The above discussion of the essentials of good design and the need for better British designers was, in fact, written nearly twenty years ago. Yet I see no reason to change its rather fierce and minatory tone. In fact there are times when, looking on at the craft world which one is glad to see is beginning to be wearied by the insistence some of its leaders have placed on the 'artist-craftsman' image, I hardly know whether to laugh or to cry.

There is a craft revival and, as with all revivals, it is not, nor will it be, the same as the last one or the one before that. It will of course have its gods and most of them will be potters. This means that there will be more potting disciples than followers of other crafts. The craft of basketmaking has no gods, not even an old Edwardian professor of Italian at Cambridge University called Thomas Okey who was the only known basketmaker to be fluent with his pen. Ours is a humble craft, too humble these days and very badly paid. Why should this be? There are a number of reasons, not the least being the value that professional basketmakers set on their own work. Again, baskets have almost no value archaeologically, though they can have as much to say about the past as potsherds. Found in digs, baskets are an embarrassment, being difficult to preserve or to identify, though not impossible, as Dr Colin Platt and Professor Yigael Yadin (see Bibliography) emphasise.

Nevertheless basketmakers are already a part of this craft revival particularly in the United States, where exquisite Shaker baskets and North American Indian basketry are now fetching high prices. The modern Indian work, alas, shows only phenomenal industry and the modern penchant for aniline dyes. But there is so much, and so much that is so good (see pp 147-148). There is also a cult, if that is not an unkind word, of highland crafts, simple useful things made behind a 200 year old curtain of time and mountains which is now dissolving (see pp 143-144). In Britain we should be proud that we were the mother country of most of these handmade mountain baskets and that their design, once ours, has grown and developed, using not willow and hazel but the trees of America.

Many books are now being written on basketry, particularly in America, lavishly illustrated and available in Britain. But not all show a very high quality of work produced. One begins with numerous examples of baskets from all over the world many of which, as one would expect, are of high quality, and most of which were made for use or at least with a purpose. These are followed by pages of instructions (mostly done in wool and string) and examples made by art students of several American universities who are now themselves teaching. But unfortunately, setting their work, much of which has taken many hours of extremely careful labour and no little skill, by the side of some of the best of the world's native and professional artifacts, only serves to emphasise the puerility and poverty of their inventions.

Much of this student work has a visceral and inward-looking depravity which points to despair and if it were not so silly, so ugly and so ephemeral some of the rest of us might be infected with the same malaise – the more so because it is beautifully photographed, printed and published.

Another more recent book is the outcome of many hours of patient and valuable research into the ways in which native baskets from all over the world are made, explaining and illustrating with the greatest care techniques which present ferocious difficulties to the average craft worker. But the attempts illustrated, using these techniques, bear little resemblance to the originals, although again they are photographed with the same loving care. The most admired of the native works are what George Wharton James (see Bibliography) called 'vicious forms', degenerate things made today to sell to tourists. No lovely shapes to train the eye, no simplicity in colour and pattern; American museums are full of beautiful things of a standard far above these. Has taste, honest good taste, vanished from the American craft scene?

No, of course it has not, but the disturbing thing about these books and others like them is how far they lead us from what basketry should be. To quote Thomas Okey, writing in *Encyclopaedia Britannica*: 'A basket is a vessel of twigs, cane or rushes as well as a variety of other materials interwoven together and used for holding, protecting or carrying any commodity'. What in the name of all craftsmen since the world began is wrong about making a work of art which is *useful* to mankind?

Many countries, still making fine baskets for their own daily use, are using their native materials in traditions which are proving unsuitable in the modern world; too laborious, taking too long to learn and dying out because there is no one to hand them on. Up to a point this is inevitable since time goes fast, but the message to fellow craftsmen everywhere is to save what you can. Compromise here and there, as one must, but try not to lose the good traditions. It can be done, it has been and is being done, and as always the onus is on the teachers.

Anyone who has lived in or visited the Far East will know of the wonderfully rich craft traditions of Indonesia and Malaysia, particularly in weaving, in the making of mats and baskets, in batik and other kinds of fabric printing. In the early 1960s, at the Batu Lintang Teachers Training College, Kuching, East Malaysia, there was a European teacher, Miss Susi Heinze, now Mrs Dunsmore. She realised how vital it was, in this newly independent and swiftly developing country, for the indigenous crafts to be written down so that they could be taught, first to the teachers, and then to the children in the schools. She is herself a talented artist with a wonderful grasp of the ways in which things are made by the fine hands of the people of Sarawak, and she wrote three books on art teaching in schools (see Bibliography). She described them as 'Handbooks of suggestions for teachers and students and all who are interested in Arts and Crafts'. They were published by the Borneo Literature Bureau, Kuching, Sarawak, East Malaysia, and they are graded for children at different stages of development. They are, though, a treasure house of lovely ideas for anyone, of splendid drawings and photographs of art and craft work so rich that one is constantly making new discoveries. The majority of the designs are indigenous, the materials entirely so, and besides pottery, painting and sculpture we can see how to make kites and hats, to fold and plait leaves, at first simply into little cooking aids and then into the superb mats and baskets of the people of Borneo. It would seem that the arts and crafts of Sarawak need never die out. These books could be of the greatest help to teachers in countries without a strong craft tradition.

Nevertheless there is need for warning about the borrowing of designs and techniques from other countries. There are those who break their hearts – hardly too strong a phrase – trying to copy impossibly difficult things, difficult because the originals were the outcome of tradition and long-inherited skills. The simple thing well made is so much more satisfactory than the bodge of something complicated, and humility is a happier state of mind – and a more hopeful and creative one – than heart-break.

Fortunately both in the United States, here in England and also in France, there are signs of a different route being taken by the young. An honesty and a gentleness and a wish to make simple things to be used in daily life is becoming evident, and these younger craftsmen do not expect their work to be treated with high seriousness or paid for with extravagant praise or equally extravagant cheques. They are not a school or a cult and perhaps the best thing about their emergence is that often they do not know each other or are only just beginning to be aware that they are not alone. They are not listening to the dead cry of 'do your own thing' but to a less strident voice saying 'small is beautiful'.

The future of our ancient craft lies with them and their belief, if they can keep it clear and unpolluted.

Glossary of Basketmakers' Terms

Back: the convex side of a willow rod.

Belly: the whole basket after the border is worked. Also the concave side of a willow rod.

Border: the finishing edge of the sides, lid or foot of a basket, made by bringing the stakes down and weaving them into a set pattern.

Bow or Bow-rod: the curved willow or cane forming the centre of a handle.

Bow-mark: a short rod the thickness of a handle put where the handle will be, and worked over during the making of a basket. Withdrawn when the handle is put in.

Bridge: a narrow piece of randing or pillaring (qv) on two sticks laid across and under the border of a rectangular basket on which half-lids are slung.

Butt: the thick end of a willow rod.

Bye-stake: a stake not inserted into the base. Sometimes used instead of the term 'liner'.

Chip: a basket, rectangular or circular, made from machine made veneer, *see* Punnet.

Coil Basket: *see* Technique, p 26.

Cover: lid.

Cram: (noun) a sharpened stake turned down at right angles, sometimes used in finishing a willow border;
(verb) to insert the above and tap down with an iron.

Creel: the general Scottish word for a basket. Now used in England for a pouch-shaped basket for river fishing.

Eel Traps: these have many names: grig, hive, wheel, kipe, ark, etc.

Fitch: the reverse twist of pairing, used when fitching.

Fitching: openwork in cane or willow basketry, formed with the stakes in the fabric of the basket, not in bordering.

Flasket: laundry or clothes basket in Wiltshire or Lancashire, large basket for pilchards in Cornwall.

Flat: a rectangular basket with a hinged lid, which stacks easily and protects the contents. Used for cucumbers, watercress, flowers and grapes.

Flow: the outward slant of the sides of a basket.

Foot: a border worked on the bottom of a basket, or the method of joining stakes to a wooden base with holes.

Frame, or Ribbed Basket: *see* Technique, p 23.

Hamper: usually a rectangular basket with a cover, made by professionals to suit special needs such as laundry, provisions, meat, theatrical and other travelling uses. The 'hamper' in Jamaica is quite different (see p 118).

Hides: strips of raw hide in various widths from $\frac{3}{4}$in (2cm) upwards, used in hamper making, usually over borders and the ends of covers for added strength and protection.

Holt: the cultivated plot where willows or osiers are grown. Also known as bed, plat, grove, hope, garden.

Hoop: a ring formed by coiling a rod upon itself, used to hold the stakes upright while the upsett, and in some cases the belly, is being worked. Also used of the ring frame used in scallomed work.

Hopper: another name for a seedlip.

Lapping: binding with skein willow or flat cane.

League: a bottom stick which continues up both

sides of a basket to take the weight.

Ledge: a small shelf worked on the inside of a basket on which a lid drops in and rests.

Liner: a rod inserted by the side of a stake for strength or decorative effect. Sometimes called a 'bye-stake'.

Listing: a decorative pattern worked with additional skeins or flat cane when lapping a handle.

Maund: a general name for a large round straight-sided basket for fish or potatoes in Britain.

Notch: a square opening at the side or border which may or may not be closed again, eg finger-holes on a hamper or the opening of a dog or cat basket.

Osier: another name for basket willow.

Packing: building up any part of a basket or base by a change in the normal line of weaving, with one or more short turns.

Pairing: two canes worked alternately over and under each other, forming a twist.

Pannier: generally a basket or pair of baskets to be carried on the back of a horse, donkey or mule. A 'pannier market' is a market selling vegetables, dairy produce and poultry, ie what can be brought in by pannier.

Picking: cutting off the projecting ends of rods when a basket is completed. A base may be picked when finished and before the belly is worked.

Pillaring: weaving up two adjacent stakes of a fitched basket in a figure-of-eight. This may give strength in one place, or be a strong way of finishing off a rod.

Plaited Basket: *see* Technique, p 26.

Pot or Pottle: sometimes a small basket for soft fruit; sometimes a trap for lobsters, crabs etc.

Pricking-up: turning up of willow stakes over the point of a knife after they have been inserted into the base. In a cane basket the stakes are squeezed with round-nosed pliers.

Prickle: a large willow basket for oysters, whelks or fruit, in Britain.

Punnet: small basket of veneer strips, usually square, with the top larger than the bottom so that many can be nested, *see* Chip.

Putcher, Putchen: a salmon trap.

Rand: a single rod worked in front of one stake and behind the next.

Randing: the weaving of single strands. As applied to willow:

Light: using only the side of the hand for compression.

Coarse: as above but with coarser strands.

Medium: using the iron to close the tips of the strands.

Close: using the iron to close butts as well as tips.

Prick: the butts are slyped and thrust down into the randing by the side of a stake before weaving in.

Ribbed Basket: another name for frame basket (qv).

Rib-rand: one rod worked in front of two stakes and behind one. The number of stakes in rib-randing must *not* be divisible by three. Sometimes called Chinese randing.

Rods: young shoots, especially of willow, used in basketmaking. Any single length of material which has not been split.

Round: one complete circular movement made round a basket, lid or base.

Scallom: method of fixing stakes to a ring of willow or cane.

Seedlip: a seed basket used when broadcast-sowing.

Sieve and Half-sieve: cylindrical market baskets. The sieve holds just over one Imperial bushel (8gal or 36l) of fruit or vegetables.

Skein: a strip of the outer skin of a willow rod, after the bark has been removed.

Slath: the structure made by the bottom sticks of a base.

Slewing: working two or more rods together in front of one stake and behind the next.

Slype: a slanting or flat cut.

Spale, Spelk or Splint: thin strips split by various methods from saplings and pole-sized trees, used in basketmaking.

Stake-and-strand Basket: the most common type of North European basket, *see* Technique, p 23.

Stakes: rods driven in with the bottom sticks to form the foundation of the sides of a stake-and-strand basket.

Sticks: short lengths of rod forming the foundation of a base or lid.

Stroke: a movement in basketmaking like a stitch in sewing or knitting.

Top or Tip: the thin end of a rod.

Trac: a simple border worked with one stake, or a stake and its liner, at a time.

Trunk Cover: a lid that fits over a basket.

Twine-weave Basket: *see* Technique, p 26.

Upsett: the setting-up of the sides of a basket, usually employing a round of 4- or 5-rod waling and several rows of 3-rod. The most important part of any basket since the shape springs from it.

Wale: three or more rods worked in sequence in front of two, three or more stakes and behind one. Or in front of two or three and behind two, using four or five rods.

Weaver: the length of material used in the weaving of a basket as opposed to the stake or rib round which it is woven.

Whisket or Wisket: a laundry or clothes basket in Lancashire and Cheshire.

Wickering: in England, the winding of tea or coffee pot handles with chair cane or willow skein to insulate them.

Wickerwork: in the USA, stake and strand, particularly willow, basketry.

Withe or Withy: a tough flexible shoot, especially of willow.

Bibliography

Allbon, Leonard G. *Basic Basketry* (Parrish, USA, 1962). Useful teaching.

Arizona Highways, Vol LI, No 7, July 1975 (Phoenix, Arizona). Excellent colour illustrations.

Arnold, James. *The Shell Book of Country Crafts* (UK, 1968). Much of interest, fine drawings of methods and tools.

Bobart, H. H. *Basketwork Through the Ages* (Oxford University Press, 1936). Much of interest.

Borglund, Erland and Hyllén, T. *Handbok i Korgflätnung* (Stockholm 1955, in Swedish). Handbook of basketmaking, with excellent drawings and many photographs.

Christopher, F. J. *Basketry* (Dover Reprint, 1952). Useful for stake-and-strand.

Coker, Alec. *The Craft of Straw Decoration* (Dryad Press, 1971). Useful teaching.

Crampton, Charles. *Canework* (21st edn, Dryad Press). The best cane teaching manual.

Curtis, Edward Sherriff. *The North American Indian* (Cambridge, Mass 1897–1927). Classic work on this subject, 20 portfolios of photographs and 20 volumes of text. In UK may be seen in library of the University of Exeter.

Dryad Leaflet No 112. *Rush Baskets and Mats*. Useful.

Duchesne, R., Ferrand, H. and Thomas J. *La Vannerie* (2nd edn, Paris, 1963), 2 vols in French. The best existing manual on willow basketmaking.

Eaton, Alan H. *Handicrafts of the Southern Highlands* (New York, 1937; Dover Reprint, 1973). History, attractive.

——. *Handicrafts of New England* (New York, 1949; Dover Reprint, 1969). History.

Evelyn, John. *Sylva or a Discourse of Forest Trees* (London, 1670, facsimile Royal Horticultural Society, 1973). History of great charm.

Florance, Norah. *Rush Work* (Bell, 1962). Useful.

Garrett, W. and Thornton, M. *Canework for the Doll's House* (Dryad Press, 1970).

Gordon, Joleen. *Edith Clayton's Market Basket. A Heritage of Splintwood Basketry in Nova Scotia* (Nova Scotia Museum 1977).

Hart, Carol and Dan. *Natural Basketry* (New York, 1975). Most useful, excellent teaching.

Hartley, Dorothy. *Made in England* (Methuen, reprinted 1974). Much of general interest, a lovely book.

Heinze, Susi (Mrs Dunsmore). *Art teaching for Secondary Schools* (1969): *Art Teaching for Upper Primary Schools* (1969): *Art Teaching for Lower Primary Schools* (1972) (Borneo Literature Bureau, Kuching). Books to keep the crafts of Sarawak alive through her children. Much for all teachers of crafts.

Hennell, Thomas. *The Countryman at Work* (Architectural Press, London, 1947). A classic; drawings of methods and tools – willow.

James, George Wharton. *Indian Basketry* (New York, 1909, reprinted, 1972). Comprehensive and authoritative.

Klamkin, Marian. *Hands to Work: Shaker Folk Art and Industries* (New York, 1972). Excellent illustrations.

Knock, A. G. *Willow Basketry* (Dryad Press, 2nd impression 1946).

Lambeth, M. and R. C. *The Golden Dolly* (1963).

——. *Straw Craft: More Golden Dollies*, Baker (1974). Folklore and teaching.

Legg, Evelyn. *Country Baskets* (Mills & Boon, 1960). Stake-and-strand; hedgerow baskets.

Martin, E. W. *The Secret People, English Village Life After 1750* (Phoenix House, 1954). History.

Mason, Otis Tufton. *Aboriginal American Basketry* (New York, 1902). History.

Miles, C. and Bovis, P. *American Indian and Eskimo Basketry, A Key to Identification* (New York, 1969). Useful.

Morris, E. H. and Burgh, R. F. *Anasazi Basketry* (Carnegie Institute, Washington DC, post-1946). Detailed study of techniques used by the Basketmaker Indians.

Navajo School of Indian Basketry, The. *Indian Basket Weaving* (Los Angeles, 1903, Dover Reprint 1971). Teaching.

Okey, Thomas. *The Art of Basketmaking* (Pitman, 1912). The classic willow teaching book in English, now unobtainable.

——. *A Basketful of Memories* (Dent, 1930). As it was.

——. 'Basket', *Encyclopaedia Britannica*, 11th ed, Vol 3, 481–3.

Paul, Frances. *Spruce Root Basketry of the Alaska Tlingit* (US Bureau of Indian Affairs, 1944). Useful, teaching twine weave.

Platt, Colin and Coleman-Smith, Richard. *Excavations in Medieval Southampton 1953-1969* (Leicester University Press, 1975, 2 vols). A few baskets treated with all respect for their historical importance.

Pliny. *Natural History* (AD 50, translated H. Rackham, Loeb Classical Library, 1938–52, 10 vols). Vols 4 and 5 recount early willow culture.

Roffey, Mabel, *Simple Basketry* (Pitman, reprinted 1953). Cane and some willow.

Roffey, Mabel and Cross, Charlotte, S. *Rush Work* (Pitman, 1952). Some history, nice rural patterns.

Rossback (Ed). *Baskets as Textile Art* (New York, Van Nostrand Reinhold, 1973).

Sandford, L. and Davis, P. *Decorative Straw Work* (Batsford, 1964). Authoritative teaching.

Schreck, Otto. *Fachbuch für den Korbmacher* (Leipzig, 1955), in German), A valuable teaching book.

Scott, O. R. *Basketry the Easy Way* (Sydney, 1954). Cane, elementary teaching.

Seeler, K. and E. *Nantucket Lightship Baskets* (Nantucket, 1972). Specialist descriptive.

Stephenson, Sue H. *Basketry of the Appalachian Mountains* (Van Nostrand Reinhold, New York, 1977). Invaluable.

Technology, Short History of, Vol 1 (Oxford University Press, 1960). Early history of world baskets.

Teleki, Gloria Roth. *The Baskets of Rural America* (New York, 1975). A most comprehensive and useful book for collectors.

Trowell, Margaret. *African Arts and Crafts* (Longmans, 1937).

Turner, Luther Weston. *The Basketmakers* (New York, 1909).

Vogt, E. 'Basketry and Woven Fabrics of the Stone and Bronze Ages', *CIBA Review No 54*, (Basel, 1947, in English). An authority.

Weygandt, Cornelius. *The Dutch Country* (New York, 1939). pp 213–33. Historical.

Whitbourn, K. *Introducing Rushcraft* (Batsford, 1969). Useful.

Whiteford, A. H. *North American Indian Arts*. Golden Guides (New York, 1973). Excellent, so much in a small book.

Wiggington, Eliot (ed). *The Foxfire Book* (New York, 1972). Student study of mountain crafts, delightful.

Will, Christoph. *Flechtwaren* (Germany). Basketware.

——. *Peddig-flechten* (Ravensburg, 1973). Cane teaching.

Women's Institute Leaflet. *Using Rushes* (1964). Basics.

Wright, Dorothy. *A Caneworker's Book for the Senior Basketmaker* (Dryad Press, 1970).

Yadin, Yigael. 'The Finds from the Bar-Kokhba Period in the Cave of Letters', *Judean Desert Studies* (Jerusalem, 1963). Analysis of early baskets.

——. *Bar Kokhba; the Rediscovery of the Legendary Hero of the Last Jewish Revolt Against Imperial Rome, 132–135 A.D.* (Weidenfeld & Nicholson, 1971). Early baskets.

Acknowledgements

While it is not possible to write a complete book of anything so multifarious and multitudinous as baskets, I have tried to bring to wider notice those works of man's skill which appear to me useful and beautiful; most of which are not beyond the range of the normal craftsman, whether young and green or older and wiser, provided he or she is not too easily discouraged nor in too much of a hurry.

Some of the photographs and drawings appeared in my previous book *Baskets and Basketry*, but more than half are new and I must acknowledge a debt to the many more kind people who have lent photographs and baskets. For the drawings I am indebted not only to David Button who made the original ones, but also to Susan Smith and Malcolm Couch. Photographs 239–42 are reproduced with the kind permission of Sue H. Stephenson and her publishers Van Nostrand Reinhold & Company, New York.

For his help with willow techniques and instructions I am deeply grateful to Alistair Heseltine as well as to those many craftsmen I have visited, watched at work and talked to about the craft. Friends in America, especially Carol and Dan Hart, Anne Murray, Sue Stephenson and Marianne Wilson, are also forever owed a debt of gratitude for letters, photographs, press cuttings and books, and for introductions to some of the great collections. Others in Holland, France, Italy and Germany have given the same help, time and interest. Not least I value the support that all these friends have given me through their belief in the vital future of our craft and in the pleasure it gives to us and to many others in a mechanised world.

I must thank Doctor W. O. Hassall, Assistant Librarian at the Bodleian Library, Oxford, for help in my early days of research, and recommend a wider use of his splendid film strips on the manuscripts in the Bodleian Library at Oxford; also the Museum of English Rural Life at Reading for allowing me to use photographs of so many of the baskets we collected together. The Council for Small Industries in Rural Areas (CoSIRA) I thank again, and also K. G. Stott at Long Ashton Research Station of Bristol University, who knows more about the genus *Salix* than anyone else.

Lastly I am grateful to my husband for his encouragement and practical help in so many ways, and for his interest and willingness to act as my memory and second pair of ears.

DOROTHY WRIGHT

Index